Expanding Disciplinarity in Architectural Practice

Expanding Disciplinarity in Architectural Practice presents an argument for the role of an architect as a generalist with a particular ability to bring spatial intelligence to bear on the significant issues of planning, settlement, and identity. The book draws on strategy and planning, landscape, infrastructure, urbanism, historical conservation, and interpretation, architecture, and the creative reuse of existing structures to encourage you to incorporate a holistic approach to your designs. Tracing a series of projects developed by his practice 5th Studio, author Tom Holbrook argues the critical importance of involving spatial practitioners in large scale strategies and designs to combine interdisciplinary thinking and concrete experience of buildings. The book incorporates interviews with prominent figures in the field of architecture, eleven UK case studies, and over 200 beautiful illustrations including the author's own award-winning designs.

With twenty years of evolving practical experience, together with associated research, teaching, and writing, Holbrook shows you how a participatory infrastructure creates a crucial bridge between strategic thinking and the reality of the built environment. This book is a must-read for professionals seeking to incorporate broader design strategy into their practice.

Tom Holbrook is co-founder of 5th Studio, a spatial design agency working across the fields of architecture, urban design, infrastructure and landscape. In combination with practice, he is Professor of Architecture and Industry Fellow at RMIT University, and directs the urban studies programme at the London School of Architecture.

Design Research in Architecture

Series Editors:

Bridging a range of positions between practice and academia, this Routledge series seeks to present the best proponents of architectural design research from around the world. Each author combines innovative historical and theoretical research with creative propositions as a symbiotic interplay. In offering a variety of key exemplars, the book series situates itself at the forefront of design research investigation in architecture.

Other titles in the series

Marcel Duchamp and the Architecture of Desire
Penelope Haralambidou
ISBN 978 1 4094 4345 2

Digital Poetics
An Open Theory of Design-Research in Architecture
Marjan Colletti
ISBN 978 1 4094 4523 4

Transitions: Concepts + Drawings + Buildings
Christine Hawley
ISBN 978 1 4724 0909 6

The Architecture Chronicle
Diary of an Architectural Practice
Jan Kattein
ISBN 978 1 4094 5186 0

Expanding Disciplinarity in Architectural Practice
Designing from the Room to the City
Tom Holbrook
ISBN 978 1 4724 8173 3

'Holbrook skilfully acts as both impresario and ethical husbander; the former at ease weaving and diving as opportunistic entrepreneur, the latter immersed in a legacy of English socialism. This is an apposite piece of research, offering spatial intelligence as a basis for synthesised thought to unpick the current conundrum of planning and governance.'

Professor Michael McGarry, Queen's University Belfast, UK

Expanding Disciplinarity in Architectural Practice

Designing from the Room to the City

Tom Holbrook

First published 2017
by Routledge
2 Park Square, Milton Park, Abingdon, Oxon OX14 4RN

and by Routledge
711 Third Avenue, New York, NY 10017

Routledge is an imprint of the Taylor & Francis Group, an informa business

British Library Cataloguing-in-Publication Data
A catalogue record for this book is available from the British Library

Library of Congress Cataloging-in-Publication Data
Names: Holbrook, Tom, author.Title: Expanding disciplinarity in architectural practice : designing from the room to the city / Tom Holbrook.
Description: New York : Routledge, 2016. | Includes bibliographical references and index.
Identifiers: LCCN 2016008429 | ISBN 9781138694323 (hardback : alk. paper) | ISBN 9781472481733 (pbk. : alk. paper) | ISBN 9781315543550 (ebook)
Subjects: LCSH: Architectural practice. | Space (Architecture) | 5th Studio (Firm)
Classification: LCC NA1995 .H65 2016 | DDC 724/.7--dc23
LC record available at http://lccn.loc.gov/2016008429

ISBN: 978-1-138-69432-3 (hbk)
ISBN: 978-1-4724-8173-3 (pbk)
ISBN: 978-1-315-54355-0 (ebk)

Typeset in Avenir and Baskerville
by Servis Filmsetting Ltd, Stockport, Cheshire

Contents

Acknowledgements

The research leading to these results has received funding from the People Programme (Marie Curie Actions) of the European Union's Seventh Framework Programme FP7/2007-2013/ under REA grant agreement n° 317325.

A generous subsidy from the School of Architecture & Design at RMIT University, Melbourne has enabled the colour printing of this book.

Notes on Contributors

TOM HOLBROOK

Dr Tom Holbrook came to architecture tangentially, co-founding 5th Studio in 1997 as a spatial design agency, working across the fields of architecture, urban design, infrastructure and landscape.

In combination with practice, Tom is Professor of Architecture & Urbanism at RMIT University, exploring comparative urbanism in Barcelona, Melbourne and Ho Chi Minh City. Tom also directs the urban studies programme at the London School of Architecture.

Tom regularly contributes critical writing and opinion to a variety of media; he is a member of a number of design advisory panels, including for London's Olympic legacy and High Speed 2 – the UK's high-speed rail project. Tom is a design advisor to the Greater London Authority.

SHELLEY MCNAMARA

Shelley McNamara graduated from the School of Architecture in UCD in 1974, where she began teaching in 1976. With Yvonne Farrell, she founded Grafton Architects in 1978. Grafton Architects were founder members of Group '91 Architects, winners of the International Competition for the Regeneration of Temple Bar, Dublin.

Grafton Architects are winners of numerous international awards including the *World Building of the Year Award* 2008 for their building for the Universita Luigi Bocconi in Milan. They are currently working on the commission for the construction of the new School of Economics for University Toulouse 1 Capitole and a New University Campus for UTEC Lima in Peru.

KESTER RATTENBURY

Professor Kester Rattenbury is an architectural journalist, critic, author and teacher. Originally trained as an architect, she completed her PhD in 1990 on the representation of architecture in the UK national press – still the only study of its kind. She has worked as an architectural journalist full-time and part-time, in both specialist, national and international press, and UK newspapers. In 1992, Kester began teaching architectural design, first on degree at the University of Greenwich and then from 2000 on Diploma (now MArch) at the University of Westminster, in a long-term teaching collaboration with Sean Griffiths of Fashion Architecture Taste (FAT).

Kester has written and contributed to many books including the *Supercrit* series, *Architects Today*, *The House Book*, the tourist guide to the London Eye, and books on architects including Cedric Price, O'Donnell and Tuomey, and Terry Farrell, as well as writing hundreds of articles, reviews and building studies. Since 2003, she has been working on research for *Another Country: The Architecture of the Novel*, which re-explores some of England's most famous imaginary environments and *The Wessex Project*, which re-explores Thomas Hardy's work from an architectural perspective.

ELLIS WOODMAN

Ellis Woodman is the director of The Architecture Foundation, architecture critic of the *Daily Telegraph* and regular writer for the *Architectural Review*. He studied architecture at the universities of Cambridge and North London, and worked as an architect for seven years before becoming a full-time architecture critic in 2003. He was formerly editor of *Building Design* magazine.

Ellis curated *Home & Away: Five British Architects Build Housing in Europe* at the British Pavilion of the 11th Venice Architecture Biennale, 2008. He is the author of *Modernity & Reinvention: The Architecture of James Gowan* (Black Dog, London, 2008) and essays in the Flemish Architecture Yearbook, and the monograph on *OFFICE KGDVS* (Editiones 2G, Barcelona, 2012).

Foreword

SHEEP AND WOLVES

Architectural books are curious animals. Think of them: the great glossy volumes of collected works; the dense, sparsely illustrated books of ideas and theories; the advertisements, the polemics, the projects. Autonomous self-contained realms for developing unbuilt ideas, and pitching them into the unknown world. Think of *Towards a New Architecture, Garden Cities of Tomorrow*. The Red Books of Humphry Repton. The Greater London Plan. Think of Palladio. Even quite reasonable, modest-looking books like this one might be a wolf in sheep's clothing. It might be trying to change the world.

As one of the examiners on Tom Holbrook's PhD by Practice, I was struck by the way that 5th Studio used books (and other publications), deliberately, to develop ideas, proposals, major – but not always visible – bits of architectural thinking, *without* a client or brief. The models Holbrook mentioned and which stuck in my mind were the Red Books and the Adam Brothers – both of them, in different ways, using books to operate in a world driven by commercial development.

That is maybe even truer now. The machinery driving any kind of major investment is principally (directly or by emulation) large scale economics. Even schools now have to look and work like something from a science park: a big shift in the way the world works within my lifetime. But those books – or speculative projects, exhibitions or whatever – can still help you operate intelligently, as designers, winning that tiny bit of space in which to turn around, and think about, and work out, how things might work differently. And then, to present them, with a certain kind of authority to a client (5th Studio often go looking for clients with their projects) – and which might just help them believe you.

That's an incredibly hard thing to do. In normal practice, the now deeply ingrained requirement for substantial commercial gain has become the DNA of any building project, affecting our *own* imaginations – not just those of the developers. It locks on to our more general architectural assumption (the one Cedric Price so profoundly, so unusually questioned): that the answer is always a building. It has fused with the driving visual aspects of our culture (what something *looks* like floods every bit of our design thinking, sometimes blocking our vision of what it *does*), to form a kind of generic cultural kerb-shot render as the tick-box genetic code needed for any idea to proceed through procurement.

5th Studio's buildings do sometimes fit (more or less) into one of the currently acceptable styles for this render (the Cambridge Commercial style, let's call it). But their thinking, their strategy, their work is always way beyond it. They seem to be profoundly interested in the parts of architecture which Price was interested in: the parts that you can't *see*, exactly, but which absolutely change your world. How easy or hard it is to cross a road to get to the riverside, say. Or how far you might have to go to get to work.

And 5th Studio seem to willingly tackle immense levels of bureaucracy to achieve that invisible, life-changing game. They seem to even relish the effort it takes, say, to get all kinds of public amenity providers to each take down a single fence to allow some normal residents to reach that riverside. Using these tactics (this becomes clearer through the forensic focus of the PhD by Practice), they've instigated complex public realm projects of a type one tends to think impossible today. Maybe their projects are less wolf in sheep's clothing than sheep in wolves' clothing: ways of introducing a gentler animal into the ruthless field of modern development.

Sheep dressed as wolves, in terms of my imperfect analogy, sound awfully vulnerable. But 5th Studio are no sacrificial lambs; they're fighters; they couldn't have done what they have otherwise. Indeed, they've become (like Price before them) used by their peers as ways of illustrating the essential bits of architecture which are in the infrastructure, the human experience or technical capacity rather than in what the building looks like. Reading this book and thinking about their work just helps remind me (the opposite of what so many publications suggest) that there's much more to architecture than meets the eye.

For books do, inter alia, allow you to imagine things that you can't exactly see. And 5th Studio's use of illustration (back to the Adam Brothers and Repton) also runs slightly over the edges of the normal frame. I'm interested in their use of tube posters or mediaeval cityscapes to do things like imagine how a park might be used; to have a stab at representing complex urban life in a masterplan; to illustrate how a bridge over a canal might change people's use of an area. To just edge our visual kerb-shot render focus into the bit that isn't always visible. Into how things work, how we can use and, hopefully, enjoy them. The things that aren't always visible. The things that renders often lie about. The things that really do change our world.

Kester Rattenbury

Preface

There is a natural satisfaction in solving problems – the precise reconciliation of an issue with a solution – nonetheless, the popular description of architecture as a 'problem solving activity' emasculates architecture's real disciplinary power: the ability to engage with complexity.

I believe that our collective patience with complexity, rather than the instinct towards its immediate correction, is necessary in an evermore multivalent world. A warming climate and rapid urbanisation present challenges that demand quite different responses from the entropic slide towards professional specialism.

Through the approaches to design illustrated in this book, I espouse the unfashionable idea of generalism in support of this richer role: of the architect as synthesist as opposed to specialist, able to observe and interpret existing situations, and to act as the impresario for what might happen next.

This book has evolved out of the research catalogue prepared as part of my doctoral submission for the invitational practice PhD program at RMIT University. The catalogue was titled *Between Furniture & Infrastructure: Expanding Disciplinarity*. The PhD began in the spring of 2011 and concluded with a public examination in Ghent, Belgium, in the spring of 2014. RMIT's practice-based PhD progresses through regular Practice Research Symposia, where candidates publicly present their ongoing research to a panel and their peers. These symposia are regularly referenced in the text.

The Research Catalogue, together with a final exhibition that accompanies the defence of the research, completes RMIT's established research in practice programme. In authoring the catalogue, I had not set out to argue for a generalist position, but rather, through the assembly of key projects, uncover points of reciprocity in the work I have been involved in over a decade and a half of practice.

In identifying the work of others – the community of practice[1] within which we locate our work – it has become clear that the discipline has surrendered much ground. While architectural discourse increasingly focusses on completed buildings within the context of the prosperous western city, many other formerly powerful themes are sublimated. The currency of spatial planning is probably at its lowest ebb for several generations in the UK, while landscape and infrastructure – formerly such strong design traditions – are at best marginal in cultural discourse. The design of infrastructure has become particularly subservient to the low-friction aesthetics of engineering, often at the expense of social integration, enriching urbanity or spatial delight.

The trajectory this book takes through the practice's work is filtered through this particular lens, leaving many alternative paths untrodden. The projects that I have selected from 5th Studio's archive tend to be those that involve themselves in some way with these lost territories, each attempting to make some reconciliation between spatial thinking at a number of scales: to create a bridge between the strategic and something physical, made and experienced within that broader context. This bridge is referred to in the title of this book.

In creating this book, I hold two great debts of gratitude: first, for the opportunity to reflect on 15 years of practice with 5th Studio, and second, to contextualise my own relationship to the discipline as a whole. In terms of the latter, despite feeling something of an interloper working on the margins of the field, I have come to appreciate just how unique and valuable is the body of knowledge it produces.

To the first part, I must here acknowledge 5th Studio as the workshop that has allowed my reflections, with a great debt to co-founder Oliver Smith and other members of the practice who have created such inspiration. The work presented here results from a rich collaboration of many hands to which I feel privileged to have been a part.

To the second part, architecture has never been an explicit choice for me but rather has been a good approximation of a discipline that matches many of my interests. My first jobs were working backstage in the theatre and on film sets, where the imperative of creating a situation with economy of effort left a mark. My transition from stage carpenter to architect was blessed with serendipity and guided by mentors along the way, to whom I owe enduring gratitude: Fred Scott, Peter Carl and Dalibor Vesely figure throughout this text in that role. The PhD program brought another guide: Leon Van Schaik, whose conception of what research in architecture can mean, and valorisation of the unique knowledge produced by the discipline, helped confirm to me that I am indeed an architect. I am very grateful for his guidance on that journey, leading directly to this book. Melanie Dodd was instrumental in opening the path to the PhD in the first place, and is a constant inspiration. Richard Blythe, Dean of Architecture & Design at RMIT in Melbourne, has provided generous encouragement, both through my PhD and afterwards through my role as professor. The support and editorial input of Melissa Horn, my wife, has been pivotal – she has helped me find my voice.

Finally, I must thank the examiners of my PhD – Professors Michael McGarry, Kester Rattenbury and Murray Fraser, for their wisdom and generosity, and for their encouragement to publish the research catalogue. Kester Rattenbury has been kind enough to write the Foreword. I have resisted the temptation to revise or update the projects presented here as case studies; clearly they are products of their time, many of which were caught by the research mid-trajectory before perhaps evolving into something quite different to the way they are described here. My decision tries to acknowledge that this book is a snapshot and those developments will be captured in other books in the future.

Tom Holbrook,
Cambridge

NOTE

1 See Leon van Schaik's discussion of this term in *Mastering Architecture*, Wiley, Chichester, UK, 2005.

PRESENCES

In the spring of 2001, 5th Studio mounted an exhibition entitled *Presences* at the Architecture Foundation's old home in the basement of Alison and Peter Smithson's Economist Building, London. The exhibition was a collaboration with the printmaker and sculptor Paul Coldwell.

The Architecture Foundation show was the first opportunity to assemble the work completed in our first four years of operation as a coherent œuvre. Some twelve years on, the themes set out for that exhibition seem remarkably consistent with strands drawn out of the practice's work through the research.

The catalogue accompanying the show included essays by the exhibitors, plus invited contributions from my mentors and former tutors, Peter Carl and Fred Scott. The essays explored the theme of 'Presences': architecture understood as an interventional activity, in dialogue both with the physical conditions of the particular, as well as the cultural milieu with which the work engages.

Two key projects framed that first public presentation of the young practice's work: Eden Street, and Fen Ditton. These projects are documented later in this volume, together with the design of the exhibition installation for *Presences*, itself an adjustment of the gallery space. Both projects involved the establishment of a rich infrastructure; on the one hand, an intervention in a semi-derelict house, and on the other, the plan for an urban extension to the city of Cambridge. This combination of design from the scale of 'transformatory furniture' through to an engagement with the very large scale of landscape and strategy in Cambridgeshire's fenlands already establishes a trajectory critical to 5th Studio's work.

The catalogue box from *Presences: The Common Place in Architecture and Art* (London, 2001, Architecture Foundation). Includes numbered prints and articles: 'The commonplace', Tom Holbrook; 'From private to public and back again', Paul Coldwell; 'Notes on new and old work', Fred Scott; 'Impresences of the world – culture as referential system', Peter Carl.

The design model of the installation, where visitors to the gallery could adjust a series of cabinets in the space.

Images from the installation for *Presences*, Architecture Foundation, Bury Street, London, 2001.

EDEN STREET

The Eden Street project was typical of that time – our early clients were, like us, surviving a recession and buying their first houses with barely sufficient funds. Projects of this period often involved a staged strategy for improvement in affordable chunks, a sequential discipline which became a key part of the practice's culture.

The project was described thus in the *Architects' Journal*:

> Working to a tight budget, the architect's first task was to stabilise the building. Long-term plans allow for an extra bedroom and a new bathroom. For the present, these have been preceded by a strategic staircase which weaves in and out of the structure like an optical puzzle by M.C. Escher. The architect describes the concept behind the staircase as 'a distillation: reduced to its basic elements of tread and riser; like the smoke-stair Mary Poppins climbs in the eponymous film,' and sees it as 'a disturbance, a ludic contamination of the division between parlour and back room'.[1]

As this passage notes, the stair was developed as a 'contamination' of the previous social divisions of the Victorian house. Set perpendicularly to the former stair (removed, before our involvement with the project, by a disgruntled builder, who then disappeared), which once rose from the lower level of the back room to negotiate three awkward split-levels towards the front of the house, the new stair begins in the front room and replaces much of the central division of the house. An intermediate landing formed in glass gives into a room which projects through the party wall into the next-door property as a flying freehold, and the future bathroom at the back of the house. A further flight rises to the front bedroom, its stepped underside reappearing in the front room below like a puzzle.

Eden Street was the first of a series of projects which, in a very direct way, explored a contemporary intervention in a house as a violent upheaval,

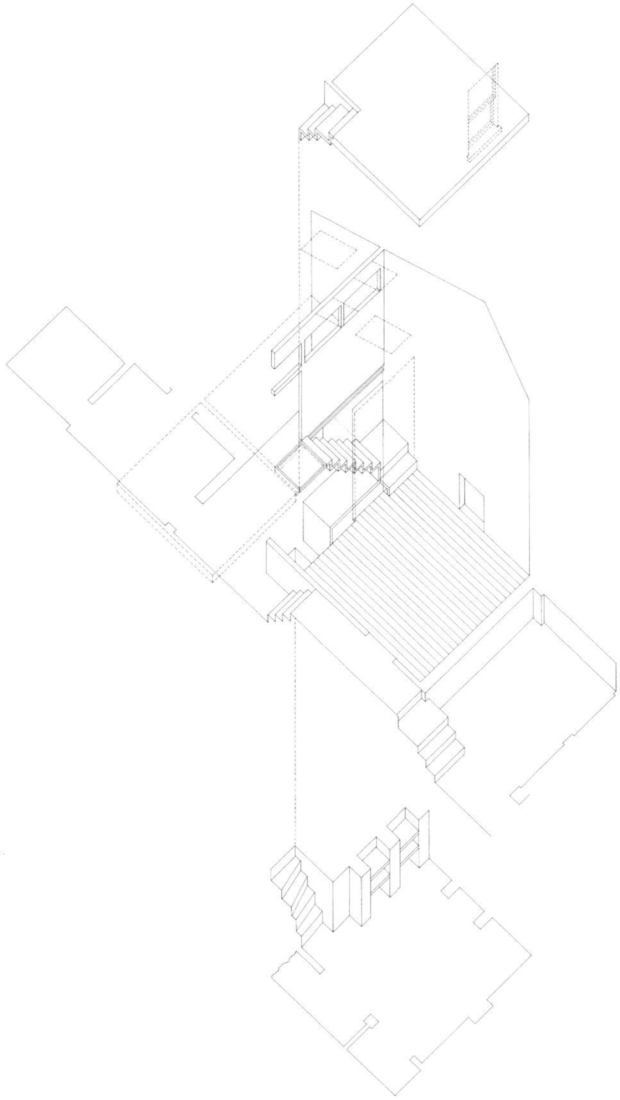

Exploded axonometric.

Living room. Photographs by David Grandorge.

introducing into the original nineteenth-century fabric quite new social and spatial relationships. In a reaction to what we regarded as clichés of modernism – the fetishisation of detail, the boutique introduction of expensive materials – this group of 'ruin' projects also bore a debt to both the theoretical work of Dalibor Vesely and Peter Carl, as well as the author George Perec's consideration of everyday elements like the staircase as a form of social infrastructure.[2] The project directly references Marcel Duchamp's savage use of wit, and his notion of 'delay': a fascination with the incomplete, the inclusion of a 'particle of ambiguity'.[3]

These early projects were quite often developed on site, combining an in-depth understanding of the host structure (historical research, measuring the physical fabric for a drawn survey, construction of study models), with an improvisatory, contingent response. In the essay written for *Presences*,[4] I describe the irony of faking up a series of detail drawings 'after the fact' to suit the publication routines of a German architectural magazine.[5]

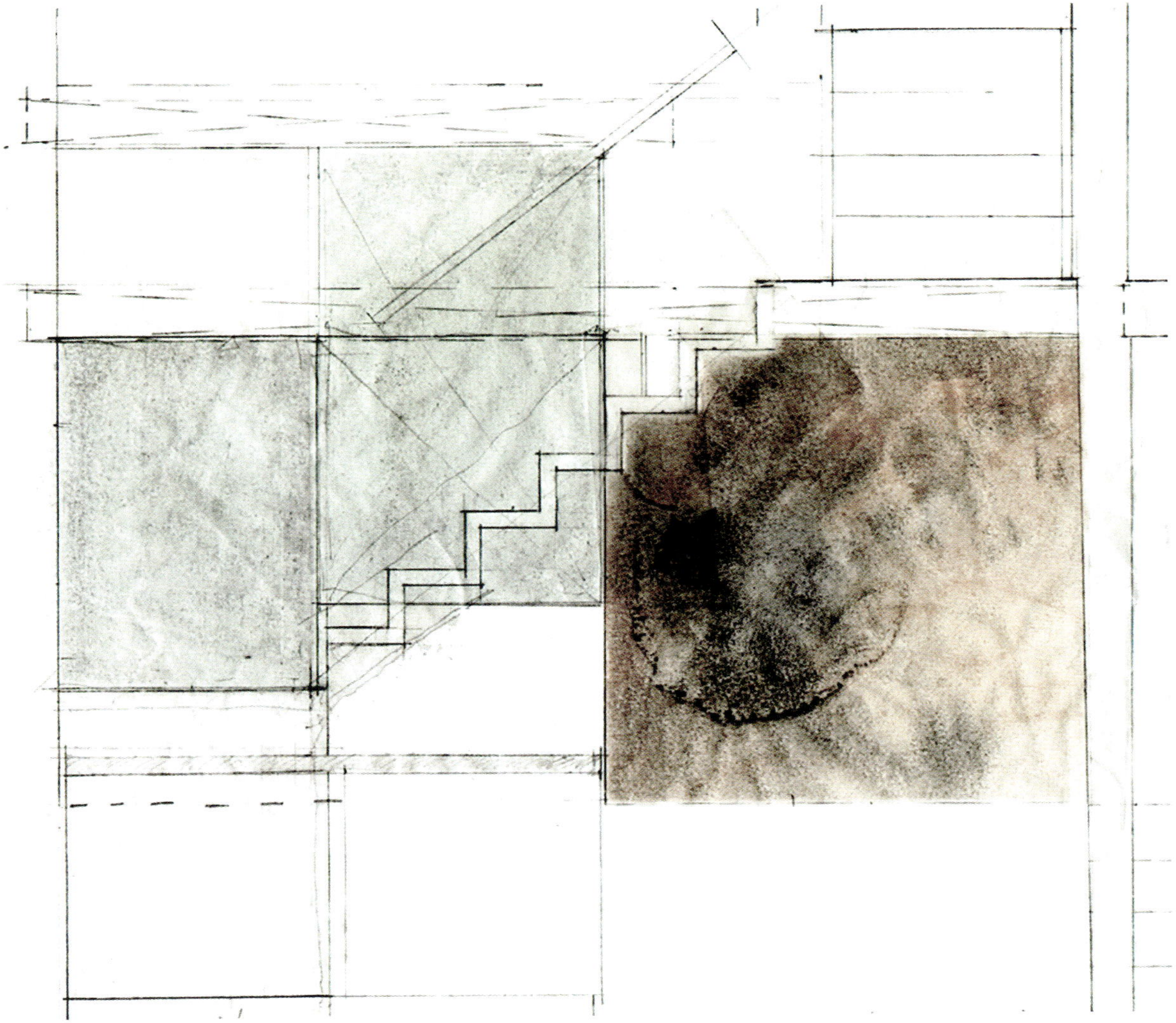

Eden Street, detail drawing overlay.

At Eden Street, the desire to condense a staircase to its essential elements required a combination of structural ingenuity and empirical testing with a joiner with whom we worked regularly. The introduction of structural glass is another motif which appears in later work, but which here, with a shoestring budget, was working right on the edge of what was possible. After completing the photographic shoot, our photographer, David Grandorge, assured us that what we were engaged in producing was 'hairy-arsed modernism' – a description that delighted us and which stuck for many years.

Eden Street, staircase from the kitchen.
Photograph by David Grandorge.

FEN DITTON

At around the same time as the project in Eden Street, the practice was approached by a national housebuilder to design some 'vernacular' house types for a mixed-use development including 2,300 houses on the greenbelt encircling the north-eastern edge of Cambridge. Knowing that their desire was for the pastiche 'vernacular' so evident on the edge of most English towns, we proposed instead to revisit their masterplan: a curvilinear parody of an organic rural settlement, with kidney-shaped enclaves of semi-detached housing.

The site is the closest that the Fenlands get to the city. Most of the Cambridgeshire Fen is systematically drained marshland at or below sea level, and we identified the relationship between water and land as being an 'authentic' vernacular of fen settlements, and that this could be used as a key means of ordering and giving identity to the new development. Having worked on the project for a few weeks, we presented a radically alternative masterplan to the client and the rest of the design team, fully expecting to be dismissed. The presentation concluded with a long silence, before a general acknowledgement from around the table that the project had been suffering from a lack of credibility, and was re-energised by our re-thinking of the strategy.

The strategy established a development grain across a great agricultural prairie at the back of the Cambridge satellite village of Fen Ditton (*Dittone*: 'the village by the ditch'), working from the remains of Fleam Dyke, an Iron Age defensive earthwork. The site was thus divided into plots, using what remained of a field grain, and the land drainage structure. Each block was bounded by a dyke, which controlled rainwater and 'grey water' drainage, the alignment of which also established cycle routes around the site and into Cambridge itself along the river.

The plots themselves were subdivided by party walls into a variety of house arrangements, from tall family houses to courtyard dwellings with mews annexes. The split-level relationships of the Eden Street house reappear in these 'party wall houses'.

One edge of the settlement is delineated by a water tower and aqueduct which, together with a 'floating park' (a landscape bounded by water), create a sequence of public infrastructures connected to one of the three primary schools. These primary ordering elements of water towers and mysterious moated structures are commonly encountered across East Anglia, from airbases to ancient monuments.

References for this work ranged from Florian Beigel and Philip Christou's 'Brikettfabrik Witznitz', published the previous year,[6] through to landscape-scaled structures such as Atelier 5's Siedlung Halen, Berne, which influenced the densest areas of the new settlement with their built topography.

The ambition was to create a settlement plan, taking the logic of land drainage and plot division as a means to create a sufficiently robust strategy to resist the vagaries of multiple house-builders developing over time. The infrastructure introduced (drainage, reed-bed remediation of grey water, a section of relief road with river crossing, bus network, water supply) is used to create a rooted landscape structure, as strong as that of the old village of Fen Ditton beside the river.

Themes from this early project reappear in current work to establish a strategic plan for the north-eastern edge of Cambridge.

Fen Ditton. Axonommetric – Party Wall House.

Florian Beigel and Philip Christou with Architecture Research Unit, 'An architectural landscape of activity fields', Regeneration Design of the Brikettfabrik Witznitz, Bornia, Germany, 1996. Design drawing of the History Field with partial reuse and rehabilitation of several large disused factory buildings, forming a public courtyard with remains of former building foundations and a new earth ramp.
Florian Beigel & Philip Christou with Architecture Research Unit

Atelier 5's Siedlung Halen, Bern.
Photograph by Croci & du Fresne.
Atelier 5

Masterplan drawing.

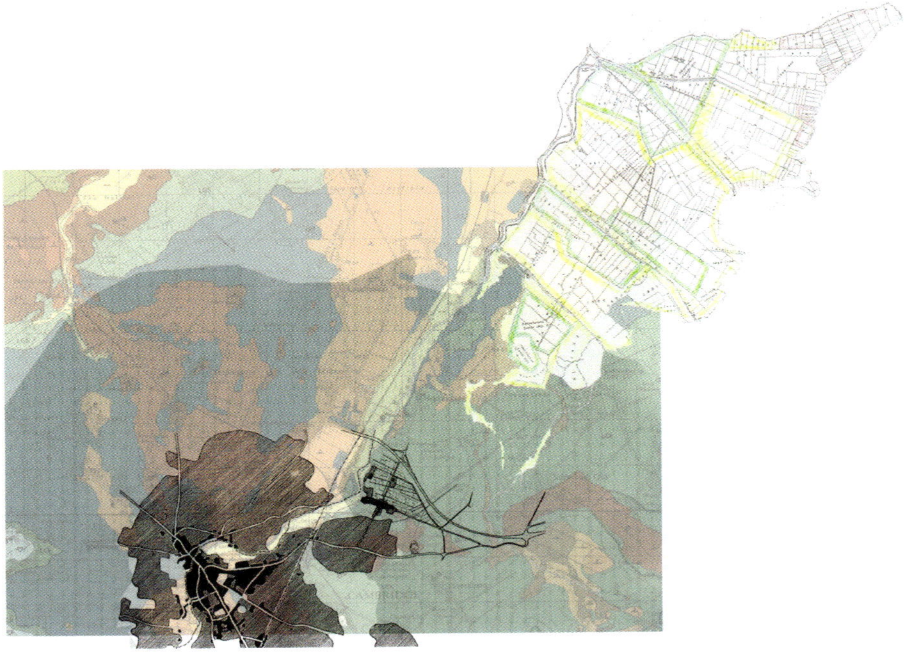

The urban extension set between the historic core of Cambridge and the fenland system to the north-east. The shadow delineates the greenbelt around the city.

View: water tower, reed beds and 'floating park'.

Typical block explored in model.

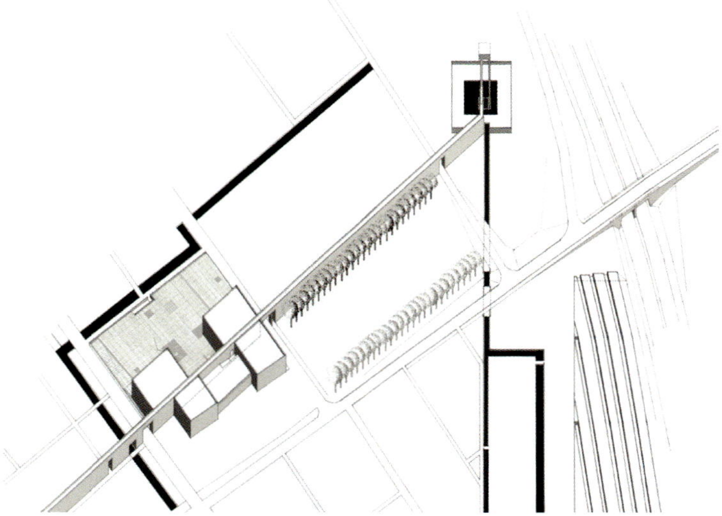

Typical block explored in isometric drawing.

Axonometric of the school, aqueduct, water tower and 'floating park'.

Exploratory view of the primary school set in an orchard with an aqueduct.

NOTES

1 Deborah Singmaster, 'Stabilising Staircase', *Architects' Journal*, 16 December 1999.

2 George Perec, *Species of Spaces*. Translation by John Sturrock, Penguin, London, 1997.

3 Explored in: Tom Holbrook, 'Marcel Duchamp & the Conditions of Experience', *Scroope* No. 5, Cambridge, 1994.

4 Catalogue accompanying *Presences: The Common Place in Architecture and Art*. Architecture Foundation, London, 2001.

5 Treppenhaus in einem Altbau in Cambridge 'Mary Poppins', *Deutscher Bauzeitung*, May 2001.

6 Florian Beigel & Philip Christou, 'Brikettfabrik Witznitz: Specific Indeterminacy – Designing for Uncertainty', *Architectural Research Quarterly*, Winter, No. 2, Vol. 2, 1996. The essay references Paul Klee's landscape drawings, so reminiscent of fen topography.

AN ENTREPRENEURIAL CULTURE

> You've talked about operating as a generalist, about working across scales, an infrastructure designer: entrepreneurial, proactive. . . In referencing the Adams' Adelphi – where they were also developers and builders – you reference a period before the discipline ringfenced itself. You are very much the architect, but you are questioning the boundaries in terms of how you would situate yourself with the disciplines around infrastructure. [1]
>
> Professor David Porter

In this chapter, I hope to demonstrate, through reference to a body of work, that my approach as a practitioner has sought to expand a disciplinary role beyond an autonomous architecture to a more provocative and plural position.

This expanded role seeks to embrace what one might call the political forces influencing a project, through openness to the contingent and adaptive dimensions that shape its progress, including economic and social narratives at both macro and micro scales.

The chapter commences with discussion of an early project, and posits the Adam brothers' Adelphi as an example of a mediatory structure between design, architecture, urbanism and infrastructure. The section concludes with the presentation of two emblematic strands of work for the practice: the Lea River Park, and a cluster of projects that explore the spatial / urban conditions for supporting creativity, most explicitly developed in the Creative Exchange project.

As a young practice in a growing city, the availability of clients with houses needing refitting was not an issue – but the maintenance of large-scale work to accompany it required the development of a propositional culture:

> The directors say that their architecture is both a 'propositional' and a 'prospective' activity that has encouraged the office to invent projects on a larger scale than the small domestic work usually available. . . What is most striking about 5th Studio, apart from its general standard of design confidence and competence, is its entrepreneurial, pro-active stance.[2]

The development of a spatially entrepreneurial outlook was partly driven by the desire to win new work at a larger scale, but also reflected and responded to a frustration with the lack of connection between the commissioning of architecture through particular projects and a comprehension of a wider landscape or strategic endeavour.

Contemporaneous with the project in Eden Street (discussed in the previous chapter) was a deepening interest in a neighbouring city park – Christ's Pieces – and in particular how the park's evident dysfunctionality might be re-thought by addressing various issues in a more holistic way. Characteristically, a broad-ranging approach was adopted, from development propositions, the use of the park as a site for teaching, through to the introduction of a seditious 'foundation myth' for the park. Responses to the local council's consultation process on the future of the park were used as the vehicle to introduce a richer reading of its history: a means to resist the municipal underplaying of its potential.[3] This project was used as the basis of a teaching studio in 2000.[4]

At one end of the park is the city's bus station, cramped onto half the site area it requires and enclosed, at that time, by a half-vacant 1950s shopping arcade called Bradwell's Court. The arcade had become the sole route connecting the two burgeoning retail centres of Cambridge, as established by the city plans of the mid-1960s. From being something of a backwater, this route had become a grim dumbbell, central to many people's experience of the city.

Realising that the potential to address the failings of the bus station lay in a holistic rethinking of this whole urban block and park edge, we invited the city's chief planning officer, the owners of Bradwell's Court, the bursars of the two adjacent colleges and the operator of the bus station to a workshop at which we demonstrated the mutual benefit and potential of a broad restructuring strategy beyond the confines of their individual estates.

This brokering of numerous divergent interests around the potential of a coherent spatial solution was clearly effective at unlocking what seemed insuperable issues – although at the time we were not regarded as sufficiently plausible agents to enact the proposals, some of which were seen as too politically contentious to even entertain. This session prompted the city planners to produce a Development Brief for the area, and the developer, Land Securities, went on to redevelop Bradwell's Court, in connection with the two adjacent colleges, using another architect.[5]

The project developed through frustration with the environments resulting from poor planning, and the strange myopia of Anglo-Saxon attitudes to development. Our perception was that understanding the context in its full complexity, and using that to establish a stronger place via a rich narrative, had the potential to resolve a number of critical problems.

THE ADELPHI AS A RECONCILIATORY MODEL

As a reconciliatory model between infrastructure and architecture, the Adams' Adelphi project has become an important precedent model and reference. It is useful to describe its relevance here in view of the light it throws on current development practice.

Emerging at a time when the profession of architecture had not yet gelled, the Adam brothers' tenacious and multiple roles in the project and in its evolution are particularly broad. What orientates the project is the potential to create a social condenser: a new piece of city which has the capacity to mediate between infrastructure and the urbane.

The four brothers (three architects and a banker) had built in Scotland and elsewhere, but were looking for the opportunity to make a project with impact in London. Robert Adam had been particularly inspired by the ruined palace of Diocletian at Split, encountered and painted by him while on his Grand Tour. A proposition emerged of an antique palace, reinterpreted for the Thames riverbank as a location for London's commerce and emerging bourgeoisie.

As the artery connecting Westminster with the City of London, the Strand is particularly fertile territory. Over its history this location has been a crucible for generating metropolitan ideas: from governance and the rule of law in the Inns of Court and the Temple, through to a notable concentration of new urban typologies and practical ideas on urban improvement.[6]

From the medieval period there had been a series of palaces along the Strand, the powerful of Europe needing representation here to be part of London's political milieu.[7] By the middle of the eighteenth century, these palaces had gone, and the Strand[8] was 'untidy and malodorous'. The Adam brothers took a 99-year lease on a piece of land called Durham Yard on which they laid out a city block with twin aspects – a quay against the Thames, and a series of streets running off the Strand, with four-storey houses, each

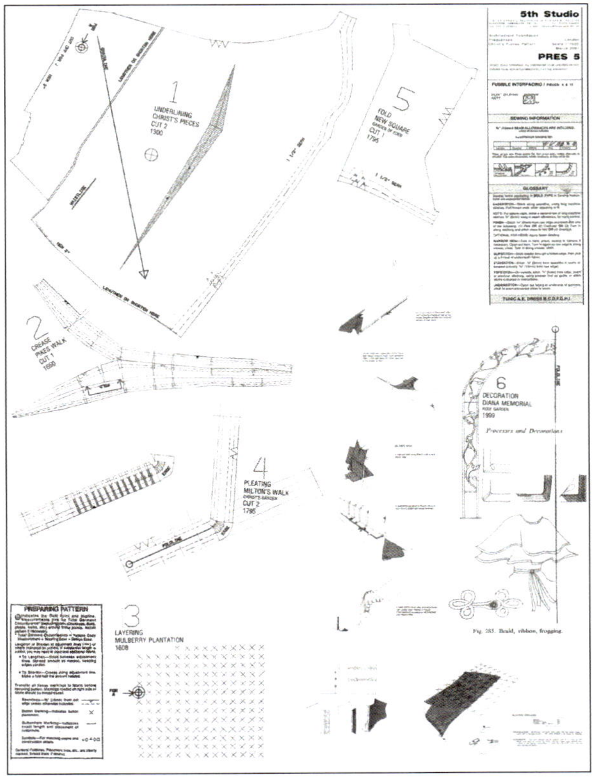

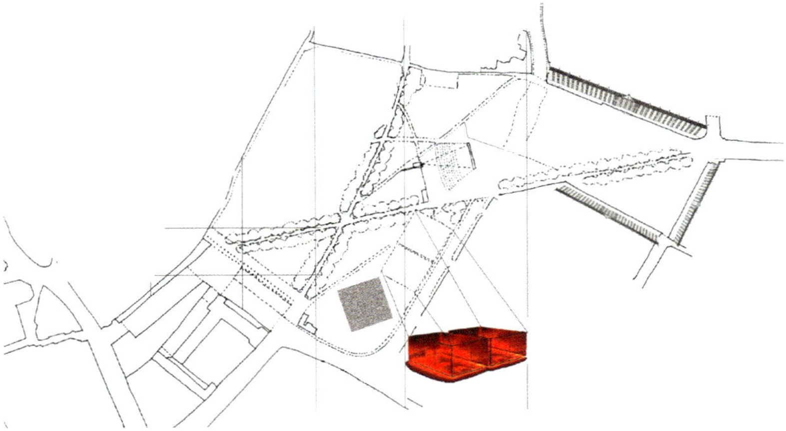

Exploratory collage, Christ's Pieces, 2000.

This 'pattern' for Christ's Pieces interrelated the park's underlying topographical form, superimposing a Cromwellian defensive line from the English civil war, the remnants of a mulberry plantation planted by King James I, a walk dedicated to the regicide poet John Milton and a monument to Princess Diana. The pattern was included as an A1 folded print on trace in the catalogue box for *Presences*, 2001.

Plan, Christ's Pieces.

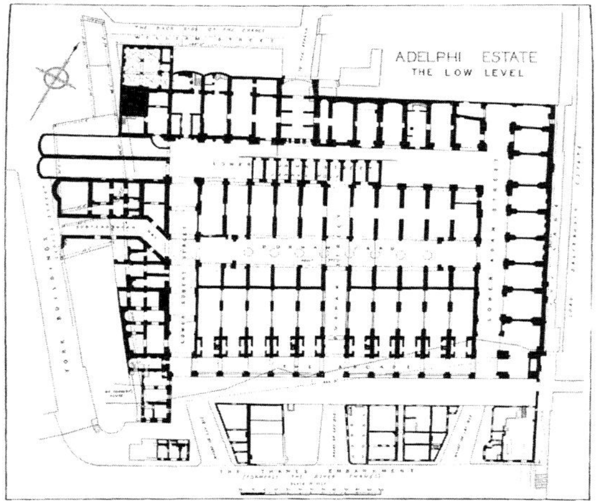

The river front of the Adelphi, from the Adams' *The Works in Architecture*, vol. III, Pl. 1, 1822.

The Adelphi – Low Level Plan.

having two stories of cellars below to house service accommodation. The Thames – then the engine of London's economy in terms of both globalised commerce and transport logistics – was edged with a series of cave-like warehouses, served by internal roads running beneath the plinth of housing.

The houses were finished and decorated by some of the finest artisans in Europe, and they were joined by coffee houses, a tavern, a hotel, accommodation for an emerging professional class and the then-youthful Society of Arts. The Adams' proposition was a very large mixed-use structure that reclaimed the riverbank, using the section like an occupied hillside to build a great deck with the warehouses below and terraced houses above of highly sophisticated refinement. In this way, it took a position between the river and the Strand and turned it into a social structure: the working Thames below and the new artistic upper class in the houses above. This development was the first time the term 'terrace' is used to describe the division of a palatial block into separate houses, perhaps inspired by the formation of what was literally a terrace above the river.

The proposition of the Adelphi depended on the Adam brothers persuading the avant-garde of London to leave the fashionable West End to colonise the working edge of the Thames – then a logistical territory, perhaps equivalent to a major rail route or airport today.

The Adelphi development is fundamentally a speculation. Steen Eiler Rasmussen, with an émigré's perceptiveness, makes this observation:

> This enterprise is very characteristic of England. It shows us a grand speculation with enormous profit in view but also enormous risk. It is quite different to speculation on the continent which are generally mere speculations in a rise of ground value. This is speculation in fictitious values. . . In the case of the Adelphi, the commercial idea is no less grand and full of imagination than is the artistic one. . . it was just as much a finance-fantasia over risk and profit: the financier was the artist and the artist a financier.

This creative speculation is something very English, and it is no less typical that when it turns out a failure, the enterprise is saved by a lottery. . .'[9]

CASE STUDY
THE LEA RIVER PARK

Ongoing work on this project – spanning over many years for a number of different clients and commissioners – connects strategic thinking with highly practical problem solving in one of London's most complex post-industrial landscapes. Our involvement spans strategy, policy-making, public advocacy, programming and curation, landscape and architectural design, project management and realisation.

The project was won through the European Union competition process at the beginning of 2007. It was immediately apparent that, despite the pre-crash optimism of the time, and a substantial budget allocation for the park, the proposition was inherently different to the concept then emerging for the 2012 London Olympic Park.[10]

The Olympic Park was already established as a thoroughgoing managerial problem. It had in place its encircling blue fence, a huge budget and special planning and land assembly powers.[11] It also had a highly defined programme of international-standard sporting topographies, and a date by which it needed to be complete. In contrast, the territory for which we had been commissioned had few of these certainties.

The Lea Valley had been identified as a potential landscape resource for London in the 1944 *London Plan*, drawn up by, among others, the planner Patrick Abercrombie: 'Every piece of open land should be welded into a great regional reservation, no open land, whatever its present use, should be built on.'[12] Some seventy years after the publication of the plan, this territory is still not possible to navigate in a continuous way. Post-games, the Olympic Park allows access to a further section of the valley. Our project – which we eventually named the Lea River Park – completes the final two-and-a-half miles of valley as the last section of the 26-mile-long Regional Park, which stretches from the outer edge of London's encircling Green Belt to the River Thames.

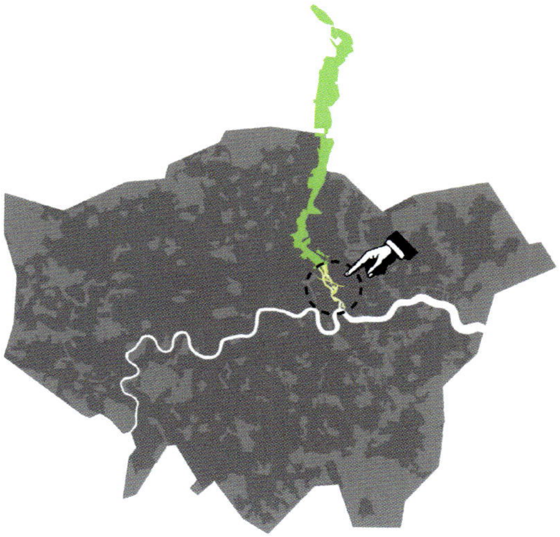

Lea River park locator.

Assembled over a few months in late 2006, the original bid panels for the project intuitively frame a set of propositions for the creation of the park which still pertain with remarkable consistency, namely:

- The idea of the valley as a cornucopia: that the park would find its animation in the role that the valley has traditionally played in provisioning London.
- That the emerging design would work with the valley as found, through 'reactivating latent and existing topography', and that 'through the interplay and synthesis of multiple concerns, a vital public ground will emerge'.

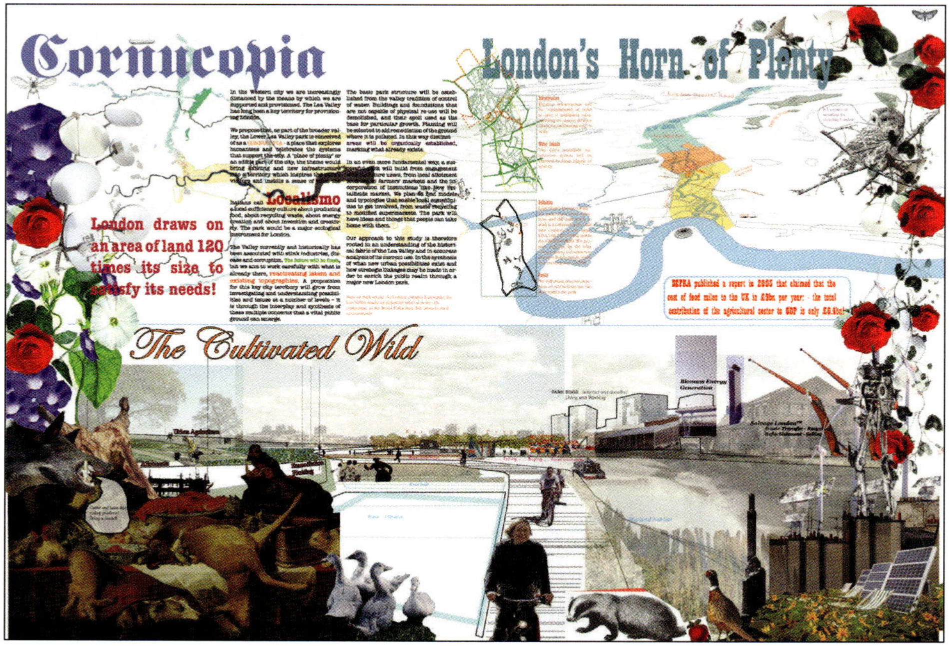

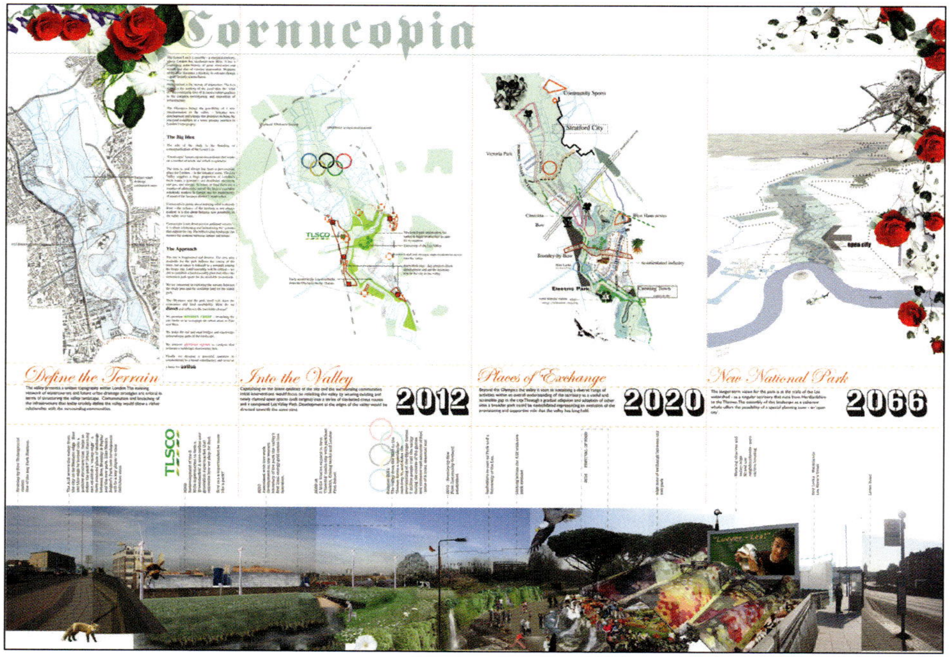

These two panels (originally four A3 format boards per image) each formed a stage of the Expression of Interest for the park. Panel 1. Stage 1, January 2007 – Cornucopia.

Panel 2. Stage 2, February 2007 – a park established over time.

- That the park will be established over time, with the inherent duration of organic landscape development, and in dialogue with change on the valley edges.
- That the park would be effectively established through an interplay between top-down activation, enabling bottom-up inhabitation.

A TRANSFORMATIONAL LANDSCAPE

From the *London Plan* onwards, the idea of a continuous parkland in the Lea Valley has been embodied in planning documents, but the physical reality on the ground is highly problematic. The Lea Valley is border country, with the river acting as a riparian administrative boundary along its length. Resulting political division has been reinforced by informal backland uses, many of which have contaminated both the ground and the river, and discouraged access to the valley.

The valley has been modified over several millennia of occupation: first by marshland reclamation and the introduction of milling by the Abbey at Stratford, then as an instrumental topography, occupied and shaped by city-servicing infrastructures over two millennia. These infrastructures have introduced physical fragmentation – a landscape of fenced, discontinuous monofunctional compounds creating docks, reservoirs, gasworks, sewage pumping facilities, electrical sub-stations and railheads. Almost all of the land identified for the new park is currently occupied by this metropolitan-scaled infrastructure.

This is where London is expected to grow: an additional 40,000 new dwellings are anticipated in the current London Plan, which, together with the Olympic Park, will completely change the valley context. Existing deficiencies in public space and connectivity in this part of east London will become even more acute, so a new park – fully integrated into the urban fabric that surrounds it – is a necessity. As with the development of other great parks in London, the strategy established for the Lea River Park does not solely address issues of landscape, but also ones of urbanism: the park must guide and set the context for new development in the valley.

The challenge of the Lea River Park is the transformation of this backland quality to create a new foreground for London, turning a working landscape into a new public space.

WORKING WITH WHAT EXISTS

In approaching the problem of a transformational strategy realised over time, we were conscious that masterplans often suffer from acting as an end in themselves, being either too prescriptive or too vague, and becoming rapidly out of date and irrelevant. Recognising that the Lea River Park is a complex project that will take many years to come together, we have established a way of describing the park which is hopefully more resilient and that has the ability to absorb change, failure of parts, and inevitable future shifts in focus or funding.

The Lea Valley is a made landscape, which plays an intimate role in provisioning the city around it. Naturalistic landscape scenography is not appropriate here, but rather park space is created from adopting and 'contaminating' elements of infrastructure and monocultural land uses which have had free reign in the valley, forcing them to culture richer, more urbane roles. Elements such as railway tunnels, by-pass structures and gasholders are co-opted into making places for a day out in the valley.

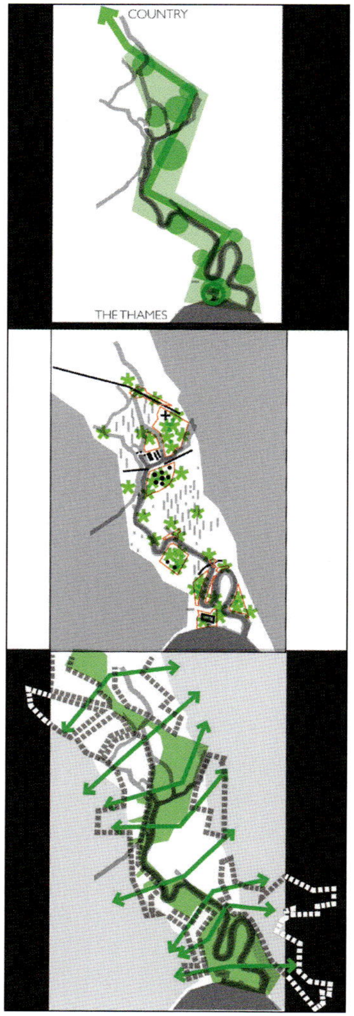

The principle of extending the Lea Valley Regional Park to the Thames; establishing critical cross-valley connections to support growth, and to develop a coherent set of landscapes; activating locations within the valley as a new public foreground.

The Lea meets the Thames.

An aerial view illustrates a highly particular topography where it is clear that normal urban rules do not apply.

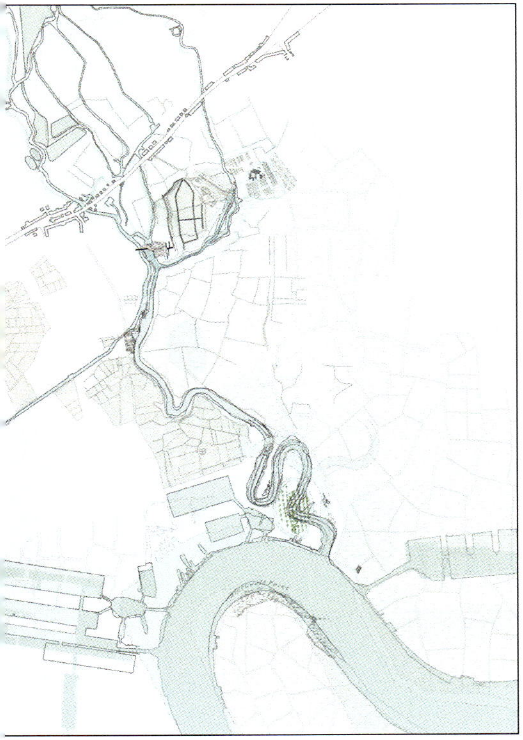

A Productive Landscape

From the early twelfth century, Stratford Langthorne Abbey began to reclaim marshland. The Abbey was joined by mills, orchards and market gardens along the fertile river valley.

An Instrumental Landscape

From the eighteenth century onwards, the Lea Valley was a key site of London's economic development. The present landscape is shaped by technical processes and infrastructure. Gasworks, power and sewage infrastructure, reservoirs, major highways and rail lines, wharves, docks and tunnels establish a purposeful topography of problem solving technical enclaves, each one fenced and autonomous.

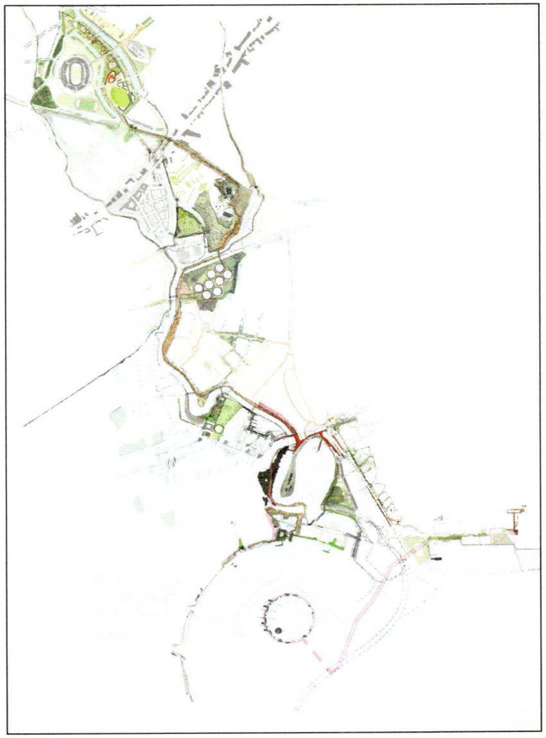

A Public Landscape

Two millennia of land-use have created a remarkable valley, but also a landscape which is inaccessible, hard to navigate, monofunctional and certainly not public. The Lea River Park will transform this working landscape into a new public foreground for London, animated by the traditions of provisioning the city.

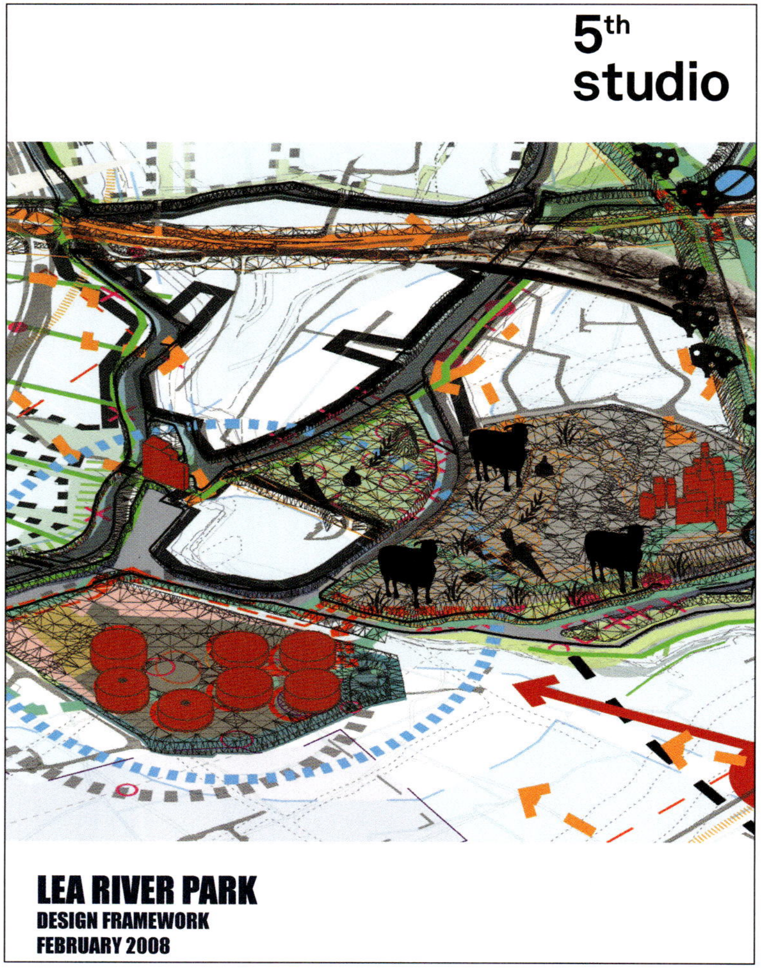

The cover of the Design Framework document, February 2008, establishing the overall strategy.

The park centres on the River Lea, the meanders of which link all its key spaces. Since London's establishment, the valley has been a provisioning ground for the city. The Lea River Park is conceived of as a cornucopia – a place that explores, humanises and celebrates the systems that support the city.

Early pieces of infrastructure are regarded as catalysts for converting what is currently land used for gas storage, sewage pumping and transport infrastructure into diverse park spaces of the Lea River Park: turning what is an industrial backwater into the foreground of a new public space which people can start to access and use.

Because of the physical fragmentation of the valley, and its occupation by enfenced technical monocultures, this is a territory with no natural constituency. Many local residents along the margins are surprised to find that they live in a river valley. With few champions, the challenge for the project is the establishment of a strong support base to ensure political momentum can be maintained.

The original client – the London Thames Gateway Development Corporation – was inclined towards a top-down managerial operation, but was less savvy when it came to developing relationships on the ground. Yet it is precisely this soft infrastructure which can be nimbler and create an impact more quickly. The resilience of the project has depended on adapting our approach from purely top-down regeneration and strategy to one of being highly responsive and able to channel available amounts of funding to solve localised practical problems.

SHIFTING ROLE

Since 5th Studio's original appointment, our role on the Lea River Park has evolved, with dramatic shifts in the context for the project. From the development boom in which we were commissioned, the financial crash has altered government funding of public projects, and the speed of development on the valley fringes. Political administrations have changed at both the national and city level, and with that has come significant shifts in policy and ideology, and rapid changes in the institutions that were acting as clients or key stakeholders.

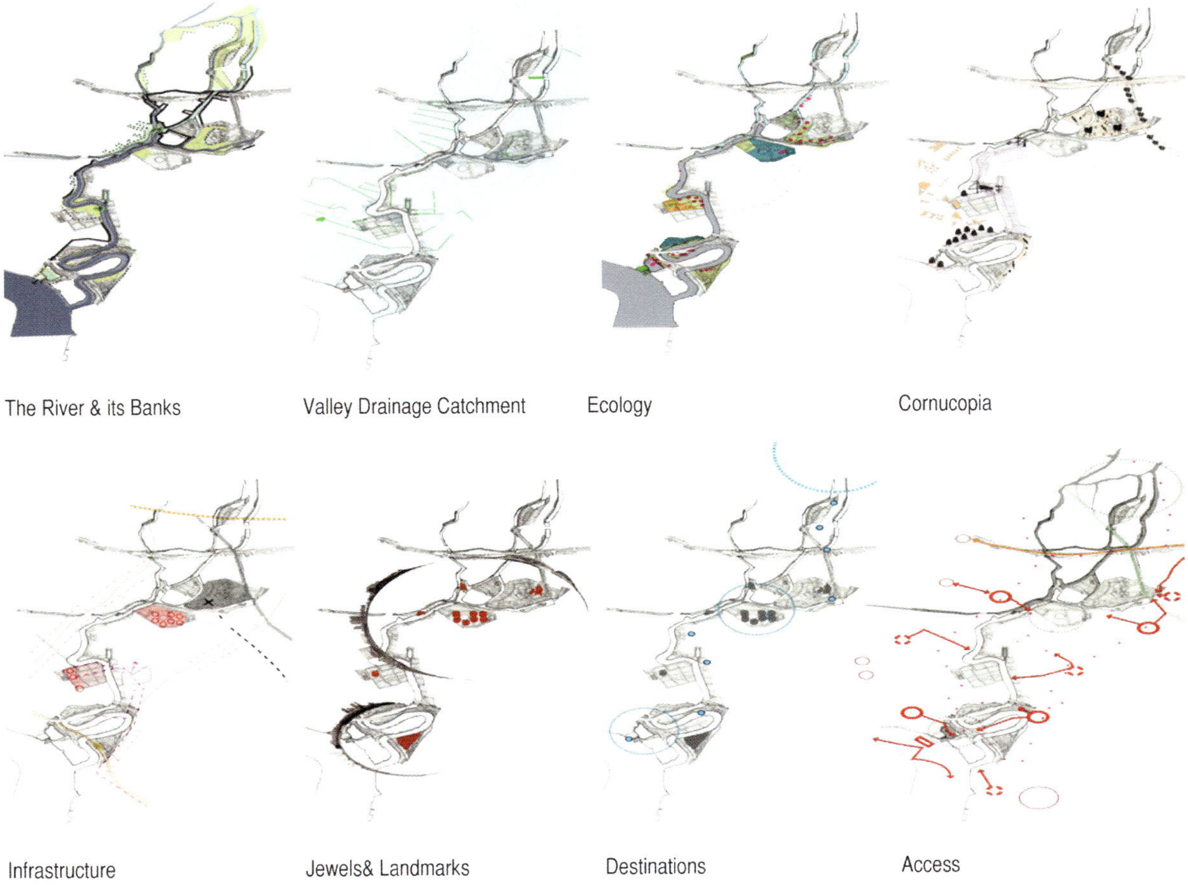

An oblique aerial view up the Lea Valley from the confluence with the River Thames illustrates the dominance of infrastructure, released from more urban engagement either side of the valley.

The image of a siege-tower is a useful analogy for how the project intends to 'contaminate'. The image is from Viollet-Le-Duc's *Dictionnaire raisonné de l'architecture française du XI*^e^ *au XVI*^e^ *siècle*, 1856.

A series of diagrams showing the co-present conditions of the river valley.

Against this background has been the waxing and waning of the political regard for spatial planning, from the powerful influence of planning bodies like Design for London and the Olympic project to the current administration's antipathy to planning towards laissez-faire policies.[13]

This extraordinary flux has been further exacerbated by work in a territory which, by definition, has no constituency: indeed, it is a landscape that has repelled colonisation. At times we have found ourselves sole advocates of the project. Perversely, procurement rules governing public financing have meant that with each new stage of the project we have had to bid in an open market situation with the continuity of our involvement threatened, or at least our legitimacy as continuing authors of the project denied.

The passage of the project has been complicated through a problematic relationship with the landscape architects we had invited in as partners. For the original bid, we invited the landscape practice Field Operations to collaborate with us. They pulled out mid–bid, and needing a plausible alternative, we approached German landscapists Latz und Partners, whose Landschaftspark in Duisburg we had referenced as an exemplar of the transformation of an industrial landscape to parkland. Initially involved as a 'critical friend' for the development of the Design Framework, the relationship was renewed for the subsequent bid to realise the first phase of projects, and at this point the client asked that the lead role be taken by a landscape architect with delivery experience of parkland.

What transpired was that the London-based team at Latz und Partners was neither adept at strategy nor nimble with practical detail – the twin skills we had developed to address the poles of this demanding project. At the same time, the complex and divergent client group became increasingly distracted by the approaching Olympic Games, the realities of budget cuts and existential threats to their organisations. These twin negatives eventually drove the project into a stall.

The original client – the London Thames Gateway Development Corporation – confident that they were dealing with a fully-funded capital project, neglected the creation of 'soft infrastructure': the construction of a constituency to evangelise and protect the project. When that client was closed by Government in its proclaimed 'Bonfire of the Quangos', the project reverted to City Hall, where it languished, its funding returned to Mayoral coffers. Without a commission, from Spring 2012 until the following year, we campaigned to keep the project alive, using press and social media and through canvassing politicians. A meeting with Daniel Moylan, a maverick politician, briefly the chair of the London Legacy Development Corporation, convinced him that they should adopt the project, despite it being largely out of their area. Subsequently the riparian boroughs of Newham and Tower Hamlets have become engaged as active clients, realising that the provision of housing on these borough fringes was dependent on the park's connective infrastructure and open space. Since that point, the project has been gradually rebuilt to its current, highly responsive state.

SPATIAL INTELLIGENCE

The images and text that formed the original proposition for the project bid embodied a series of intuitive insights on the terms in which this particular landscape might be transformed into a new park for London. Over the course of the project's development, a number of different sorts of knowledge have been necessary to develop and bring to bear on the project, together with the evolution of variety of means to structure, represent and communicate our design thinking.

In his book *Spatial Intelligence*,[14] Leon van Schaik argues for the importance of reintegrating disciplinary knowledge with the conscious use of spatial intelligence in the built environment. Over the course of the research that has led to this book, I have become aware at how multiple our role has been, in particular on the Lea River Park project, and yet how located it has been to the particular conditions of the valley. The breadth of this role necessarily combines, to adopt van Schaik's triad, 'acute observation, respect and wit'.[15]

At the largest scale, the project rests on the establishment of a clear strategy: the construction

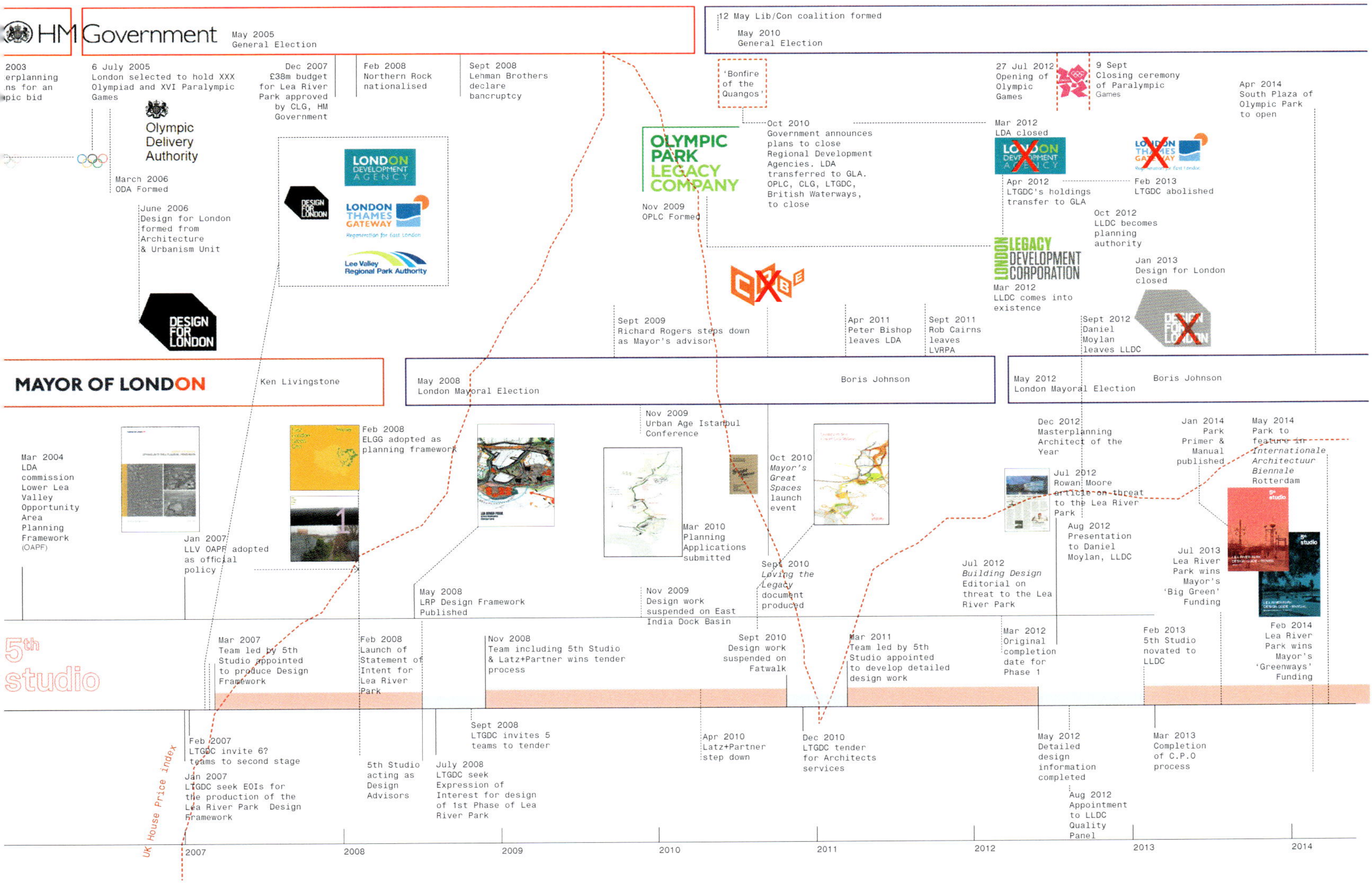

Mapping of critical events across the lifespan of the Lea River Park project. The upper band illustrates institutional change and national events, the central band records key publications, and the lower band maps the design programme, with a red bar indicating a formal commission for the practice.

The cover of a publication produced by the practice in Autumn 2010 in an interregnum in our appointment, to promote and generate the next set of commissions flowing out of transformation of the lower Lea Valley, post-Olympics.

of a narrative with sufficient depth to establish an overarching approach. The strategy – which is constantly re-stated – sets the ambition for the project and how that is enacted over time. It interrelates how the various elements contribute to a coherence 'greater than the sum of its parts'. Because this strategy is not tied to a totalising formal idea, it is highly adaptive and can be realised in many stages.

The project is rooted, and continues to be enriched by, an intuitive, tacit understanding of the task of creating a public landscape in the Lea Valley. This tacit knowledge operates alongside the development of a comprehensive knowledge about a particular place, created by various forms of research over time. This patient accumulation of knowledge towards what we might call a 'connoisseurship of place' encompasses a wide spectrum: ground conditions, land ownerships, thwarted plans, desired change, latent development, technical constraints, practical dilemmas and un-grasped opportunity.

A particularly rich strand of research has been the revealing of a complex, layered flora. This flora comprises the highly localised colonisers of derelict or post-industrial land (London Pride; *Saxifraga urbium*), the exotica that was first introduced through escapees from dock cargoes and ballast, plants established in allotments and gardens in the area by a long-established immigrant population (Capsicum) and self-seeded flora flowing into the river from the sewage outfall at Abbey Mills (fig trees). The valley is a site critical in the development of an international exchange in plants, from John Tradescant's first plant-collecting voyages, to the East India Company's trading of Indian opium in exchange for Chinese tea out of Blackwall. Each of these strands co-exist, presenting a plurality of possible landscape narratives

Frans Snyders (1579–1657), *Pantry Scene with Servant*. Oil on canvas, 135 x 201cm. Alte Pinakothek, Munich. An image of Cornucopia.

which fit very well into the intuitive sense that the valley has a complexity which intimately mirrors London's own development in microcosm.

Somehow we knew at the outset that this sort of depth (presented here in terms of various dimensions of flora, but these narratives are multiple) existed in a latent sense in the valley for us to discover. The philosopher Michael Polanyi identified this tacit intelligence in, for example, the feat of medical diagnosis, or in the trajectory of scientific discovery:

> We must conclude that the paradigmatic case of scientific knowledge, in which all faculties that are necessary for finding and holding scientific knowledge are fully developed, is the knowledge of approaching discovery.
>
> To hold such knowledge is an act deeply committed to the conviction that there is something there to be discovered. It is personal, in the sense of involving the personality of him who holds it, and also in the sense of being, as a rule, solitary; but there is no trace in it of self-indulgence. The discoverer is filled with a compelling sense of responsibility for the pursuit of a hidden truth, which demands his services for revealing it. His act of knowing exercises a personal judgement in relating evidence to an external reality, an aspect of which he is seeking to apprehend.[16]

This close, intuitive understanding of the territory extends into an encyclopaedic familiarity with practical conditions – for example, the sectional challenges of connecting one piece of land to another. Here, highly practical knowledge has

The presence of fenced-off infrastructure enables a wild co-existent culture of colonising plants, which the writer Richard Mabey has called the 'unofficial countryside'.

allowed us to identify effective approaches or to be adaptive, knowing where things are too difficult to achieve the desired results, or where effort or funding might be applied to greatest effect.

The bridge design at Poplar Reach is a good example of this synthetic knowledge, where technical requirements and constraints are absorbed into the aesthetics of the approach. The form of the bridge developed from the requirement that the structure needed to be highly responsive to a number of site conditions, including the presence of high-voltage underground cables, the potential presence of unexploded ordnance from wartime bombing, complex land ownership and boundary issues, the operational requirements of the navigation, the avoidance of complications with costly river wall structures and flood risk considerations. All these technical demands are consolidated into a structure with an appropriate and contingent character, which also references the pragmatic traditions of bridge-making in the Lea Valley: part of close observation of ubiquitous bridge structures carrying utilities across the Lea Valley, but clearly a step away: not a pure structure from engineering, but something more public, more generous.

Furthermore, the bridge structure has physiognomic connection with a number of other park structures along the valley which are part of a

The bridge in the foreground, in a view looking south towards the Thames.

The bridge uses an offset Warren truss to minimise mass, allowing passage within the structural depth with an air draught set by navigational requirements.

On the bridge, with views on either side of very different river reaches.

recognisable family of interventions. The design of this early family of public infrastructure is discussed in more detail as a case study in the next chapter.

PROGRAMMING THE PARK

In terms of representation, the use of the perspective collage allows the testing and communication of proposals for particular sections of the park, through their form underlining the transformative character of tuning an existing landscape towards a particular prospective role. These collages have been used, for example, to explore appropriate introduction of programme and to help negotiate and establish a brief, and – at times – even a client.

Diagrams and cartography of various sorts have been critical as a means to abstract a complex topography to allow the exploration of particular aspects at any one time. The narrative strip has emerged as an effective way to combine a close-edited narrative with precedents and various images as a condensed way of communicating a proposition. We have used this representational form to attempt to orientate and agree a hierarchy across multi-headed commissioners, each with different agendas and priorities. Narrative drawings are also used to articulate and propose a balance between contradictory demands on particular places: for example, spatial conflicts between ecological value and cultural importance.

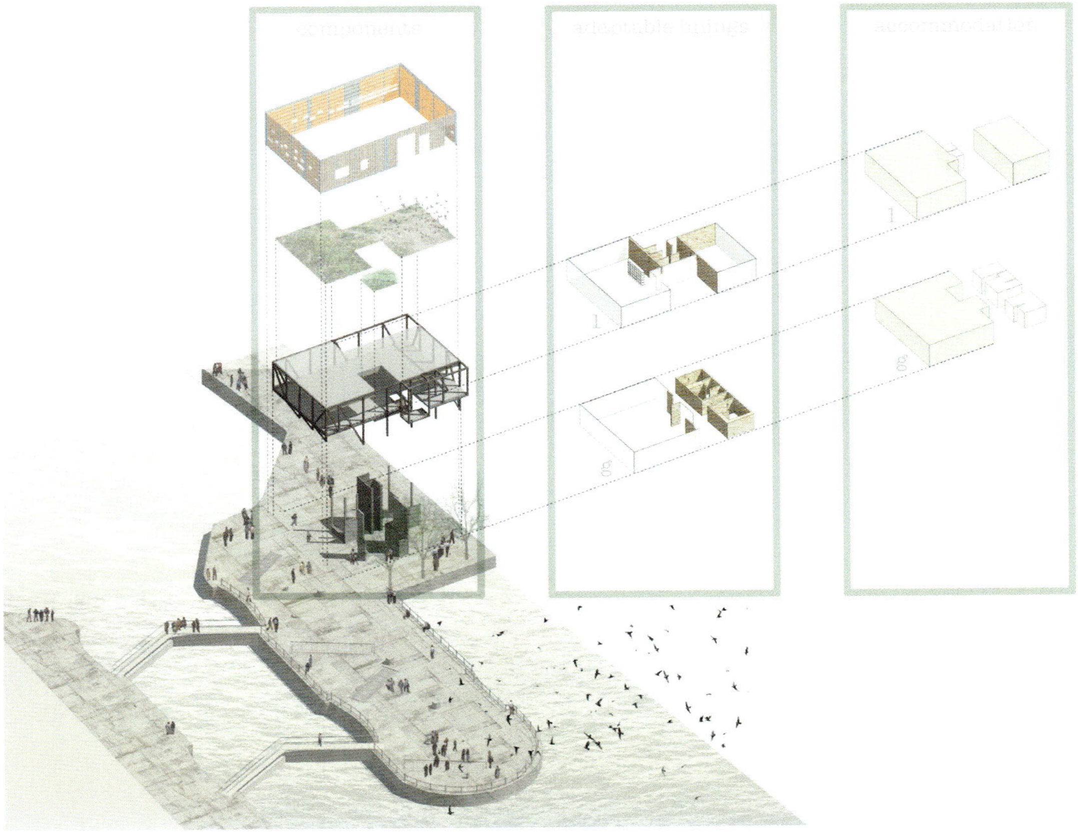

View of a visitors' centre for East India Dock Basin.

The components of the visitors' centre exploded to propose use and mix of accommodation to the client group.

"The vision for East India Dock Basin strikes a balance between retaining and improving existing assets - both ecologic and historic - and introducing new functions and attractions to this unique site. It identifies areas of individual character and opportunities and seeks to tie them together into a holistic, well-measured design response that will reintegrate this gem into the fabric of East London."

A/B Report, May 2009

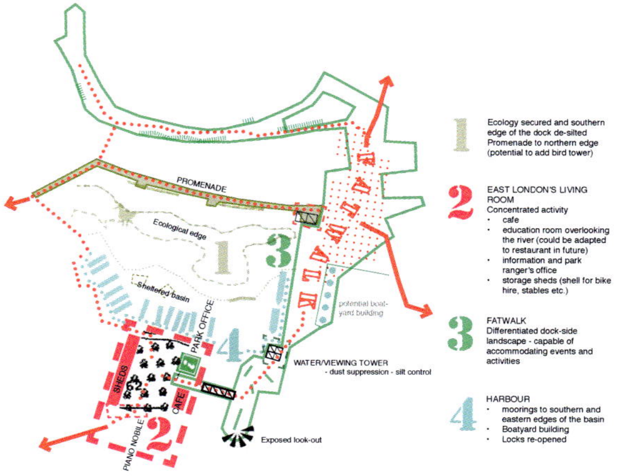

_ A Regional Park
_ A Local Park
_ A Heritage Park
_ A Playable Park
_ A Creative Park
_ A Learning Park
_ A Healthy Park

Highly adaptable, seasonal, playable, fun, set up a table and a barbeque, pull three tables together for a family gathering, use it as an orientating structure the valley, climb on it, support four people or 1,000, it all away for events, add new elements every seaso move it around, get introduced to the Fatwalk ...

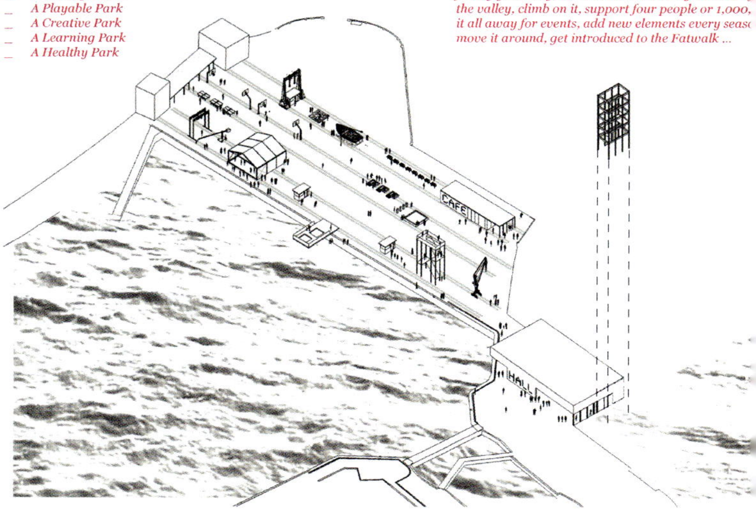

14 JULY [?]

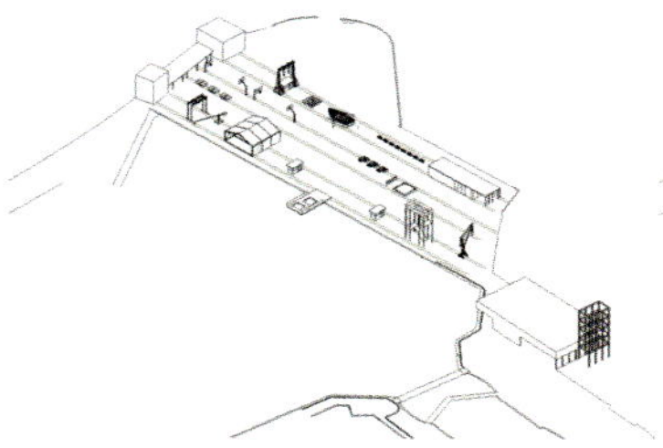

Full summer deployment provides visitor infrastructure for enjoying the whole Lea River Park. Facilities range from formal education /event spaces (the Park Hall) through to fountains, slides, zip wires and barbeques.

LATE SEPTEMBER

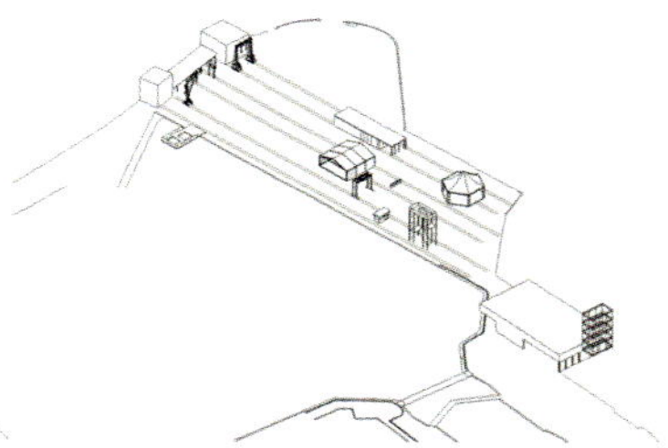

Quay partially cleared for events.

The Fatwalk provides key visitor infrastructure (WCs, catering, lighting).

FEBRUARY

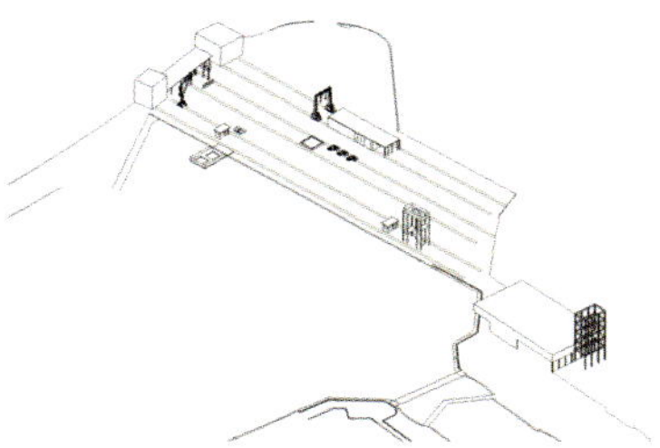

In winter, the quay arrangement would reflect programmed events and work with schools. The Park Hall provides a heated space for much of this.

The quay is set up for a variety of activities, particularly at weekends.

Various drawings were produced to explore and negotiate programming for East India Dock Basin, where conflict existed in the client group between needs of conservation versus facilities for visitors.

A narrative for how objectives might be aligned, and the budget allocated, at the basin.

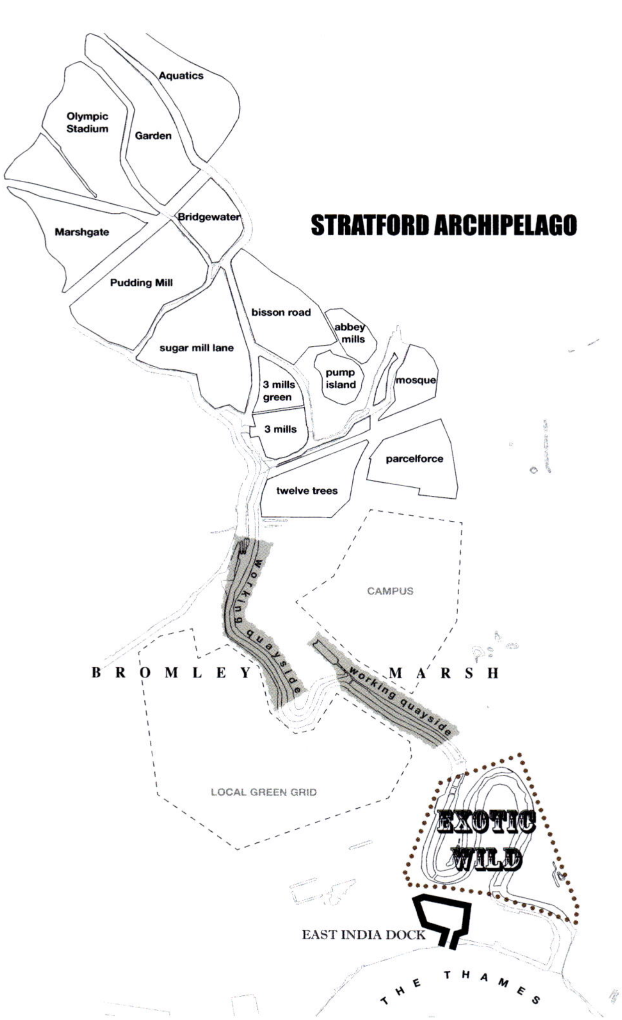

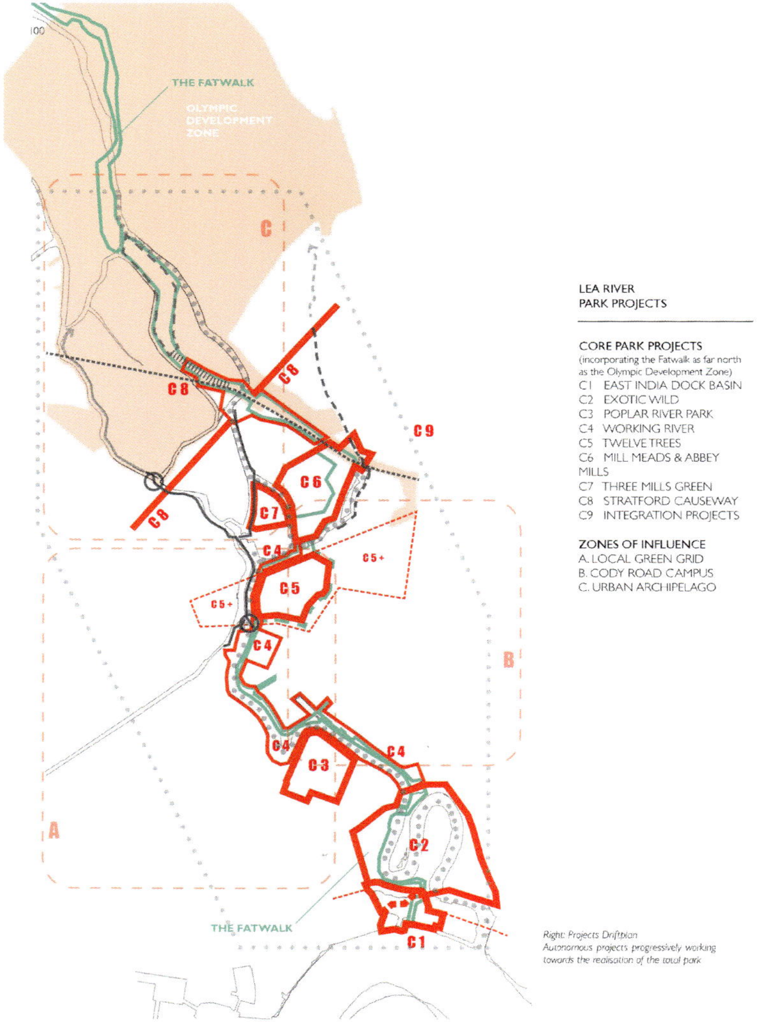

Right: Projects Driftplan
Autonomous projects progressively working towards the realisation of the total park

The close observation of the changing land-use and topography down the valley developed an awareness of what programme was appropriate where, through the establishment of 'character areas'. This enabled the project to fall into a series of autonomous projects.

These independent projects, linked by the skewer of the Fatwalk, will happen over an extended timeframe, enabled by infrastructural change and funded by enabling development on the valley edges. C5 is the only section to have been completed.

The park areas drawn as a topographic grain with the river at their centre. The areas east and west, while outside the park space proper, are nevertheless regarded as 'borrowed landscapes', and reinforce cross-valley connections and the orientation of housing estate open space (west) and generic business park landscaping (east) towards a more coherent role within the watershed of the river valley.

View down the valley connecting the Olympic Park with the Thames. The darker 'figure-ground' illustrates projected development in the valley fringes, generating a new edge to the park, much as imagined by Nash at Regent's Park.

An oblique view of East India Dock Basin. An intervention in this former entrance basin to the East India docks negotiates a delicate balance between nature conservation (the silting up of the dock through neglect has created an important inter-tidal habitat) and a hidden visceral history. The basin is the key Thames-side public space at the southern extremity of the park.

Mill Meads. Bazalgette's ornate sewage pumping station (and Allies & Morrison's 2004 replacement) were built in what was a meads – a floodable river pasture. Our proposition here is to follow a major capital project to upgrade London's underground drainage system with public access to the mature landscape of the Meads. As a potential terrorist target, security is provided through a ring of fenced allotment gardens.

Canning Town. The fragmented landscapes, caught between the busy A13 road, the river Lea and the Docklands Light Railway offer the chance to form a key entrance to the park, acting as a manifold to the multiple routes south to the Thames and the Royal Docks. A new ramp adopts this space left over after transport planning and will provide improved access to Canning Town tube station. It is populated by structures to mark the maritime history of this part of the valley.

Silvertown Viaduct. Silvertown Viaduct was built as Britain's first flyover to cope with the traffic using the Royal Docks in their heyday. The viaduct is now underused by traffic, presenting an opportunity to adopt it as a connective public resource, exploiting its pier-like qualities, and the views that it offers of the Lea Valley and the Thames at Blackwall Reach.

CASE STUDY
KNOWLEDGE ECONOMY

5th Studio's propositional culture has been important in the establishment of certain themes in the practice over time. One of these has been a concern with the spatial manifestation of Cambridge's 'creative cluster', and the consideration of what sort of built form supports this creativity.

Since the very early days of the practice, various self-initiated projects have attempted to establish a more urbanised, polyvalent model for this economy that seeks to establish a civic culture within the city, as opposed to the high-tech business park sprawl that surrounds Cambridge.

One of the first of these projects was made as a proposal to Cambridge University Press, to use a one-kilometre–long strip of land they own between a current and a former rail line. The proposal sought to create more contingent, low-cost working space for start-up firms – a type of space not available in the corporate science-park mode – bringing back into use redundant land trapped in an infrastructure corridor.

Much of this thinking was later refined in the Creative Exchange project in St Neots, and then in a project on the edge of Cambridge entitled the Future Business Centre. Similar concerns are evident in the City Silo project, which as a self-generated and undeveloped proposition, has a certain direct quality, discussed next.

CREATIVE EXCHANGE, ST NEOTS

St Neots is an agricultural market town on the western edge of Cambridgeshire, strategically located on the Great North Road (the A1), the East Coast Mainline and the River Ouse.

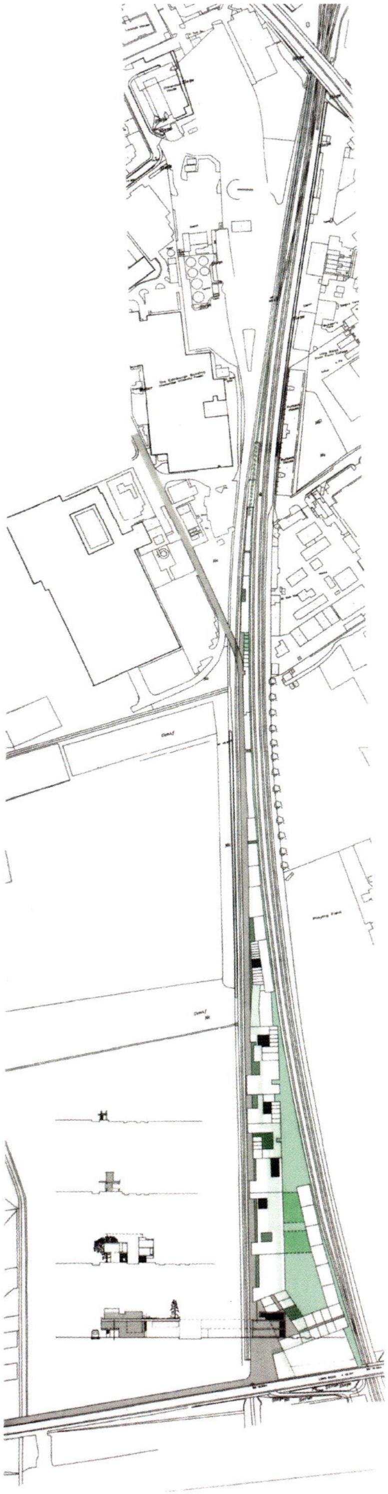

One-kilometre proposition plan. The proposition here was to use the residual space between two railway lines as a dense 'field system' of labs, studios and workshops. The low value of the land would allow more contingent uses.

City Fringe: the Future Business Centre's working courtyard. We worked with a charity who rent cheap work space to start-up firms to establish an incubator building on the fringes of Cambridge. The project brings together physical making (workshops) with more virtual creativity, and shares common resources such as meeting and lecture rooms, and front of house facilities.

The street frontage. The building is the first to create a frontage onto this road, which generally is backed onto by large sheds.

The decline of agriculture and associated manufacture has affected the town, with much of its workforce commuting instead to service jobs in London; what was a thriving market town is increasingly becoming a London dormitory. Within the 'growth area' the local authority has been expected by government to expand housing provision, and the town is growing on its eastern fringe. As a reaction to the town's growing dependence on London, the district council developed an economic strategy structured around a desire to catalyse a local creative culture, more orientated to the Cambridge innovation phenomena.

Once appointed, we reviewed a number of potential locations in public ownership across the town to house creative workspaces in support of this economic strategy, including a decommissioned fire-station, a historically listed house and a former mill. We were also invited to design a bespoke new workspace building which the council planned to rent to new creative firms on advantageous terms. The building was mostly funded by government as a form of infrastructure to support housing growth.

The council had identified a partner in the local school, who had begun teaching related courses on entrepreneurship to their older students. The school is set in mature parkland, once forming an estate around a house which was demolished in the 1960s, at which point the remaining estate was given to the town as a park.

The school has grown significantly owing to the urban transformation of the town, as it grows away from its original marketplace foundation towards the rail station and points east; it had also flipped its entrance towards this direction, from where most pupils now arrive. We felt that locating the new building in this context could be used to reconcile the school's relationship with the park – atrophied by ad-hoc extension of the school's buildings – and to improve the experience of arrival, which was effectively from the back, through the staff car park. In a typical act of mission creep, this led to us developing a spatial strategy for the school as a means to locate the new building within its estate in a coherent way.

The limited budget and defined spatial requirements resulted in a very tight 'net to gross': the ratio of net income-generating space to the total area of the building. We were interested in the fact that in a shared creative building it is precisely this 'net to gross' space that promotes interaction and serendipity, as well as enabling the internal economy of interactions between tenants implied in the term 'creative cluster'.

Rather than providing rooms structured along a fire corridor with inevitable resultant division and isolation, we stacked the accommodation and created a single enclosed fire stair. What would have been general circulation was condensed and coerced into becoming a shared room on each floor, orientated to the park. Structuring the building with a vertical order also allowed the creation of more public rooms for events and interaction on lower floors, with shared studio space and rooms for individual firms above, and a working garden on the roof.

We were very conscious of the economy of the building, spending the budget on raw volume, to create contingent, loose-fit and generous space for the clutter of 20 young firms. A critical issue in the project was the reconciliation of a neglected landscape with an idea of a productive economy. This continuity between landscape and building was implicit in the former house and estate which stood on the site, and in the model of the English country house, at one point an equivalent typology

The site (yellow square) located with respect to the proposed parterre reorganising the school's relationship to the park. The River Ouse is to the left, the original marketplace bottom left and the rail station to the right.

Model of the parterre as an entrance avenue to help reorientate the school to the town's eastern expansion, establishing public buildings (library, Creative Exchange, sports hall, theatre) to the park edge.

Easington House – the image of the English country house with its relationship to landscape understood as an economy: a form of husbandry. Drawn and engraved by Johannes Kip for *The Ancient and Present State of Gloucestershire* by Robert Atkyns, London, 1712.

A mapping of potential sites across the town which could be inhabited by a burgeoning creative economy.

MARKET SQUARE

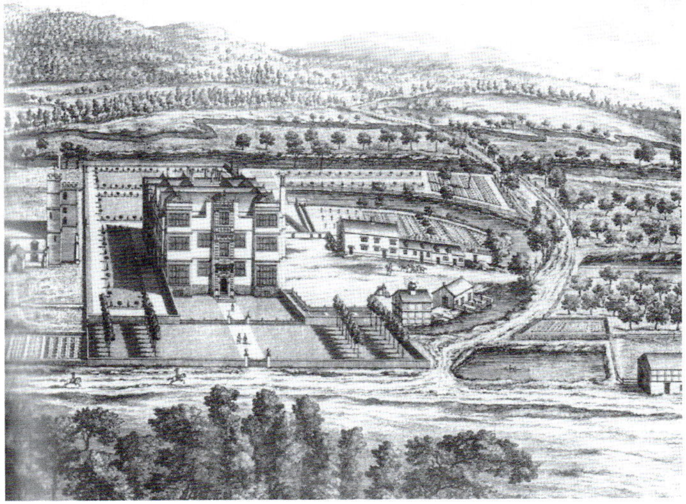

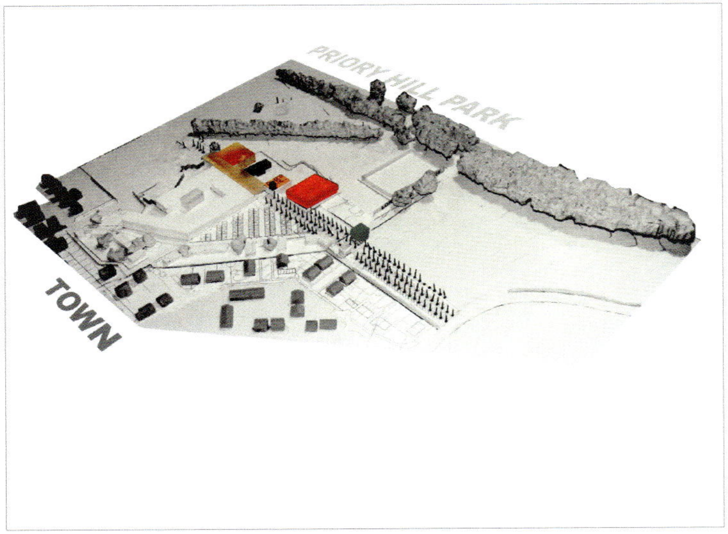
PRIORY HILL PARK
TOWN

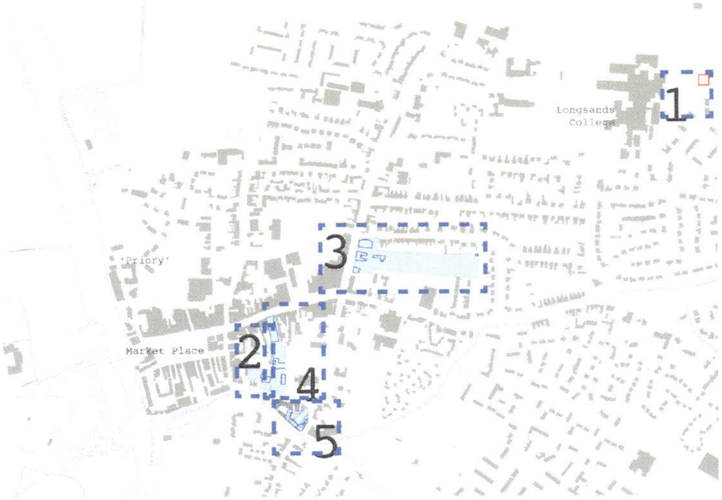
Longsands College
'Priory'
Market Place
1
2
3
4
5

for concentrated creativity and invention, with a range of public and less public rooms close to those demanded by the building brief.

The generic condition of a dormitory town, which had transformed St Neots, from its position as a strategically placed town with a powerful connection with its surrounding context to a banal, subtopian condition, also seemed deeply problematic in terms of the establishment of a creative economy. The building therefore proposes a critique of its surroundings towards something that seems to have been lost – a reminder of a more vital urban condition.

This was recognised in a review of the building by Peter Carl, who talks about the project establishing an 'incipient urbanity':

> It is remarkable how consistently the building plays on three registers at the same time: it is part of an incipient urban transformation; it is a prominent element in a landscape configuration; and it has its own business to accomplish, as the Creative Exchange. These registers are sustained on the interior, according to a diagonal organisation with entry from the east and the public rooms oriented north, to the park. The south facade above the first floor is blind, to prevent overlooking the neighbours' gardens.
>
> The pillars of the reinforced concrete armature avoid the corners, allowing the glass to determine the primary envelope. At the same time, the exposed concrete constantly recalls the earth and, thus, the park, which is always in view from the public rooms. The ground and first floors frame the double-height reception, which is scaled to the site and allows access to the stair through its back wall, as if stepping outdoors before ascending. This gives on to a space that acts as a reception, exhibition room and seminar room. Like the open-plan office on the first floor, this room opens to the park.
>
> The upper rooms extend beyond the armature, gaining space, shading the rooms below, and creating a public room that acts like a small forum (in which a spigot for coffee and tea plays the role of town fountain). . .
>
> The several forces that the Creative Exchange elects to negotiate – urban and rural, natural and technical, education and service, economics and ethos, making and politics – are not, so to speak, added value. Rather it is a matter of basic honesty – these forces acknowledge the conflicts inherent in the proposition.
>
> Once it was common, but now it is rare for one to be able to hear in a rural building the urban resonances – the deep consistency of town – of civic praxis.[17]

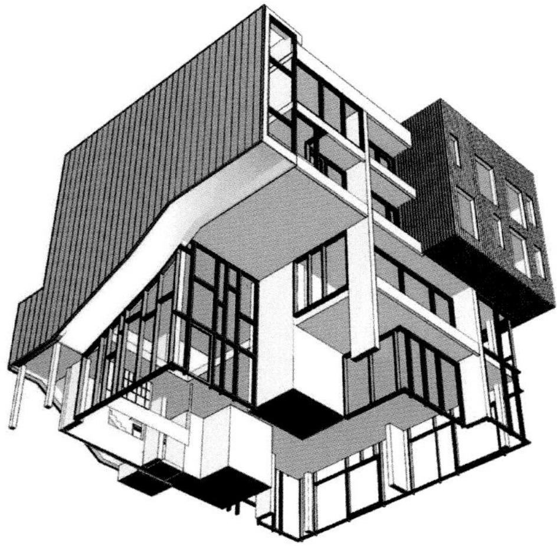

Up axonometric of the Creative Exchange, used as the building's sign.

Shared kitchen facilities in a 'hall' at second floor level, viewed from one of the rooms.
Tim Soar

View of the surrounding park from the roof garden. The roof garden allows continuity with the landscape without the disturbance of football games and school lunch breaks at ground level.
Tim Soar

The blank south elevation encloses the staircase – the building's only fire compartment – allowing the rest of the volume to be open. This view illustrates our desire to establish what Peter Carl called 'an incipient urbanity' on this suburban edge of St Neots.
Tom Holbrook

The planning and materiality of the building is discussed in more detail in the following chapter.

CITY SILO

This project developed as a speculative critique of the major redevelopment of land around Cambridge's railway station, and embodies a deeper conversation in the studio about the re-urbanisation of

Creative Exchange, west elevation.
Tim Soar

Creative Exchange, at the end of a new avenue of lime trees, establishing a formal access to the school from the east.
Tim Soar

Creative Exchange, south west corner.
D Grandorge

Creative Exchange, first floor studio.
Tim Soar

Cambridge's 'Silicon Fen' research and development topography.

Foster Mill is a striking example of a grain silo and flour mill located, as is customary across East Anglia, on the rail-line: a prominent concrete industrial building marking a point of mediation between the 'fat of the land' and the city. Le Corbusier in *Vers un Architecture* described the giant grain silos of North America as the 'splendid fruits of a new era'.

The mill finally ceased operation in 2000, and was slated for conversion into flats, as part of a masterplan by the Richard Rogers Partnership.[18] The masterplan itself we felt to be very weak, being highly formal, and establishing an urban grain which was too coarse and too resistant to changes in economic fortune. When the financial crash came, the plots were too large for the residual market, and the realisation of the masterplan slowed to a crawl.

At the heart of the masterplan, structured around the station, is proposed a large urban square. The mill buildings form a lynch-pin of the southern edge of the square. The silo building of the mill caught fire one night in July 2010 and was largely destroyed, leaving only a 7-metre-high enclosure, like the root of a molar.

The mill is a listed structure, and discussions immediately began between the developers and the city authorities about rebuilding the former structure in facsimile, but as apartments, omitting the obsolete industrial role in all but a formal reference.

We had concerns about the square, which was illustrated as a vibrant urban space, but which seemed to lack sufficient elements that might help to animate it in this way. We were suspicious of what we coined the 'lazy cosmopolitanism' of the masterplan, which promised a congested urban culture, while illustrating an urban grain of corporate boxes with little public life.

Foster Mill, Cambridge.

'Lazy cosmopolitanism': the square as imagined by Richard Rogers Partnership. © Rogers Stirk Harbour + Partners

The fire seemed to provide the city with an opportunity to grasp this urban square, and to bring to it a structure which could embody some sense of the city's ambitions and prospective vision. If this was the opportunity for an act of curation, what might be brought to this most visible of Cambridge's public spaces, at a threshold to Cambridge from the station? How might the city as a whole represent itself to this public threshold?

One of the more successful coups of the developers had been to persuade Microsoft Research to swap a site on the edge of Cambridge for a more urban location near the station. Although this has been embodied within a boxy corporate shell, it is nevertheless a welcome reverse of the marginalisation of the research world.

To accentuate that – and as a provocation – we proposed a structure on the silo site which would house a dialogue centre: a central resource which acknowledged Cambridge's global connection, and which brought together the worlds of university, business and commercial research in the context of dialogue about future global change.

Structured as a series of auditoria and seminar spaces conceived of as a continuous landscape through the building, it would also house local exchange and city events, as well as accommodating, on a short-term basis, particular thematic interchanges on global issues. A dense residential stack would allow short-term residential sojourns in the heart of the city while participating in conferences and events.

At its base, within the ruin of the burnt-out building, would be a bar and lobby, radically open to the square, allowing an encounter between a passer-by and the highly specialised world of global research. Rather than the blandness of private apartments, the City Silo proposition attempts to restore the mill as a place of work while structuring exchange between the city and the world beyond, creating a public theatre of conflict, negotiation and collaboration. It is thought of as an expansion of the public domain.

We found that the reaction to the proposal was polite interest, but with little sense of the urgency of finding a spatial embodiment of what is a big political and social issue for the city: how to maintain momentum and relevance in a globalised and fast-moving market of research.

The concerns of this project have been extended into ongoing work to revisit Cambridge's north-eastern edge, which includes Europe's first Science Park, as well as the residual land which deals with the city's sewage and solid waste.

GREATER NORTH CAMBRIDGE

The city's Science Park, now fifty years old, faces a number of threats to its continuing primacy as the centre of the 'Cambridge Cluster'. A new railway station is planned on former rail sidings, providing a fast link to London. Hard won, this station will provide critical new infrastructure to the north of the city, in an area which is the last opportunity for major urban growth. The station will act as a catalyst for long-term change, but arrives in a strategic vacuum on the border of two local authority areas. What could be a vital reappraisal of the potential of the city's northern edge for ensuring the city's continuing vitality is in danger of being missed.

As a proposition about revisiting this marginal landscape of city servicing and anonymous research, we propose an urban retrofit, which seeks to radically urbanise this topography over thirty years, welding together a territory around public space, and a connection to the strongly figured landscape of the Fenland, which comes into the city fringe along the River Cam. From a current series of monofunctional land uses (sewage remediation, research, railtrack, highway infrastructure, parking), a complex urban form needs to be grown.

This project emerged directly out of the PhD research as one of three propositional 'exegetic projects'.

City Silo as a framing corner of the station square. The bar occupies the brick remains of the burnt silo, while the auditorium and rooms for dialogue help animate the square.

Plans at key levels.

Exploded axonometric identifying the parts of the proposition and how it relates to the new public space in front of the station. A truly public space resolves infrastructure, civic framing of the square and streets, and the contributions of the surrounding architecture.

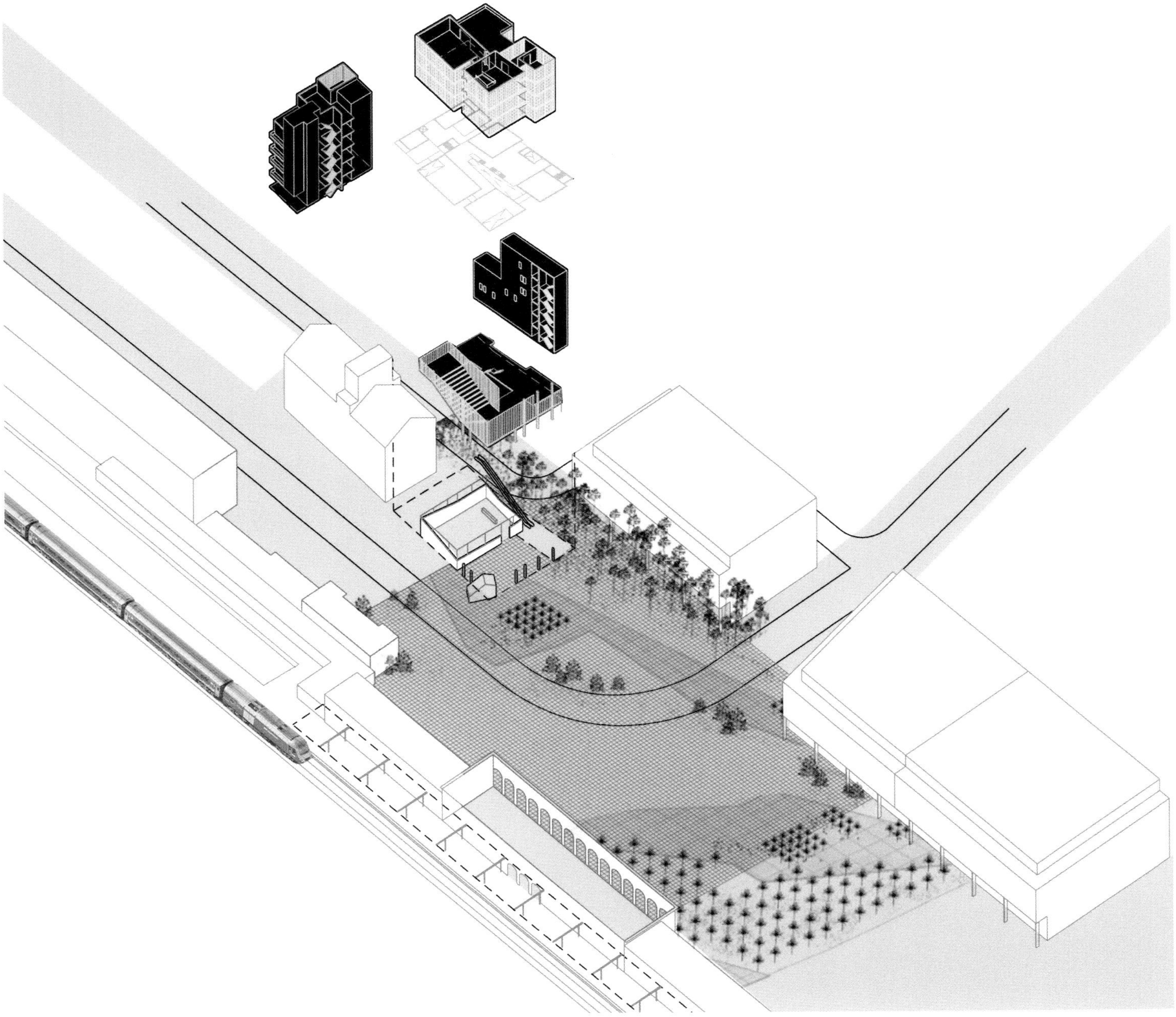

NOTES

1 Professor David Porter, panel observation, Practice Research Symposium, Ghent, Belgium, April 2012.

2 *New Architects 2: A Guide to Britain's Best Young Architectural Practices*. Architecture Foundation / Merrell, 2001.

3 This project features in my essay for the exhibition catalogue for *Presences* and was accompanied in the catalogue box by a drawing developed with Helen Stratford exploring a playful connection between defenses on the site from the English Civil War and a memorial garden to Princess Diana.

4 Tripos Studio One, tutored by Tom Holbrook and José Esteves de Matos, University of Cambridge Department of Architecture, 2000.

5 The architects were Panter Hudspith. See *Architecture Today,* September 2008. The scheme is well described in this article in the context of Cambridge's urban planning, but omits our involvement as catalysts, of which the author – curiously the same one who supplied the quote on our propositional nature, referenced above – was probably not aware. The bus station remains an unresolved problem for the city.

6 For example, Joseph Bazalgette ran his great sewer parallel to the Strand, sparing London the cholera epidemics that decimated other European cities. The sewer project was combined with the world's first underground metropolitan railway, and an early example of a relief road in the form of the Victoria Embankment.

7 There were peculiar dispensations: one could escape pursuit for debt by moving within the precinct of the Savoy, which only lost its special judicial status in the last century.

8 'Strand' means beach or shore.

9 Steen Eiler Rasmussen, *London, The Unique City.* Jonathan Cape, London, 1948.

10 The Olympic Park design team at the outset was an uncomfortable alliance between Foreign Office Architects, Allies and Morrison, and EDAW.

11 The Olympic Development Agency was established by Act of Parliament in April 2006. The budget for the games was £2.4 billion, rising to £9.3 billion.

12 Patrick Abercrombie, *Greater London Plan*, HM Ministry of Works, London, 1944.

13 'This government means business in delivering plans to help people build new homes and kickstart the economy. We're determined to cut through the bureaucracy that holds us back. That starts with getting the planners off our backs. . .' UK Prime Minister David Cameron, September 2012.

14 Leon van Schaik, *Spatial Intelligence: New Futures for Architecture*, Wiley, Chichester, UK, 2008.

15 van Schaik, op. cit., in reference to the work of Venturi Scott Brown at the National Gallery, London, Sainsbury Wing, p. 74.

16 Michael Polanyi, *The Tacit Dimension*, Anchor Books, New York, 1967, p. 24–5.

17 Peter Carl, 'A Civic Endeavour', *Architects' Journal,* 13 November 2008.

18 Now Rogers Stirk Harbour and Partners.

LOCATED PRACTICE

Landscape is important to the way one thinks and one's notion of what is natural or not. Your working territory is a made, engineered landscape, fabricated around water and infrastructure; what is natural in that landscape is not the English thing to be natural – to do with hills and sheep and thatched cottages with roses – but rather, there is a strangeness, an otherness in that landscape, which one can pick up in your work.

Professor David Porter[1]

WORKING GEOGRAPHY & OTHER INFLUENCES

The two projects described at the outset of this book as an introduction to the work – a staircase, and a new piece of city – stake out the span of a working territory which is sustained through the œuvre of the practice: on the one hand, incrementally adjusting or intervening within existing buildings in urban centres, while on the other hand, making propositions at a strategic scale around the margins of cities and towns.

5th Studio has its roots in East Anglia: a dense, highly urbanised landscape, which conversely also contains some of the critical establishing settings for the idea of the English pastoral in broader culture, with its highly entwined and complex interrelationships between the natural and the man-made. This territory contains one of the highest concentrations of infrastructure anywhere, and at its margin is London, with the simultaneously destructive and nurturing gravitational pull of a great star.

One of the defining factors of this working geography is the variety of different urban and rural conditions packed densely into approximately 650 square miles. The region includes Roman settlements, ancient cathedral cities, the particular 'knowledge economy' of Cambridge, marginal seaside towns, major ports, experimental new towns (the garden cities, Harlow), market towns and dormitory suburbs on metropolitan lines to the capital. The interstitial territory is similarly variegated, with high ecological-value habitats often created in what were formerly industrial or agricultural workings (the Broads, the Fens), creating conflicts between ongoing production and nature conservation. These landscapes are fundamentally constructed and natural.

In terms of a pastoral tradition, one might reference, for example, John Constable's Stour Valley, John Clare's Helpston or Humphry Repton's landscape work. The synthetic condition of East Anglia has attracted a close concern for the reality of people's lives in a landscape, evidenced by Ronald Blythe's *Akenfield*, the close account of the life of a post-war Suffolk village, or the work of the anarchist writer Colin Ward. My father, the Norfolk-born poet David Holbrook, was very much part of this writing tradition and it suffused my childhood.

The sense of landscape as a project perhaps goes somewhere to explain the coincidence of the 'New Nature Writers' to East Anglia, including Roger Deakin, Richard Mabey, Robert McFarlane and Mark Cocker, or the attraction to the territory of émigrés such as the novelist W. G. Sebald.

Humphry Repton (1752–1818), who was born in Suffolk and lived in Norfolk and Essex, was the first of the new class of professional consultants, in contrast to his contemporaries: the aristocratic Uvedale Price, or the contractor 'Capability' Brown. Repton's approach was via his 'Red Books', where

A mapping of 5th Studio's working geography, which also illuminates a field beyond traditional architectural concerns: the city-supporting infrastructure which critically defines this region of the UK.

Wisbech
Norwich
Yartoft
St. Neots
Cambridge
Hadleigh
St. Albans
Hemel
LONDON

he employed 'before and after' eye-level perspective images as a highly propositional tool to establish projects. His projects, like our own, tended towards the peripheral land on the edges of cities, responding to urbanisation and a newly emerging relationship between city and countryside at that time. Repton was one of the first landscape designers to include infrastructure as a key component of reshaping topography.[2]

Describing the work of the practice through the course of the PhD in the international context of RMIT University's Practice Research Symposia in Ghent and Barcelona, it became clear that this working setting was highly particular, and has allowed us access to an unusually broad spectrum of concern, spanning urbanity, marginality and the pastoral.

The sites on which we work tend to be divergent: either extremely engaged and rich, or peripheral and banal. Our working territory is one undergoing radical change: a change that is perhaps as profound as that encountered in Britain during the industrial revolution.

The restricted availability of land in the south-east of England – and the multiple claims made upon it – create dramas which, while played out through extreme demographic and economic phenomena, are nevertheless sublimated in contemporary architectural discourse, in its current tendency to focus on established urban centres.[3]

To retrieve a broader conception of the intellectual realm of the discipline it has been enriching to identify an older 'community of practice'[4] in a generation working in the late 1960s and early 1970s who were concerned with the role of a wider, non-urban landscape. This generation – including James Stirling, Cedric Price and the Smithsons – also extended through critical writing: for example, Ian Nairn's advocacy of the visceral experience of landscape in the 'Outrage' series of the *Architectural Review*.

The work of this period formed a particularly English contribution to architectural discourse, keyed as much to landscape traditions, such as the picturesque, or the scholarly historical archaeology of Rudolf Wittkower and his pupil, Colin Rowe.[5] This period in architecture was also particularly rich with respect to working with context, as part of an emerging critique of modernism's utopian and universalist claims. The concerns of establishing an adaptive, non-dogmatic urbanism, exploring a more negotiative and heterogeneous approach to reality 'as found' through techniques of juxtaposition and bricolage, were an attempt to discover an alternative to the antiquarian approach to history.[6]

Central to this project to enrich and critique modernism was the notion of differentiation – of working with the found qualities of a place in all its complexities. The extraordinary pedagogical exchange of Colin Rowe and O. M. Ungers' period at Cornell University in the 1970s, included both Hans Kollhoff and Rem Koolhaas among the student body,[7] and one can trace from this period the emergence of interest in what Koolhaas framed as a 'culture of congestion' and in the development of bounded conditions.

As an example of an extension of architectural pedagogy into the realms of urbanism, planning and landscape, Rowe taught design studios during the 1970s that took infrastructure – such as New York State's Parkway system – as a landscape instrument used to generate differentiation between urban and non-urban conditions.[8]

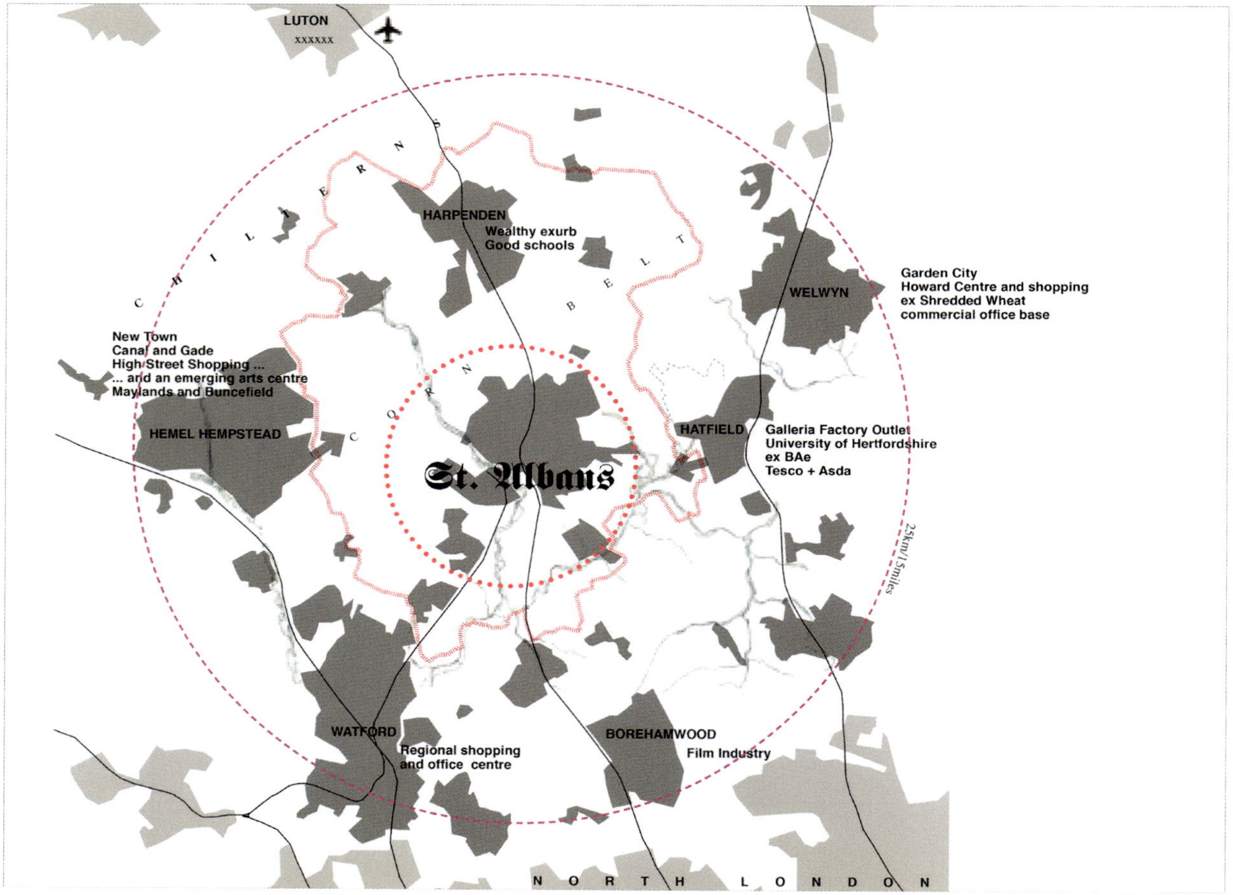

Our mapping of a cluster of towns on the north-western edge of London's periphery, each developing a very different economy and identity. This periphery maps precisely to the new locations Repton was drawn to in the late eighteenth and early nineteenth century.

Outrage: On the Disfigurement of Town and Countryside (*Architectural Review* special 1955; book1959). My parents owned this and its follow up, *Counter Attack Against Subtopia* (1957), and I was fascinated by them.
Tom Holbrook

Drawing from a Charrette held at King's Cross, London, in 2008 in which I unwittingly mirror the observations of Grahame Shane, a student of Rowe's at Cornell, whose drawing Field Analysis of Central London (1971) is reproduced below.

The drawing investigates the interrelationship between the latent natural topography with the built topographies of infrastructure. Shane's drawing relates stream beds to property boundaries, and the morphology of London's Great Estates.
David Grahame Shane

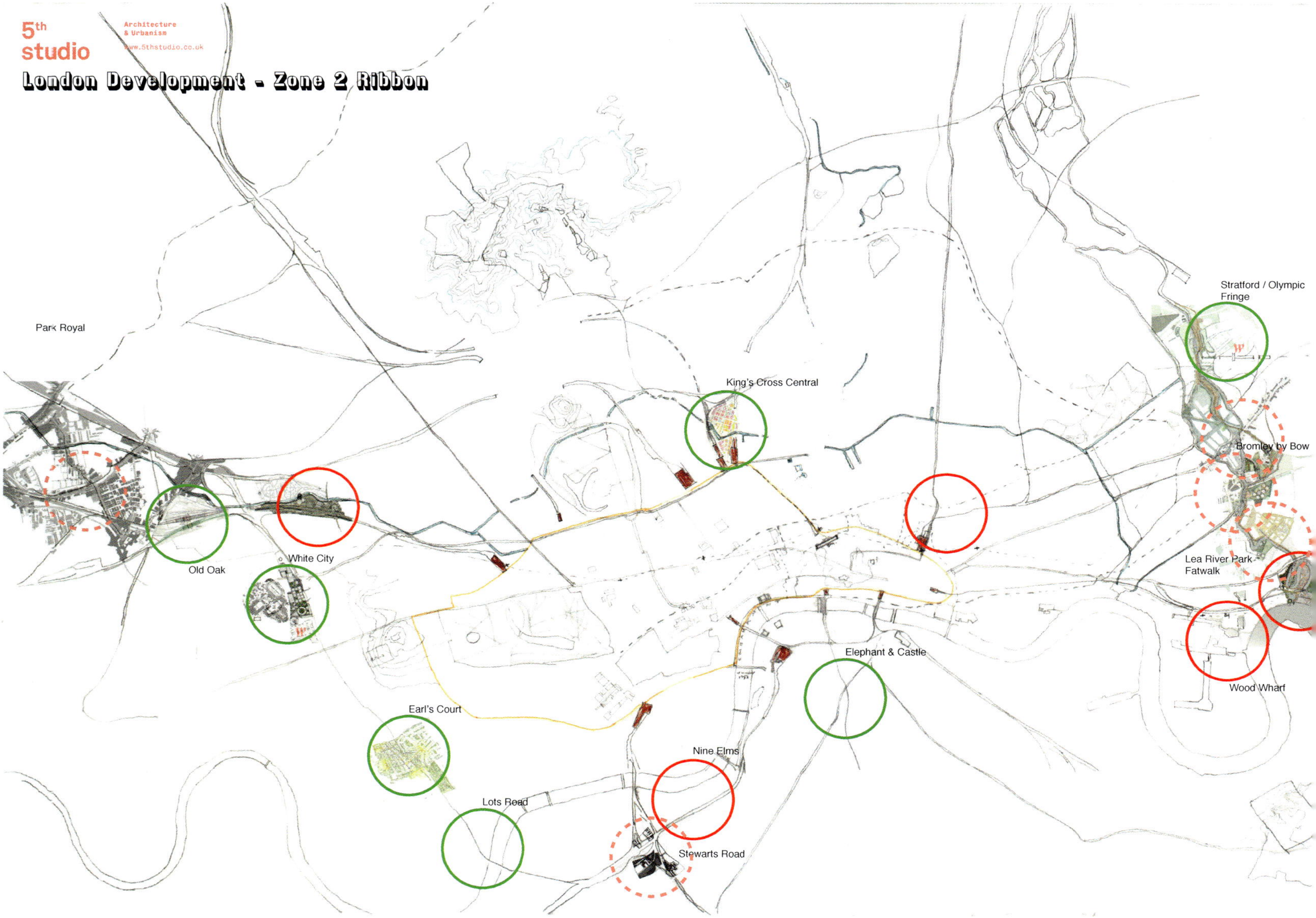

5th Studio projects mapped against major urban change, observed to be following the 'Zone 2 Ribbon' (Zone 2 being a transport fares designation which coincides with, for example, the location of key Victorian termini in the city). This exercise was undertaken to identify potential future locations for involvement on projects – a prospective mapping.

EDUCATIONAL INFLUENCE

My approach as a designer is informed by two strong influences from my educational background. I studied Art & Design at Kingston Polytechnic, where Fred Scott was teaching.[9] Following my degree – and conversion to architecture – I was attracted to the University of Cambridge as a graduate student by the reputations of Dalibor Vesely and Peter Carl.[10]

While there is not the space here to do more than summarise the work of these three teachers in the briefest of terms, it is important to acknowledge their continuing influence as mentors, both in terms of the expectation that a designer should operate across the culture, and that action would recognise the complexity of the world as a starting point. To each, the role of the designer is understood as interventional. When understood in these terms, the designer operates in the role of interpreter, situating current concerns in a superimposition or archaeology of other meanings, either evident, or latent, but also bringing into play the possibility of new meaning.

Scott's approach, articulated in his book *On Altering Architecture*[11] (two chapters of which are developments of the essay written for the catalogue of our 2001 exhibition *Presences*), is towards a craft of alteration which commences with the process of 'stripping back':

> Stripping back in its extended manifestation is the process by which the interventional designer acquires an understanding of the host building with which she or he is engaged. It is to the end of developing a structured affinity as a preparation for the correspondence between their work and the existing. . . the process of delineation of the qualities of the host building, an analysis of the given.[12]

Scott's theoretical foundation lies in structuralism, particularly in the reference to typology, where structures can be related to an ideal or archetype in a work of interpretation. Scott insists that type cannot be understood in purely formal terms:

> Stripping back may be thought of as consisting of an examination of four aspects: firstly, material. . .of what and how the building is made; secondly, spatial, concerning entrance, circulation, hierarchy and proportion; thirdly, the style of the building and the exemplars from which it derives; and fourthly, the building as palimpsest. . . being the marks of previous successive occupations.[13]

Scott explains his intention in writing *On Altering Architecture*:

> As I came to understand it, intervention had tended to be a broken-backed activity: work on an existing building, to make good and to prepare it for a new intervention, was seen commonly as merely preparatory, and as such exempt from accusation, one way or the other; the purpose and outcome of this approach was to highlight the singularity of the new design. My counter argument is that the designers' attitudes to the host building are a central component of their work, and because of this, the structured understanding of the context for the work is essential.[14]

Dalibor Vesely and Peter Carl had been teaching at the University of Cambridge Department of Architecture since 1978, and I joined the school in 1991, at the height of their influence there, attending the infamous MPhil seminars, which often ran late into the night.

Vesely develops typological understanding towards the deeper cultural model of the typicality of situation:[15] the hermeneutic understanding of the typicality of particular experience, described as: 'a rich depository of experience and the result of a long process of reconciliation between complex and contradictory tendencies in contemporary urban life'.[16]

Elsewhere, Vesely contrasts engineering – with its abstraction of the phenomenal world to systems – to architectural design:

> Architectural design begins always with a vision, not of a system, but of the situational structure of the anticipated space, as well as the quality and purpose of the space seen in simultaneity and reciprocity. Architectural design remains an open dialogue between the initial conditions and the emerging configuration of space. The process is in many ways similar to interpretation in other areas of culture.[17]

Vesely and Carl's insistence that architectural design should be regarded as a practical skill, in dialogue with concrete situations in the world – in praxis – has been fundamental to how I understand and approach projects. This approach can be evidenced explicitly in the Lea River Park project, which directly addresses the results of several centuries of instrumental thinking, and puts into place a series of strategies for the erosion of that abstraction to create a landscape more available for human interaction and imagination.

Each of these educational mentors locates architectural intelligence as a practical interaction with radical context. In the discussion that follows, I interrogate this a little more and follow a typical design approach through a series of case studies at various scales.

CLIENT FOUND AND LOST

> *Design for London amounts to the most important city architects' department in the country. . .a group of design-led individuals who promoted a dignified public realm for all Londoners.*[18]

Looking back through the archive, there is a thread through the work which constitutes a critique of the discipline of planning, as currently experienced in the UK. This frustration with planning cultures – fatally disconnected from the concrete, fixated by management routines and squeezed between the short-term cycles of politics and capital – is shared by a generation of architect-urbanists, many of whom have chosen to become clients as a means to introduce alternative, more spatially connected discourses. Most significant of these agencies was Design for London, the mayoral urban planning unit, which for just over a decade exemplified an alternative approach to planning. Design for London were a significant client for our work, and this coincidence of outlook requires acknowledgement.

The Greater London Authority Architecture and Urbanism Unit originated in 2001. London's first mayor, Ken Livingstone, appointed Richard Rogers, (fresh from completing the *Towards an Urban Renaissance* report for the UK government),[19] as the unit's head, and the early team included Richard Burdett, Mark Brearley and Eleanor Fawcett, a former student who then became a client for our work in the Lea Valley. In 2006, the unit was merged with the London Development Agency's design team to establish Design for London, which was run by former borough planner Peter Bishop. For a period, Bishop was also Deputy Chief Executive of the London Development Agency (LDA) and built valuable political support for the unit until his departure in 2011. Thereafter, and with the disbandment of the LDA in 2010, Design for London were increasingly marginalised and finally wound up at the beginning of 2013.

Design for London typically worked as a catalyst on the interstices of London's thirty-two boroughs, negotiating between agencies (including the boroughs, the mayoral transport agency Transport for London and numerous other public sector and business organisations). Their involvement was tripartite: first, in originating and guiding projects, establishing design briefs and developing cross-border masterplanning and area strategies (with a particular focus on east London where the challenge of managing rapid change in the capital is greatest). Second, they directly delivered physical projects, particularly in terms of London's public realm. Finally, the unit developed mayoral spatial policy and strategy: for example, the Mayor's *Housing Design Guide* and *Climate Change Strategy*.

Their sensibility was to reveal and work with what exists, and to situate themselves between the familiar planning tropes of 'top down' and 'bottom up'. Mark Brearley, the former head of design at the unit, locates their role thus:

> We are in the middle, because we are identifying possibilities and then trying to build them into a constituency, to make them bottom-up, even though we might have actually seeded the idea. Not enough ideas for positive urban change come fully from the bottom up. There are just not enough people around who have a clear notion of what can happen. Thoughts do need to be introduced, but I wouldn't see this process as top-down; it's not a crude imposition, it's an offering up, and then building a constituency, nurturing a momentum.[20]

Contrasting Design for London's role with contemporary planning, Brearley clearly identifies the centrality of the proposition:

> I do believe in the idea of following an agreed plan that has democratic endorsement, and using the leverage of public ownership of development rights to influence outcomes. But these days that's a slightly eccentric belief, and it is far removed from the day-to-day practice. In fact, planning of that type has limited influence today as there are so many obstacles to actually getting anywhere with a whole concept for a locality. So we have migrated our efforts to where we think we can still have a good effect more readily; through a more entrepreneurial, opportunistic approach, pitching ideas and getting support for them, persuading, telling stories, marshalling resources, and helping seed enthusiasm. This is a more productive way than the idea of planning familiar since the 1940s.[21]

This theme is echoed by the editor of *Building Design*, writing in response to the breaking up of CABE – the Commission for Architecture & the Built Environment:

> . . .what we most desperately lack is local planning of a propositional kind. If we had planners capable of offering a three-dimensional vision of the city to which architects and developers could respond, the need for a design watchdog like CABE would be much diminished. At present, there is only one planning agency operating in the UK that has proved itself capable of steering the city's development in that proactive manner, namely Design for London. [Design for London is] instrumental in establishing a collective vision for the town's regeneration and in ensuring that commissions for individual projects are awarded to some of the best architects in the country.[22]

Some of 5th Studio's projects with Design for London: The Lea River Park Design Framework (2007); Park Royal Public Realm Strategy (2008); Stitching the Fringe (2012); Royal Docks Vision (2012); Mayor's Great Spaces (2009); Ideas for Mabley Green (2013); Crossrail Atlas (2012); East London Green Grid (2006 on).

Design for London gathered a number of like-minded practitioners: including East (the practice originally established by Brearley), Muf, David Kohn Architects and the landscape designers J&L Gibbons. The amount of work addressed by this group was contentious, often attracting criticism from the press, with accusations of cronyism and conflicts of interest. The existence of a unit that wanted to support long-term and careful commitment to a place, around what were often modest projects, demanded fresh skills from the discipline, and few practices were able or willing to sustain that sort of involvement. In the early years of the Architecture and Urbanism Unit, these skills were so rare in the UK that much masterplanning work went to Dutch practices, such as West 8 and KCAP.

Design for London actively grew a more local pool of architectural talent who had the sensibilities and skill to address the emerging spatial agenda in London at that time, and it was interesting to see the resentful reaction to that from the more traditional quarters of the architectural profession.[23] Sustained involvement by professionals is actively countered by the requirement that the public sector competitively tender services at regular 'milestones', removing their ability to positively *commission*, replacing that with the risk-averse regimes of *procurement*.

Design for London acted like a guerrilla movement, seditiously implanting design ambitions into local authority work. This clandestine operation was simultaneously a strength and a weakness. With a team of under twenty and a small budget, the unit nevertheless made a disproportionate impact on planning in London, influencing policy and public investment in the capital. Its guerrilla status perhaps prevented the assimilation of the unit into a more permanently acknowledged place in the Mayoral administration.

Our own involvement crossed the whole span of Design for London's activities, from the work on the London Olympic Fringe, numerous masterplans (for example, the public realm framework for Park Royal, discussed later), through to policy level projects: for example, the London Green Grid, the *Crossrail Atlas* and policy advice to the Mayor on climate change strategy.[24]

The diaspora from the break-up of the agency continues to provide critical clients for the practice – including Eleanor Fawcett, now Head of Design at the London Legacy Development Corporation, and client for the Lea River Park project. Beside ourselves, Fawcett is the sole person to maintain continuity with the park project across its lifetime.

THE CONTAMINATED FIELD

> All of your work is in an area that has been worked and reworked and reworked. Everything you do is in a majorly contested field: there's no such thing as a greenfield site in any of your projects. . .Across the scales you seem to break things down into a certain scale of block, forming assemblages in contested fields. Is it the contested field that forces that way of thinking?. . . I'm interested in how you have built up this painstaking way of understanding complexity in this way: the coherence of the grain that you have developed as a response to this condition.[25]
>
> Professor Leon van Schaik

In acknowledgment of the multiple claims made for land in our working territory, and a desire to make this phenomenon more explicit, most of our work involves the negotiation of what we refer to in the studio as 'contaminated fields'. This term

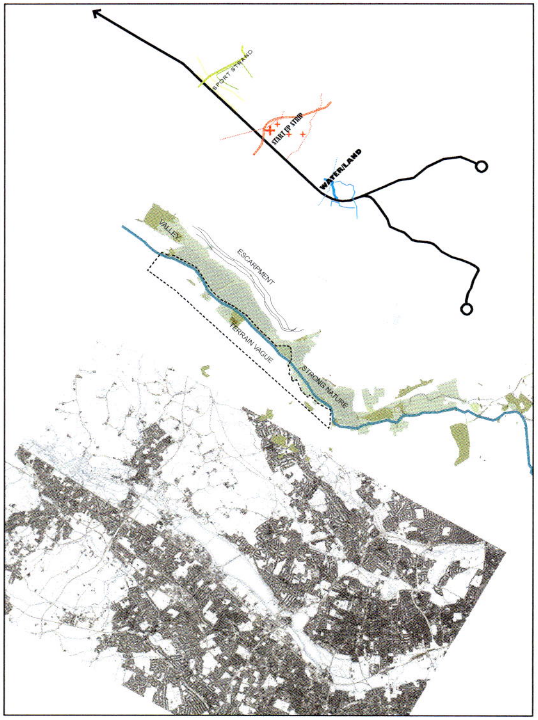

A drawing exploring the topography of the Lea Valley, for which we act as Green Grid Area Advisors.

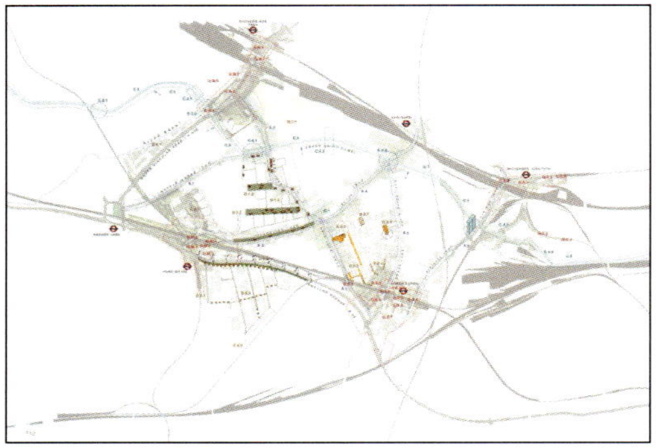

Park Royal Masterplan (discussed as a Case Study later). Park Royal is a series of distinct pieces of urban fabric whose diversity is critical to its economic operation and urban character. To support this richness of place, and fit with the reality of what would make sense on the ground, the strategy proposes a number of small-scale interventions which respond to specific local conditions. This 'toolkit' plan assembles the different proposals, ranging from sign painting the walls of anonymous sheds through to an off-road cycle network.

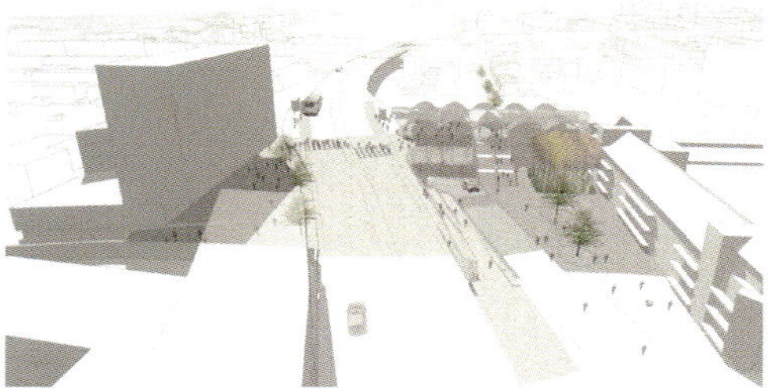

5th Studio were commissioned to investigate the integration and impact of the new Crossrail station at Abbey Woods. Here adjacent development and public realm interventions combine to create an elevated station square which radically alters the nature of an existing flyover.

The Crossrail Atlas attempts to provide a comprehensive description of the regeneration potential of the Crossrail project. The Atlas describes the new geography of urban change and regeneration along the Crossrail route.

emerged very early on in the studio as a means to situate a desired relationship of design work within rich context. The contaminated field acknowledges a multiplicity of claims on a particular landscape that can be brought into juxtaposition. These layers might include the uncovering of literal and physical objects (for example, the incorporation of Fleam Dyke as a means to structure the landscape in Fen Ditton), but might also reference the unrealised, the lost or the latent.

A number of projects dealing with interventions in rich contexts characteristically commence with the editing of the host context with some violence: first by a version of Fred Scott's 'stripping back', as a critique of the situation as found, then through the introduction of fragments as a means to establish a provocative dialogue between the host and the intervention.

In my graduate dissertation,[26] I appraised the work of the Veneto designer Carlo Scarpa, the

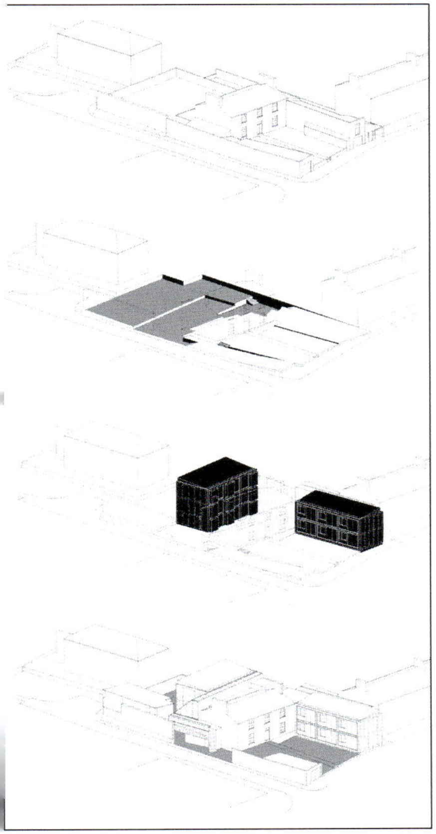

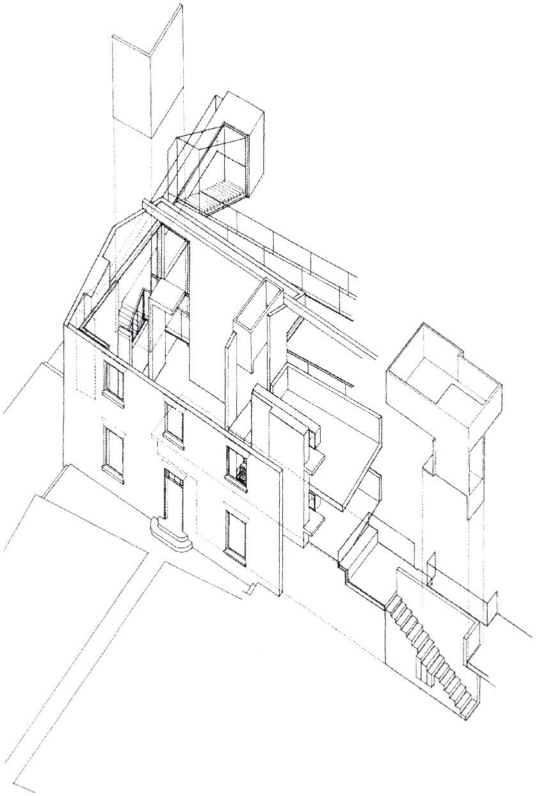

A project to enlarge a pair of Georgian houses to form a graduate hostel for St John's College, Cambridge. Site axonometric, illustrating: a. the found condition of a doubled house and carpenter's workshop; b. the creation of new grounds; c. fifteen study rooms are brought into a concentrated relationship with the original house, which provides the common social spaces of the hostel; d. the ensemble.

Axonometric exploring how the original 'doubled house' remains the hostel address, with an intervention creating a 'superdomestic' condition for shared social spaces.

A model of the hostel.

critical appraisal of whose work I felt had been over-aestheticised, therefore missing its essential power: the violent upheaval integral to the work. A series of early projects in 5th Studio's oeuvre are disruptive, using assemblage techniques to emphasise a certain awkwardness; a provocative position of the intervention with respect to the host building. A later cluster of projects – which tend to be at the strategic end of the spectrum in terms of their scale – extends this project of differentiation, seeking to uncover and amplify particular characteristics as interventions in landscape.

Typically, projects start with an investigation of what exists, seeking to emphasise essential qualities while stripping away those aspects which obscure or normalise the potential of the site. This initial stage explores how a particular context has evolved: what forces have shaped it over time and how its particular characteristics have come about. The site's evolution is revealed through sequential maps, historical research and physical experience of the site, and this process includes both the successive physical realities of its archaeology and frustrated potential.

The combined analysis is embodied in abstractive recordings of the site, towards a summary of its character. From this tectonic and social reality, a narrative is constructed to both accentuate the situation and to bring into dialogue the potential new reality of the project. The spectrum of judgements used to select what might be valuable in a contested field range from the most pragmatic and empirical to more fugitive qualities, and as such the design process typically ranges from assembling hard site data through to a more tacit understanding of what is at play. In terms of re-use of physical artefacts, one might be alert to fabric which is too precious or tough to erase. This encompasses work to listed (historically protected) buildings for example, or to the prioritisation of labour to achieve the desired effect with the least resistance.[27]

As Koolhaas has noted,[28] the trajectory of conservation and heritage is inextricably bound up with the modernist project and an integral component of it. The confrontational position of critics like Ian Nairn in the 1960s, to propel the conservationist instinct towards a richer cultural involvement in the particularity of settings, and the ingredients of place, has settled into a banality of conservation closely allied to the particular economics of property ownership as investment. What began as a radical movement (i.e. the fight to save London's Covent Garden market from re-development) has become a deeply reactionary impulse, closed to the discipline except on the highly defined terms of established conservation practice.

The extraordinary adaptive ability of much of London's Georgian fabric – the terraces of Westbourne Grove for example – may be ascribed to their non-deterministic grain, allowing them to be subdivided into bedsits when times are hard, and to act as single mansions when in turn the area becomes more prosperous. A client of the practice selects London buildings to purchase for redevelopment by assessing whether they have 'good bones', allowing adaptation in relation to the orientating armature of the host.

Implied in the project of differentiation – the resistance to homogeneity – is an enjoyment of the scenographic qualities of juxtaposition, and the acknowledgement of the picturesque tradition of English landscape as a series of experiential conditions, to be encountered sequentially. The sequential or episodic understanding of a project also becomes evident in the culture of understanding a project – in particular a large-scale project – as something that evolves over time, rather than aspiring to a fixed, ideal formal condition or end-state. This attitude, familiar to landscape practitioners who have to work with the long timescales of planting, lies behind the most distinctive work of the practice.

The opportunistic and staged realisation of a project has many roots in the culture of the practice, from the experience of theatrical production of situations through to an interest in how things might 'come off' – an entrepreneurial attitude to spatial possibility discussed earlier. These twin temporal dynamics – sustained long-term commitment and more expedient 'can-do' responses – also map to the distinct sorts of knowledge developed through the typical design process.

PARTS AND WHOLES

We maintain that the œuvre of the practice is purposefully heterogeneous and not driven by formal concerns; however, it is certainly the case that our working approach to design has had consequences which exhibit a surprising consistency between projects, and that discussion of this continuity has been somewhat sublimated. One response to emerge very early in presenting the work at Practice Research Seminars was that discourse of the aesthetic dimensions of projects had been neglected. This challenge arose at the first presentation in response to my positing of the Adelphi, and Easington House, as exemplary models of mediatory structures

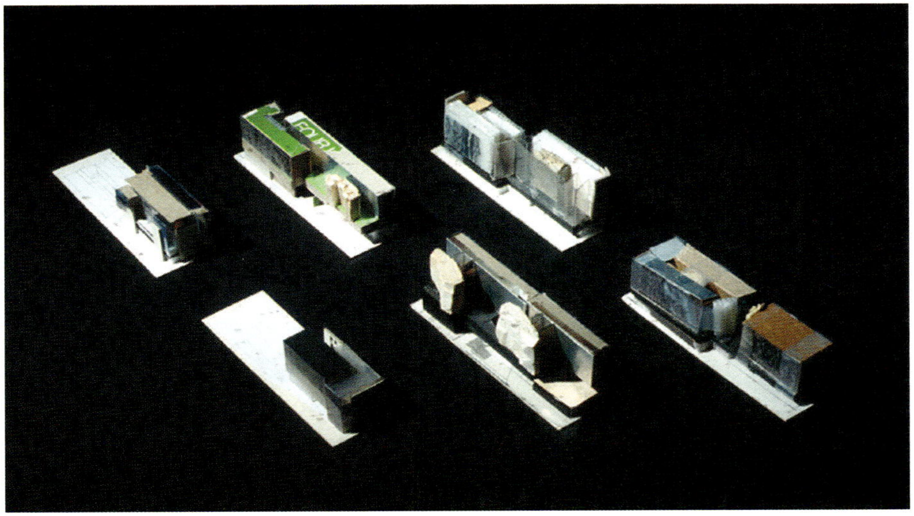

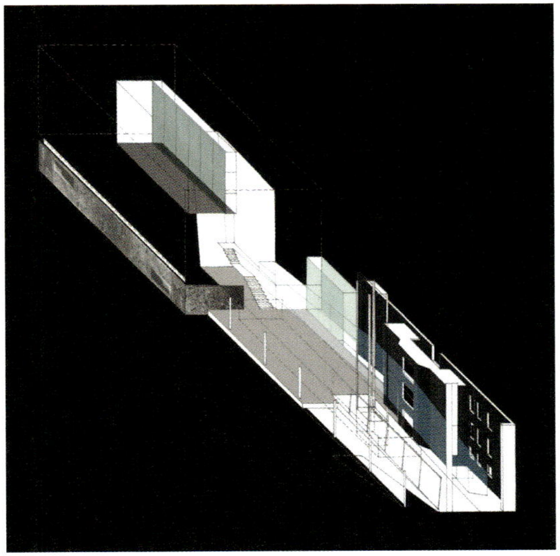

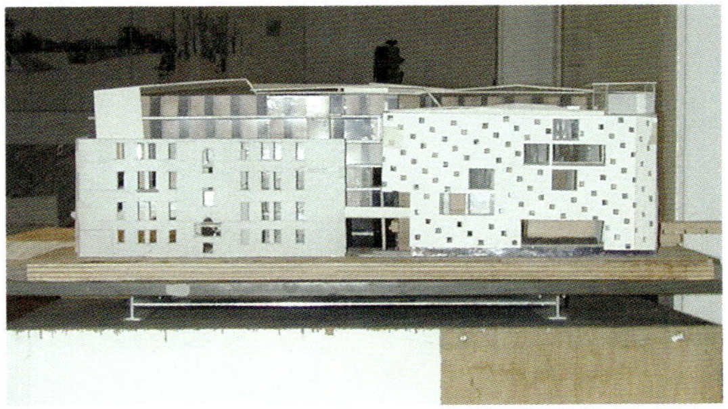

Typical design trajectory of a project: in this case the re-working of a pair of buildings to create a hostel for disabled students, together with a university polyclinic. A series of 1:500 sketch models test the potential 'topography' of the project.

In parallel, collage studies explore the potential of intervention to create key spaces – in this case a foyer and street entrance/elevation.

Axonometric projection drawings explore sequences through the building and help establish hierarchies of spaces.

Sketch models at a larger scale are used as tools to develop and adjust the design.

More finished models follow at key points in the process: This model was produced for dialogue with the client and the planning and conservation bodies.

operating between architecture and infrastructure, and referenced in the design development of the Creative Exchange project.

The architect John Tuomey, participating on a Practice Research Seminar panel, accepted the relevance of these precedents while noting that the distinctive character of both was the un-fractured, singular element of their form:

> In your own work, you are not strongly pushing the sense of the whole. Your work comes across as being assembled out of fractured parts rather than being comparable to those precedents that you cite. Why is your work not more singular, if the things you love are like that?[29]

This challenge has been significant, and ultimately it is only possible to address the question through a more explicit understanding of how critical projects have developed. This chapter therefore concludes with an examination of this phenomenon via a series of case studies. However, Tuomey's question also prompts two associated and more general responses which I would like to rehearse: 'Is the Adelphi really so singular?' and 'In any event, is it possible in contemporary culture to produce a singular architecture?

In many ways, one can see that the aesthetic upheaval emerging from the English Baroque and the Enlightenment signals the emergence of themes that continue to haunt contemporary architecture: primarily, the separation of aesthetics as a philosophical mode distinct from the rest of culture that one encounters, for example, through the work of Hume and Burke. The Adelphi was, after all, imagined as the locus of precisely those emergent Enlightenment structures that Habermas calls 'the bourgeois public sphere',[30] housing numerous coffee houses and the great room for the Royal Society for the Encouragement of Arts, Manufactures and Commerce.

It is immensely significant that the Adelphi, with all its surface continuity, guaranteed by the Romantic attachment to plaster and stucco, was modelled not on Diocletian's Palace, but on the *ruin* of that palace, and that the superficial continuity of its surface is not 'all that meets the eye'.[31]

The Adelphi project clearly responds to contemporaneous ideas emerging from a reappraisal of the work of Vanbrugh, who 'possessed a sense not only for the arrangement and piling up of masses but what might be called architectural drama to a larger degree than any other English architect'[32]

The Adams brothers would have been exposed to radical landscape theory as expounded by figures like Uvedale Price, who, in his *Essays on the Picturesque*, identified its characteristic association with broken or fragmented forms, weather stains, irregularity of effects and the disposition of boundaries.[33]

In response to the second question, as Ignasi di Sola Morales acknowledges in his essay *Terrain Vague*, we no longer operate with the certainties of the Enlightenment but rather through the estrangement of the '*unheimlich*':

> Not the individual endowed with rights, liberties, and universal principles, not the subject of the Enlightenment and of the Declaration of the Rights of Man: on the contrary, here is a politics for the individual in conflict with himself, despairing at the speed at which the whole world is transformed yet aware of the need to live with others, with the other.[34]

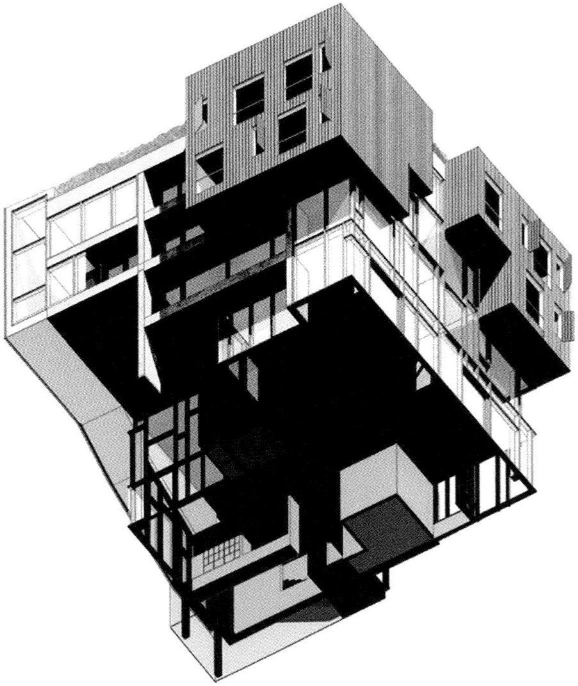

Axonometric of the Creative Exchange, 5th Studio, 2009.

Robert Adam, print, *The Ruins of the Palace of the Emperor Diocletian at Spalatro in Dalmatia*, 1757.

The discussion of the retreat from the singular facade in modern architecture is picked up by Anthony Vidler in his own discussion of the architectural uncanny.[35] To plot the dissolution of the facade he picks up on Colin Rowe's critique of Stirling's Staatsgalerie as a reworking of Schinkel's Altes Museum but 'without a facade'. Vidler follows a thread from Schinkel's already dissolving elevation through Le Corbusier's Chandigarh Assembly to the Staatsgalerie, referencing Rowe's critique of that building which 'in other respects seemed to reply successfully to his general criticism of modernism, especially with regard to its replication of a fragmented urban discourse that to all intents and purposes echoes the formal project of Rowe's own *Collage City*'.[36]

BRICOLAGE

In earlier discussion of the practice's domestic projects, I referenced the notion of 'contamination' as a – sometimes violent – interventional critique of the original host. This translatory attitude to existing fabric appears as one of the roots of what otherwise might be read as a 'punk' aesthetic, establishing as it does a vocabulary of materials which, in their nature, are fragments assembled as bricolage.

In one Research Seminar, I noted the practice's decision to cease work on domestic projects as a significant moment, and this caused some discussion. This decision was not driven by distain for the small projects on which we cut our teeth, but was rather in recognition that the trajectory in that world, as our reputation increased, was towards the 'boutique' and it was precisely the edginess and essential incompleteness of the work which we valued that became less possible in that context.

The sensibility of bricolage reflects in a very direct way the desired bridge between the different sorts of knowledge in play in the design process, from the strategic through to provisional and engaged operations on the ground. Irenée Scalbert's essay *The Architect as Bricoleur* acknowledges the practical wisdom inherent on the bricolage process:

> Bricolage cannot have a form because, to the bricoleur, it is a life process. Nor can bricolage have a philosophy, insofar as it does not lend itself to concepts and theories. Instead bricolage values flair, wisdom and forethought, resourcefulness, deception and vigilance, opportunism, skill and experience. Bricolage is a form of cunning. . . the bricoleur is always waist-deep in practical situations, nowhere more comfortable than between the sensible and the intelligible, between the earthly and the aerial.[37]

It is certainly the case that the design process and the tendency of projects to develop over long periods of time extend the contingent effects of the peripheral forces shaping the project. This temporal extension, together with the interest in multivalency, is well-matched to the episodic generosity of collage. To quote Florian Beigel:

> In the discussion about the relativity of parts to the whole, the compositional technique of collage is useful as it puts emphasis on relationships of separate but dissimilar events and rather less on the ending. It has the elements of suddenness, free association, multiple meaning. It can capture the infinite. Each part has an integral value within the whole, and at the same time retains its own episodic value. There are no latecomers to a collage.[38]

CASE STUDIES

These case studies illustrate the continuity of 5th Studio's design process, from the scale of a room through to a strategy for a complex landscape.

KENSINGTON CHURCH STREET

This project involved the reuniting of two maisonettes in a house clumsily extended and partitioned into three separate properties in the mid-1980s. The planning process was very difficult, with the Royal Borough of Kensington & Chelsea's planning officers relying on formulaic rules of development: an early scheme to extend the back of the property was unsuccessful and the final scheme concentrates largely on internal modifications. The project is therefore interesting to discuss here as it solely operates within the interior of the host building, but nevertheless embodies a number of ideas about landscape.

Within these tight parameters, we were interested in re-discovering some sense of the scale of the house – both in terms of the obscured hierarchy of primary spaces and the original materiality, lost beneath bland partitioning.

Working around an existing stair that provides access to the top floor maisonette (under separate ownership), the new arrangement seeks a spatial openness absent from the cellular subdivisions of the earlier refurbishment.

The basement has been opened up into a single space for family living. The kitchen, laundry and shower room are enclosed by a layer of placed elements along one party wall. Transitions between public and private areas of the house are developed through layering of screens and light enclosures, rather than partition walls.

Two new staircases were introduced: an external stair, which allows access from the front garden to the basement, and a new internal stair, linking the basement, ground floor and the first floor. The staircases at basement level are twins – one internal and one external. They are both made from concrete, with support walls made from board-marked in-situ concrete, into which are fitted precast concrete treads.

Concrete was selected as a raw, homogenous material. With an in-situ finish, it would evoke the garden that we were prevented from building in, and with a precast finish, it would reference the lost elegance of the original house: a combination of two types of careful making. We worked with Sam Price of the engineers Price & Myers, who has extensive knowledge of the cantilevered staircases often seen in Georgian houses, where the ability of the treads themselves to transfer forces to the ground allows a delicacy of structure. This allowed us to make something visceral and substantial, yet light and perforate.

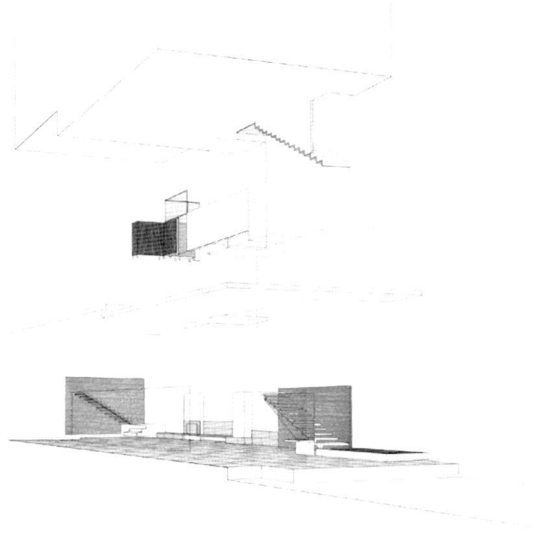

Perspective 'pop-off' identifying the interventions as a series of furniture screens within a cleared primary architectural space. The drawing also identifies the twin stairs at basement level, one internal, one external in the 'area' which provides access from the front garden.

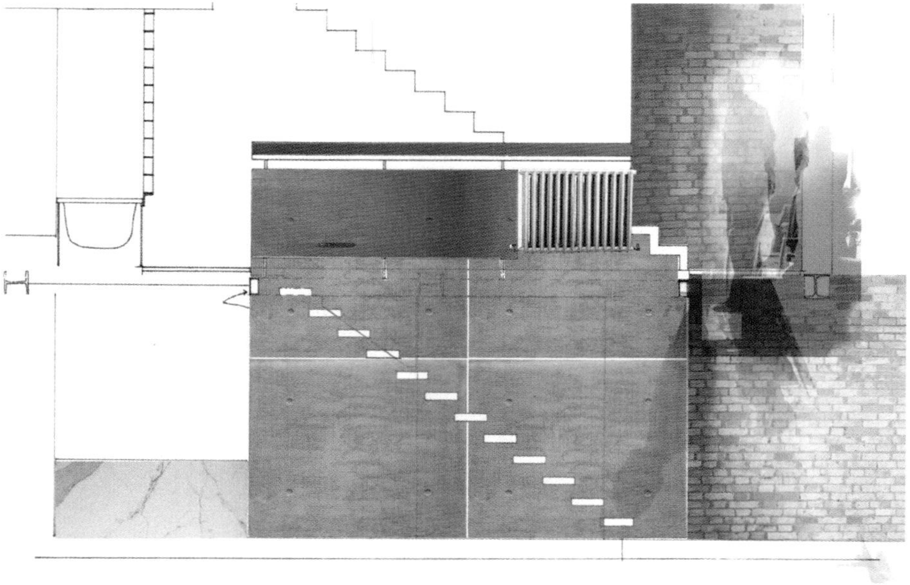

An early sketch section identifies the desired quality of light and material to create a more visceral connection between house and garden.

The internal stair in elevation, contrasting board-marked in-situ concrete on the party wall with in-situ concrete treads.

Floor plans at basement, ground, first and second floors.

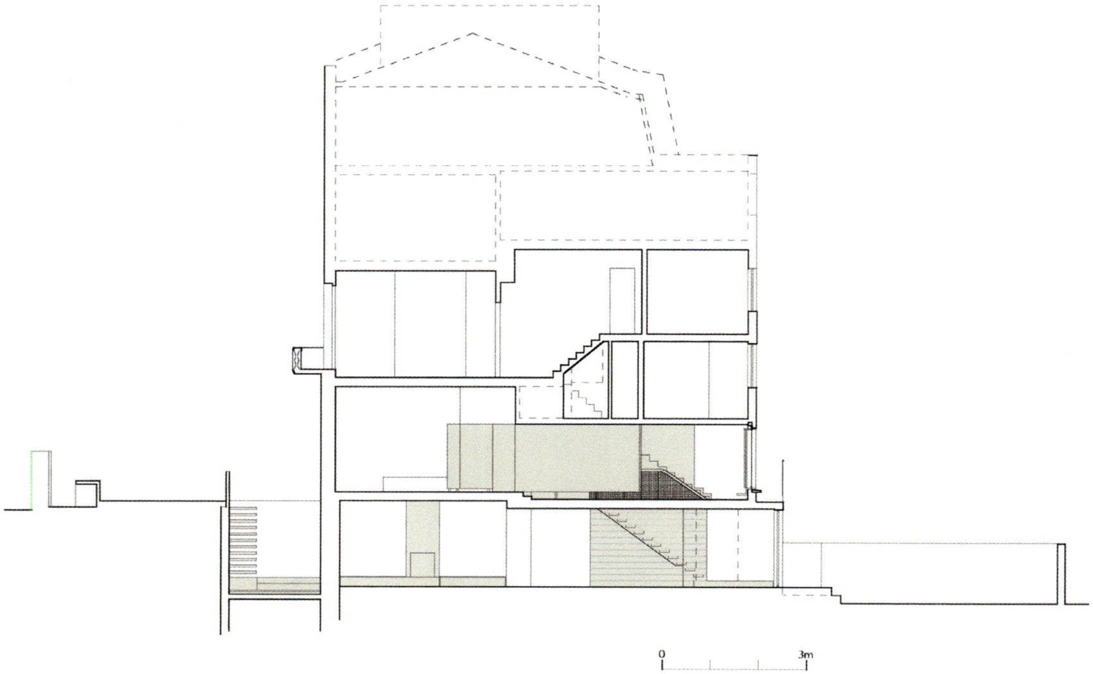

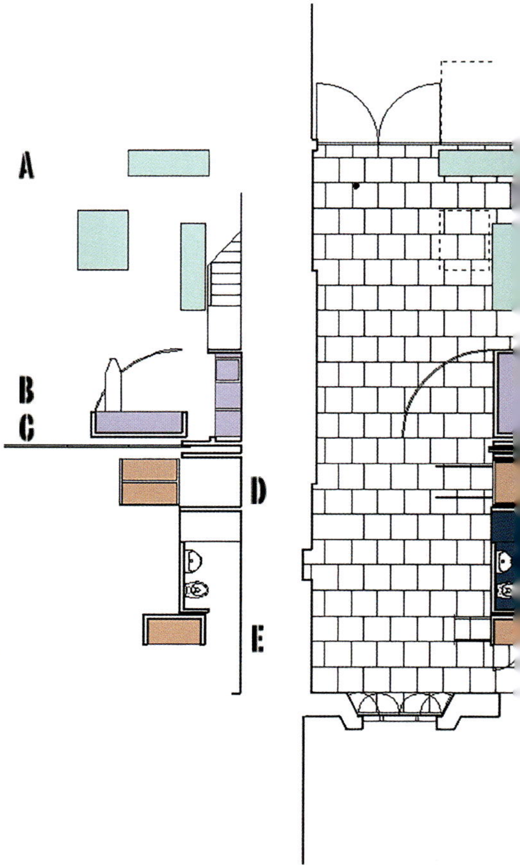

Section through the house showing the two reunited maisonettes. Kensington Church Street is to the left.

Early diagram. The basement opened up into a single space. The kitchen, laundry and shower room are enclosed by a layer of hinging, folding elements along one party wall.

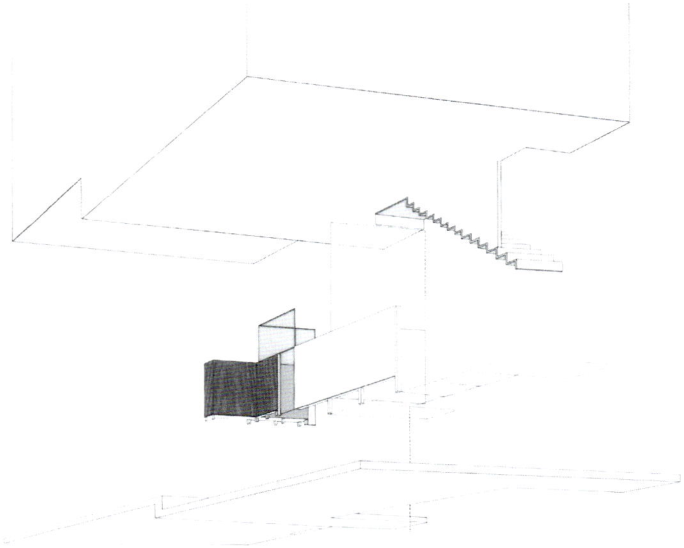

Axonometric, upper ground floor – a furniture piece establishes a dressing room corridor and en suite bathroom as a vitrine behind the headboard for the master bedroom, allowing the main volume of the room to be read at upper level.

Photograph by D Grandorge.

Photograph by D Grandorge.

Photograph by D Grandorge.

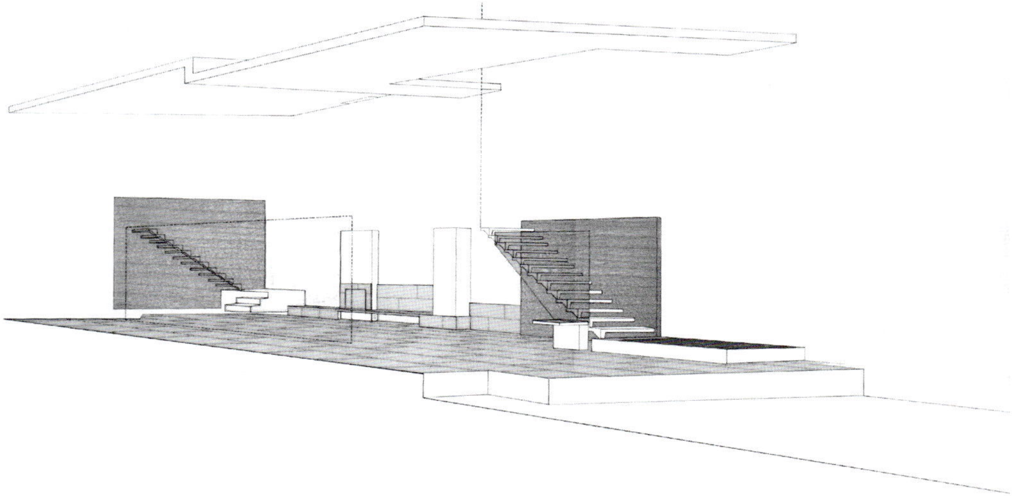

Axonometric – basement – the kitchen and utility room are enclosed behind a timber screen. A concrete staircase reunites the basement with the ground floor internally. Its twin, illustrated over, connects the basement to the street.

Photograph by author. Tom Holbrook

Photograph by D Grandorge.

Basement – the screen also encloses a shower room and WC. Photograph by D Grandorge.

The front window opens to an excavated area, with a stair up to the front garden and street. Photograph by D Grandorge.

The Kensington project was informed by work on my first house, featuring a wall-scaled door, which became a feature of a number of subsequent projects, such as Victoria Street.
Tom Holbrook

Victoria Street – the framing of internal spaces draws inspiration from paintings of Dutch interiors and from the adjustments to my own houses.

The pavilion as we found it.
Tom Holbrook

THE GEORGE V PAVILION

The use of collage techniques at Kensington Church Street can be seen even more explicitly at the George V Pavilion. In contrast to the interiority of the Kensington project, this project primarily involved the wrapping of a building's exterior.

We originally became involved in Trumpington – a village directly to the south of Cambridge on the edge of a major growth area – through the development of a community infrastructure strategy. The local authority became conscious that, alongside the development of new schools, health facilities and other community facilities for the new urban development, the existing community had been neglected. We were therefore invited to extend our very large-scale strategic work to include some highly practical hands-on community engagement and to consider where funds could be spent on the village's pavilion, as they became available.

Originally built in the early 1950s, the pavilion forms a gateway onto the local recreation ground, but the building had been poorly treated and maintained for many years. Vandalism and neglect had led to all but one of the many connections between the

After the work – the tall window to the kitchen/café acts like a beacon. The front canopy proposes a sheltered place for local kids to hang out. On the right is the over-clad, ready-made changing room. Photography by D Grandorge.

recreation ground and the pavilion building being blocked up. The hall's French casements to the field had been removed and replaced with blockwork.

Because of the blocking off of the outer doors, football teams had to walk through the main space to the changing rooms, pockmarking and spreading mud onto its parquet floor, further reducing the building's usefulness to the broader community. Over time, the remaining glazing had been replaced with translucent polycarbonate and steel doors guarded access doors. The building was dark and unloved and, to local kids and users of the recreation ground, seemed outdated and irrelevant.

BETWEEN SECURITY AND DELIGHT

From the building's history of neglect and defence against damage, we became interested in how to develop an aesthetic which worked with the materials generally encountered retrofitted over exposed buildings to prevent vandalism. An art and architecture fund enabled us to develop a collaboration with an artist – Michael Tuck – who had formerly worked with the practice as an architect. Early thoughts about defensive buildings and use of camouflage or dazzle patterns were developed into a method of colouring standard multicell polycarbonate sheets. Combined with a sprayed steel mesh, this gave us a layered robust but beautiful composite to wrap around both the existing pavilion, and the new addition of an 'off the peg' changing room block. The mesh unifies the original and new structures, unifying their exterior while making something new and contemporary from the old building.

Part of the wider strategic work we were developing, which led to our appointment on the very practical upgrading of the pavilion.

This included much consultation with the local community groups on what they would like the building to provide.

The front canopy and entrance.
D Grandorge

The re-glazed elevation to the playing field, protected by a sliding security gate. The changing rooms are to the left.
D Grandorge

"... the building has one final trick in store: the grille running along this elevation has been designed as an enormous retractable security gate. With the push of a button, 8m of steel mesh is sent slowly motoring along the facade until the full expanse of glazing is exposed . . .. It is a moment emblematic of a scheme that balances the demands of accessibility and fortification with considerable invention and a great deal of charm." *Building Design*, 29 January 2010.
D Grandorge

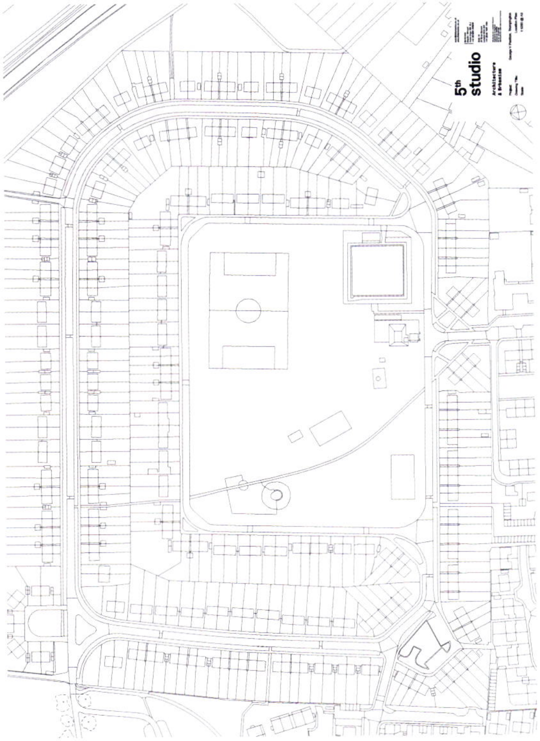

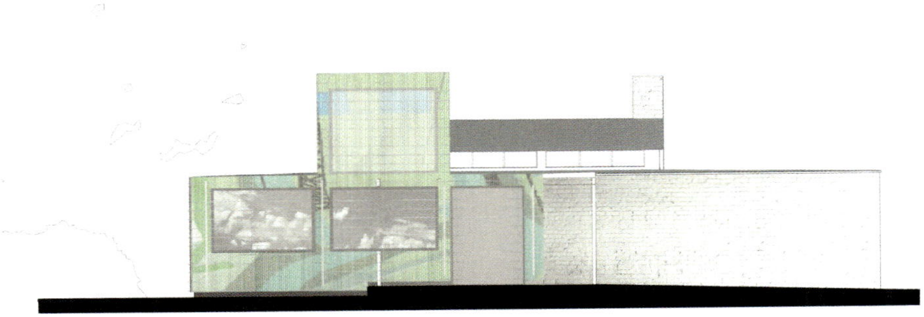

Site plan of the pavilion on its playing field, surrounded by council housing from the 1950s.

Details of the layered cladding of original building, new extension and off-the-peg changing room block.
D Grandorge

Road elevation.

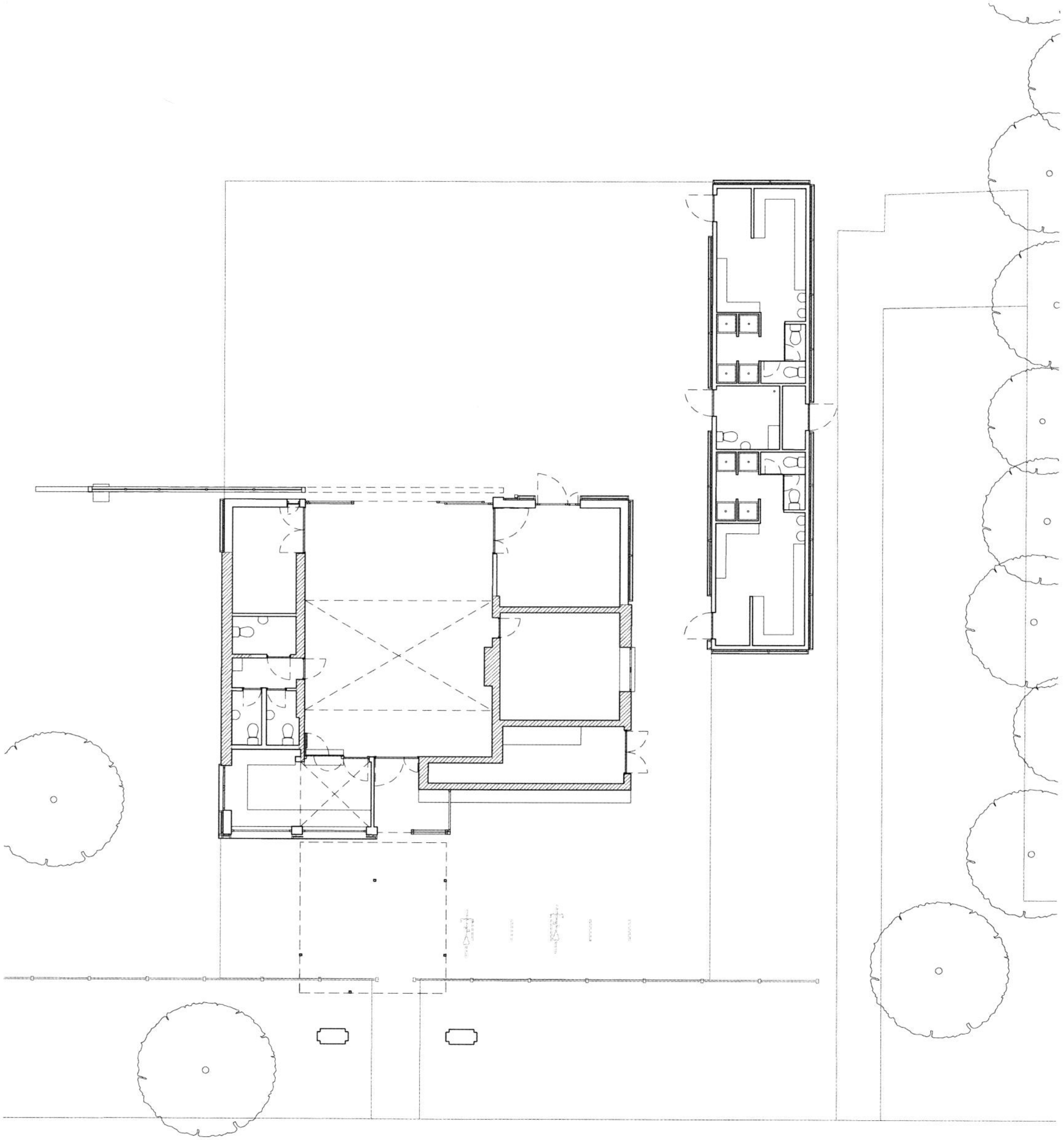

Plan of the ensemble.

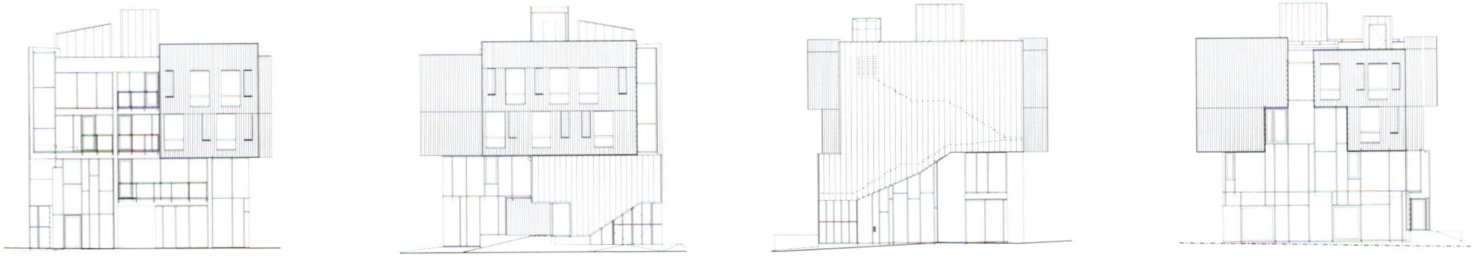

Model of the Creative Exchange.

The roof garden.

Elevations.

CREATIVE EXCHANGE

The Creative Exchange project has been discussed earlier in this document in terms of its wider urbanistic scope, but the project appears again here in terms of its ambition to create a generous structure from a highly predefined and restricted brief and budget.

Our research of the typology of shared workspaces revealed a tendency towards elongated low-rise forms with sets of rooms structured along a fire corridor, resulting in a series of silos offering little chance of interaction and serendipity. We wanted to find space for interaction and mutual support, but this did not appear in the brief, and there was no leeway in the budget for additional area.

The defined areas of the programme were made into a series of scaled volumetric blocks, and it was soon apparent that stacking the programme structured the building with a vertical order: public rooms for events and interaction at ground level, a shared studio space at first floor, then individual spaces for fourteen different firms on the upper two floors, with accommodation on each floor clustered around a public 'hall', orientated to the park. This hall space was created 'free' from concentrating what would have been a circulation corridor into a room. More useful 'free' space was found by creating a working garden on the roof, accessed by the lift.

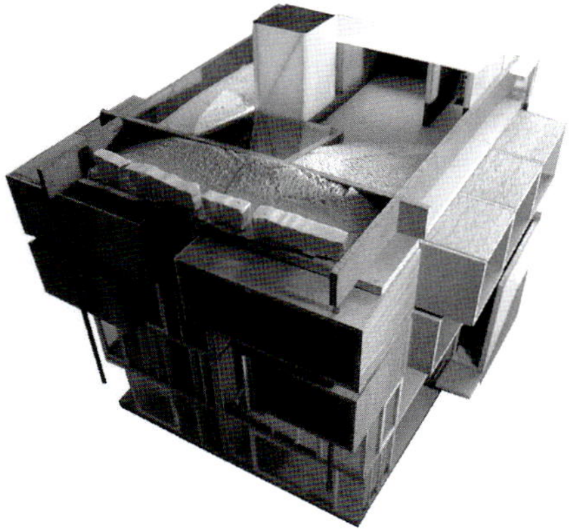

The brief – itself derived from a business plan commissioned by the local authority client – cut into volumetric blocks.

The blocks deployed as the client imagined them – as a range of rooms along a corridor in a single-storey building.

The programme stacked vertically condenses the corridor into a central hall, ultimately used for social interaction, ventilation and for dropping light into the middle of the plan.

Model made at various stages of the design process, from 1:100 to 1:20.

Model made at various stages of the design process, from 1:100 to 1:20.

Aware that the success of the project lay in the building's ability to accommodate the detritus of around twenty creative firms, we wanted to direct the budget to making a generous armature, rather than obsess about seeking to control the fit out by users of the building. I was delighted when a passer-by asked me 'is it finished yet?', as clearly, until occupied and under the direction of its inhabitants, the building is unfinished.

The limits of our control were brought home by the lack of comprehension by the local authority client on how to properly market the building. They ultimately delegated this role to a building management business, who let the spaces

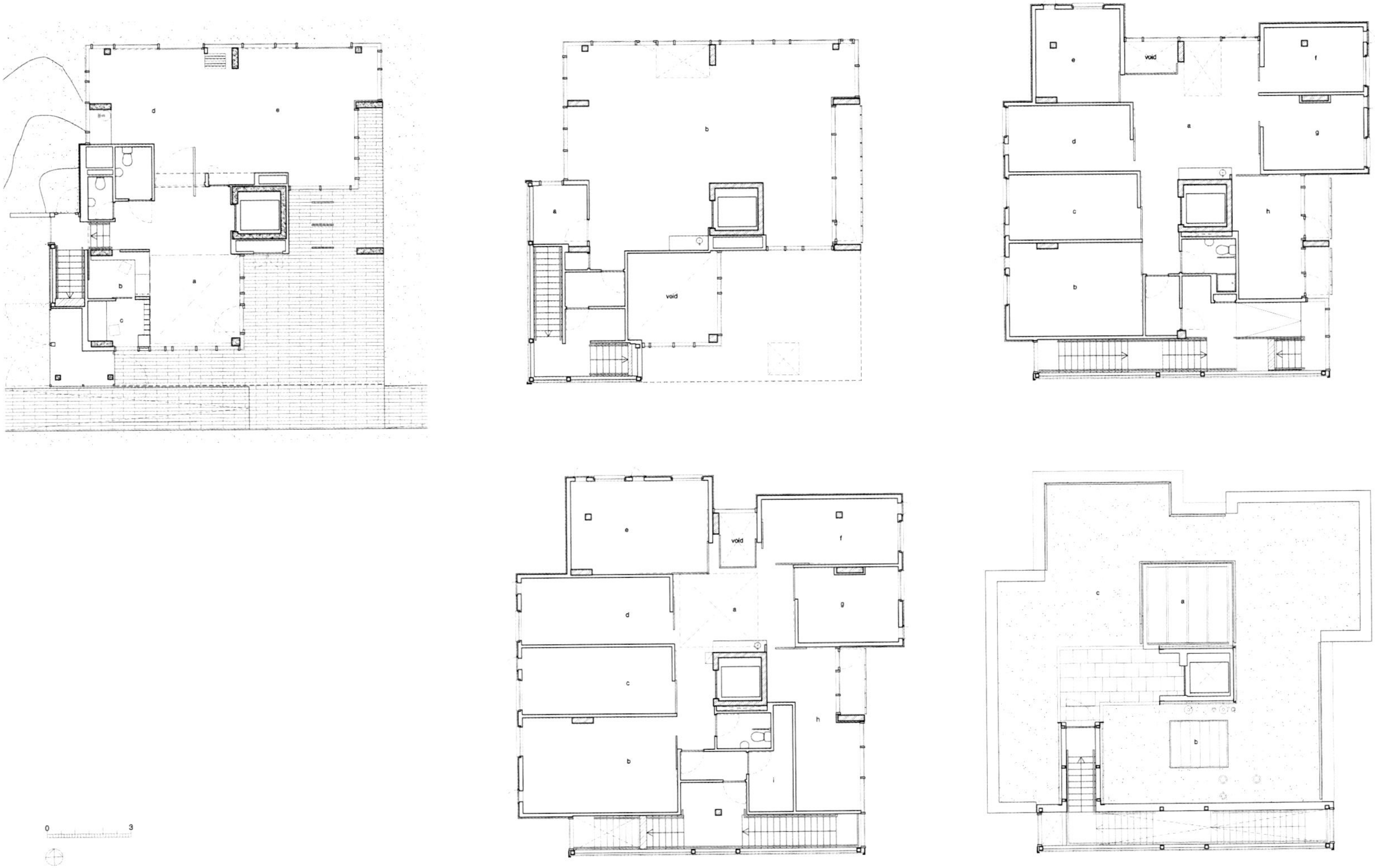

Plans at key levels.
Top row: Ground floor – concierge, meeting and exhibition rooms; first floor – shared studio; second floor – seven workrooms around a hall.
Bottom row: Third floor – seven workrooms around a hall; roof garden.

The use of concrete forms a self-finished armature which is then subdivided by partitions and linings using the ply formwork. This reference to the making or craft of the building seems an important connection to the otherwise elusive notion of a 'creative economy', as does creating a meaningful connection with the landscape beyond.
Tim Soar

Tim Soar

not to creative start-up firms as intended, but to general businesses looking for cheap office space. The unfinished quality of the building was not understood by these residents, and we were told that carpet tiles, suspended ceilings and the other generic ingredients of the standard office have since been introduced.

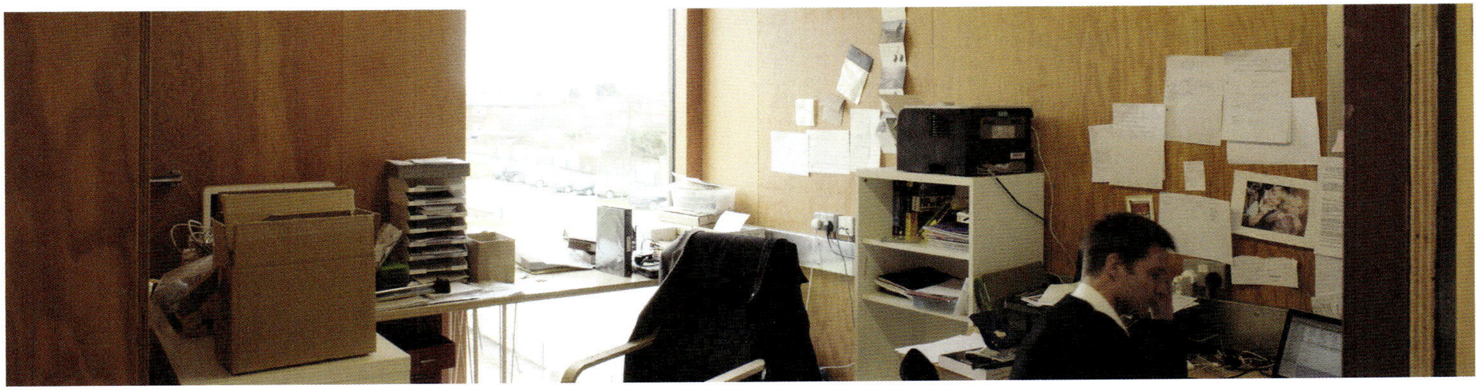

Drawing of a speculative fit out of a workspace.

Inside a workspace.
D Grandorge

5th studio

Architecture
& Urbanism

mail@5thstudio.co.uk
www.5thstudio.co.uk

Sent from

Darkroom
Gwydir Street
Cambridge CB1 2LJ
t +44 (0)1223 516009
f +44 (0)1223 566010

Unit 14
21 Wren Street
London WC1X 0HF
t +44 (0)20 7837 7221
f +44 (0)20 7837 7065

Creative Exchange
A Note on the Architecture

In designing Creative Exchange we were faced with a number of questions: What is it that makes a workspace 'creative'? How do we make judgements about how best to spend the tight budget for the project? How do we make sense of the building's position on the edge of Priory Park, St Neots?

With the intention of maximising the value of what the architecture contributed, we looked at our own experience, and the sorts of spaces that we have chosen in the ten years since setting up our firm. We have always had the sense that the work we do comes from a studio, rather than an office - the clue is in our name! We would always choose an unheated wreck with nine-foot ceilings over the easy comfort of a ready-fitted office. Looking across the world's cities, artists of all kinds are always the first to populate the fringes, looking for unusual and inspiring spaces, often left over from industry.

At Creative Exchange we have tried to create a generous building, making the floor to ceiling heights as high as we can, opening up between each floor, and between the building and the park beyond, so that the light animates the building. We have made a space which is purposefully very different to the domestic space of a house - an alternative to the spare bedroom where many businesses start up. Despite that, we did have a super-domestic model in mind - that of the English Country house, the location of so much invention over the centuries, with a mix of public rooms on the lower floors and more private rooms above, sitting in a remarkable park.

We have condensed the building, and made it vertical, turning what are often fire corridors into useful shared hall spaces on the upper floors - here we hope that different firms can have a shared space where they can support each other over a cup of coffee, or get advice on a late-night layout for a deadline. The materials we have used to make the building are left exposed - a reminder that this building is about making and crafting.

Creative Exchange has a big character: we hope that its new inhabitants will love it, and add their own layer of occupation, so that each workspace develops its own unique character within the larger community.

Tom Holbrook
Director

5th Studio is a Limited Company
Registered in England
Company No. 3373123
VAT No. 711 206 489
5th Studio is a RIBA Chartered Practice

A letter to new residents.

View into a workspace from the hallway.
D Grandorge

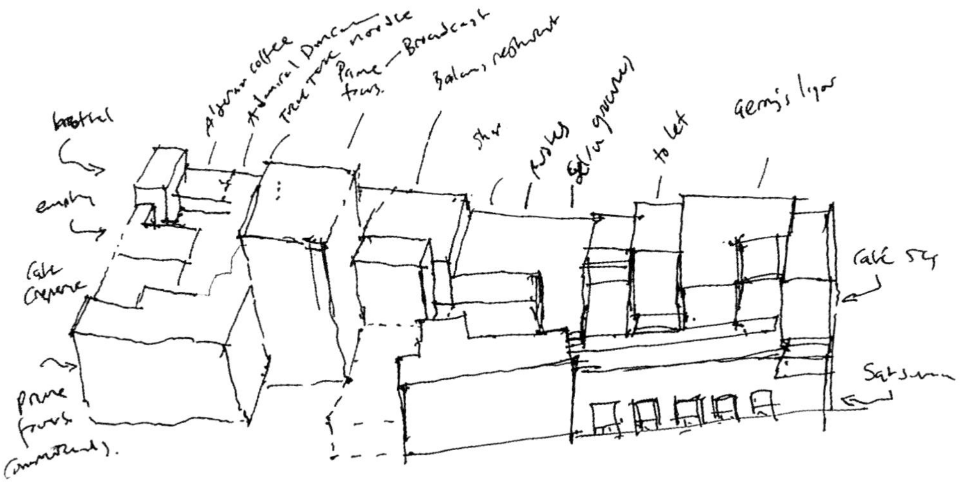

Part of an extensive audit of the block and current uses.

AN URBAN BLOCK IN SOHO

This project explores a strategy for the incremental transformation of a complete urban block, bounded by Old Compton Street, Wardour Street and Bourchier Street in London's Soho.

Soho is on a trajectory from being the seedy heart of London's sex industry towards prime value land. Sex shops are steadily being converted into restaurants, which command astonishingly high rents in return for their location. Former brothels now house an expansion of Wardour Street's film post-production world. As Soho's gentrification continues apace, planning regulations of this conservation area resists change to the external appearance of the street. Opportunities for altering the built fabric exist almost solely in the replacement to damage from wartime bombing, mostly dating from the 1950s.

The model identifies these moments of opportunity – both in terms of the perimeter of the urban block and the less protected spaces of the bock interior, which – as they are now in common ownership – may now work across former plot divisions as a singularity.

Using extensive physical modelling to understand the complex grain, the study explores the potential for intensification of a whole urban block, with the aim of enabling the interior of the block to work as effectively as the successful street frontage, and to provide complimentary scale and type of volume to the cellular rooms available in the seventeenth and eighteenth century buildings lining the street.

Large technical spaces are required by Soho's burgeoning media and film special effects community, and we proposed that these form a deep block interior, with access from two new internal courts. The changing vertical grain is also recognised, with a transition from street front up to a variegated roofscape. The strategy allows for incremental transformation of the fabric as leases expire, allowing building work. Opportunities for new buildings and for spatial expansion are identified.

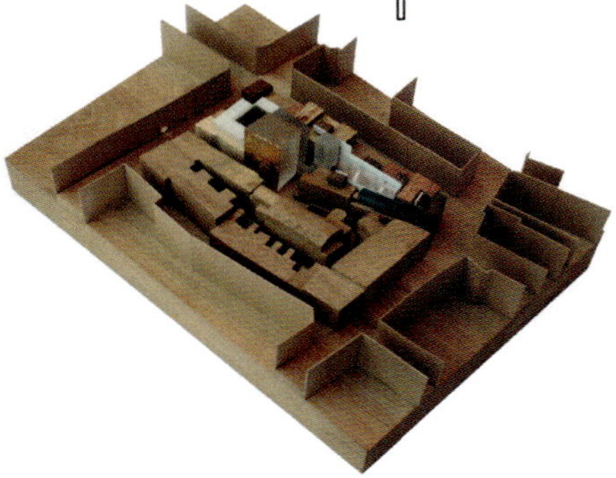

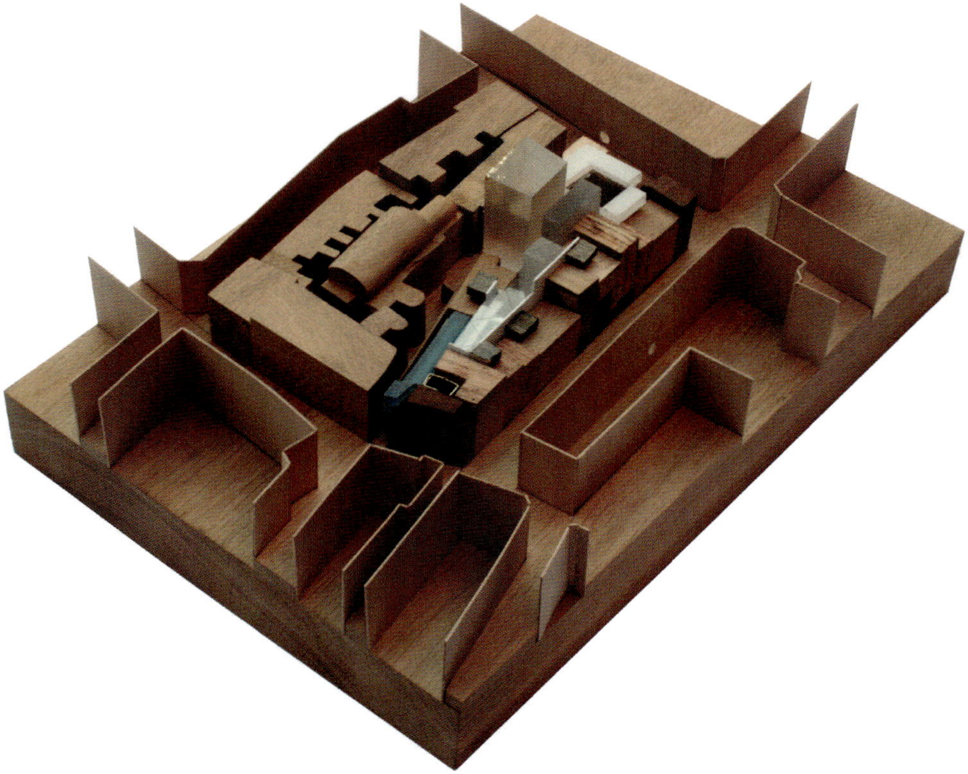

Design model exploded: 6. Hotel 'special' with rooftop pool makes a corner with a long view along Brewer Street. 5. New living spaces envisaged as a vitrine-like tower over Bourchier Street, the only area of the site not currently occupied. 4. A series of 'garrets' created along the block roofline. 3. The less useful 1950s infill on Old Compton Street are replaced with bespoke buildings which also configure a relationship with the block interior. 2. Internal court and connective tissue aimed at catalysing an effective block morphology. 1. Large-scale internal volumes in cleared block interior create highly technically controlled spaces providing sound stages for media use for instance. Base. The edited state which acknowledges the high value of the existing street frontages of shops and restaurants, together with a useful grain of rooms at higher level.

The model of the block, assembled.

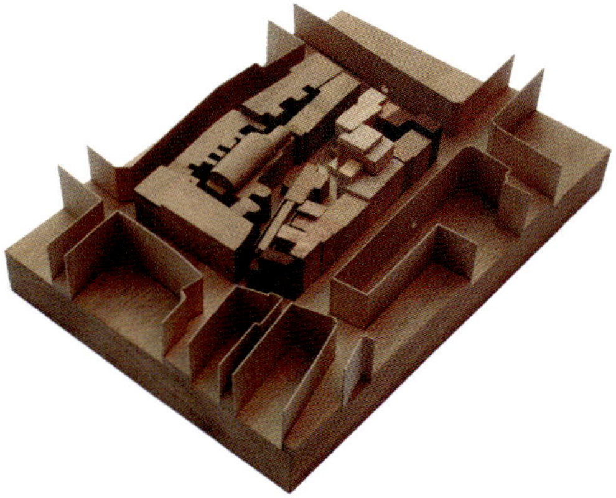

The block modelled as it exists. The various ages of buildings are reflected in the tone of the wood used. Since Soho has become a carefully protected conservation area, this coding also identifies where intervention might be possible, and where it would be resisted by the planning authorities.

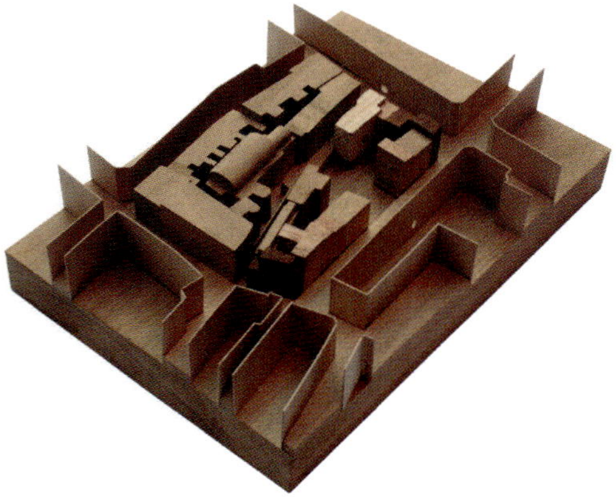

'Soft' fabric removed from the model includes two properties on Old Compton Street which were rebuilt in the 1950s, replacing buildings damaged during the Blitz. The frontages to the block are very high value, and work well in terms of accommodating various uses that need well-proportioned rooms. The interior of the block, being largely an ad hoc extension to the original fabric, is less contentious in conservation terms, as well as being the least fit for contemporary needs.

The interior of the block is made more accessible by the first intervention – a new arcade running from Old Compton Street to Bourchier Street. . .

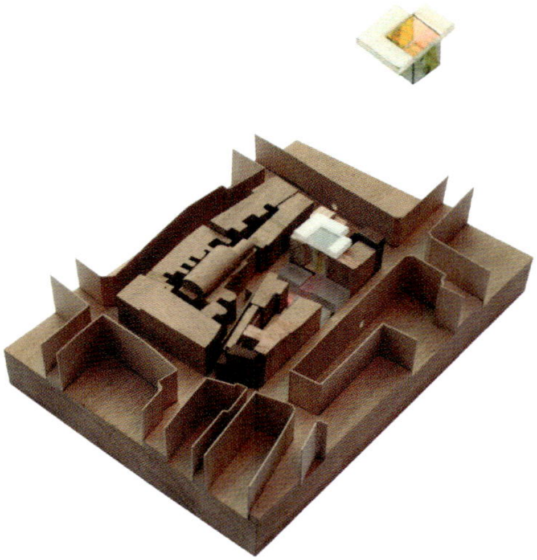

. . .which gives access onto a court, providing a connective 'address' to the block interior at the east end, together with new larger scaled 'infrastructure' found in the heart of the block, providing a soundstage and bluescreen post-production facilities.

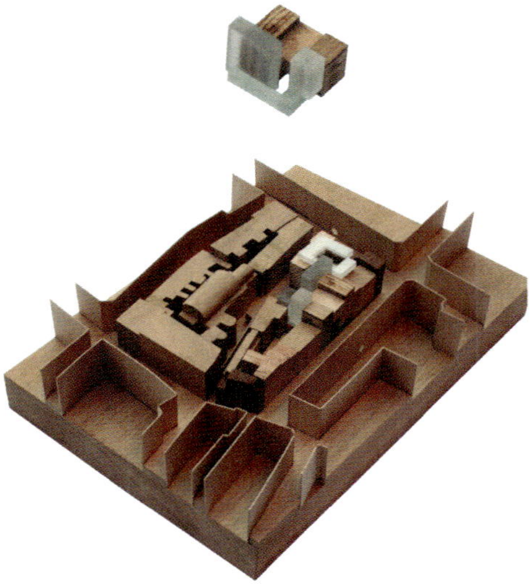

The 1950s buildings are replaced with new buildings that create more bespoke facilities, while maintaining the street line.

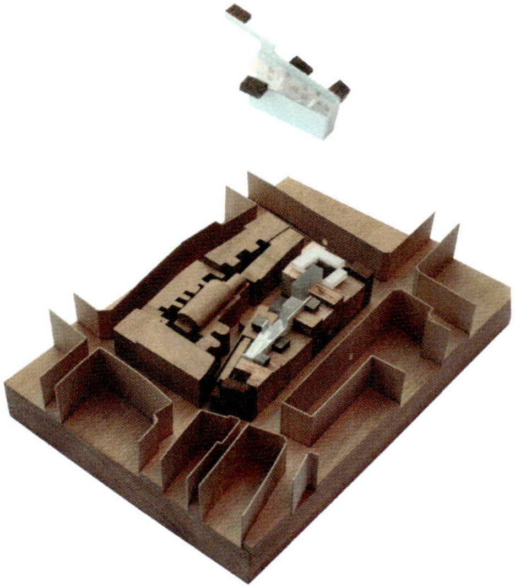

The block interior works much more vertically to complement the cellular spaces of the original fabric of the houses. A series of studios and penthouses appear at the highest level above the technical space in the middle of the block.

A yard, currently used for car parking and refuse, is identified as the location for a nine-storey residential tower. New frontages onto Bourchier Street aim to make this a more active street.

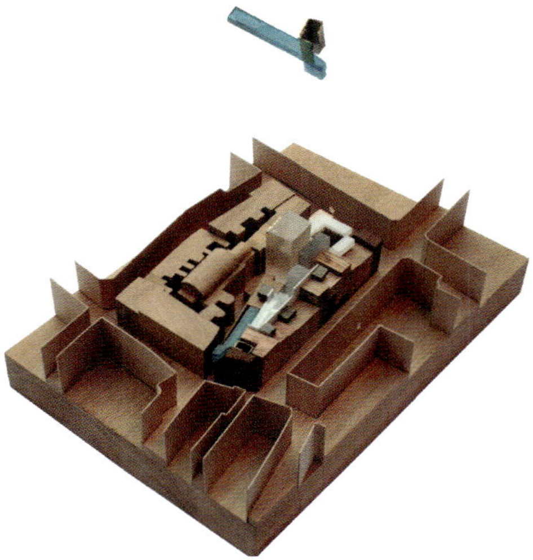

At the West end of the block, where it meets Wardour Street, a hotel is formed, with a rooftop bar and pool joining a family of attic-level fragments with connections across the upper horizon of Soho.

A 'seige-tower' connection at Twelvetrees Crescent, providing a link between a towpath and a privately-owned listed bridge.

THE LEAWAY, OR FATWALK

The Leaway is the primary project in the realisation of the Lea River Park, connecting the Thames and the Olympic Park, as well as establishing critical cross-valley routes.

Funding for the first phase of works to create the Lea River Park was originally set at £28 million. Part of this funding was used to establish a continuous route through land assembly, as the backbone of the future park and was therefore directed at addressing physical severances and obstructions: establishing a route connection at Bow Locks, a new crossing over the Lea at Poplar Reach and a means of crossing beneath the A13 motorway flyover near Canning Town.

These early pieces of infrastructure are regarded as catalysts for converting what is currently land used for gas storage, sewage pumping and transport infrastructure into diverse park spaces of the Lea River Park: turning what is an industrial backwater into the foreground of a new public space which people can start to access, use and enjoy.

The Leaway engages with the central concourse of the Olympic Park, ensuring continuity between the two park areas in a continuous but changing environment.

We originally named this project the *Fatwalk* to reflect that it was a manifold of routes that converged in this part of the valley, and to emphasise that it is a place in itself rather than just a linkage between points: one that aggregated all the leftover fragments of land next to infrastructure. The idea of 'fatness' also acknowledged the many intended users, from cyclist to horseriders, but also referenced a tradition

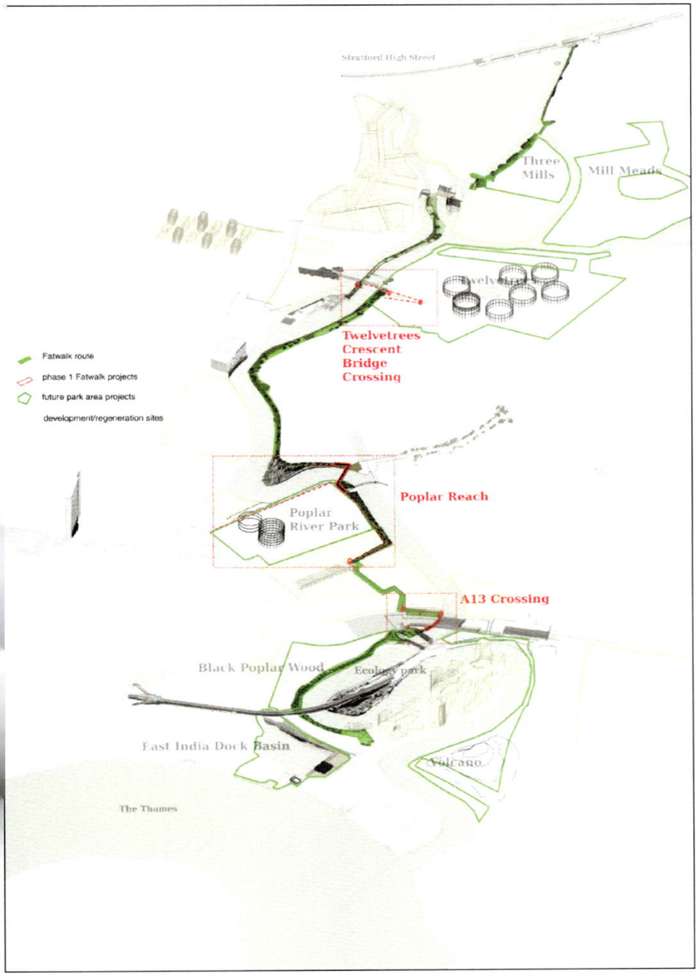

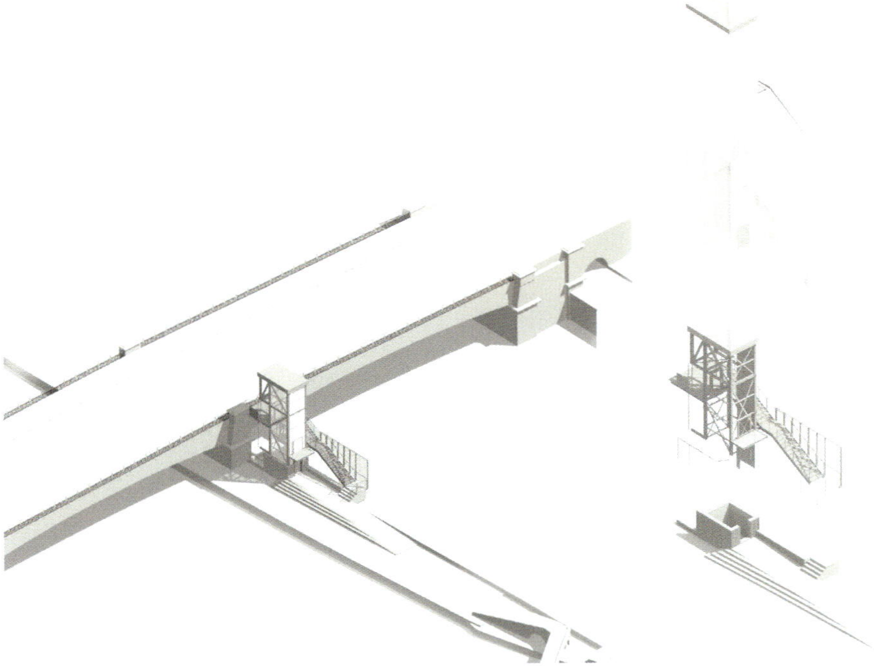

Mapping of phase one interventions in the valley indicating (in red) points of fracture in the ability to access the valley.

The components of the lift and staircase 'seige-tower'.

in London to name places in a resonant way: we used the example of Rotten Row, the well-used riding path in Hyde Park, originally the *Route du Roi*, but corrupted with typical English antiauthoritarian wit. Ultimately, the name Fatwalk proved too contentious for risk-averse commissioners, but the way it stuck in peoples' minds and provoked a response certainly helped us keep the project alive in times of trouble, preventing it slipping from memory.

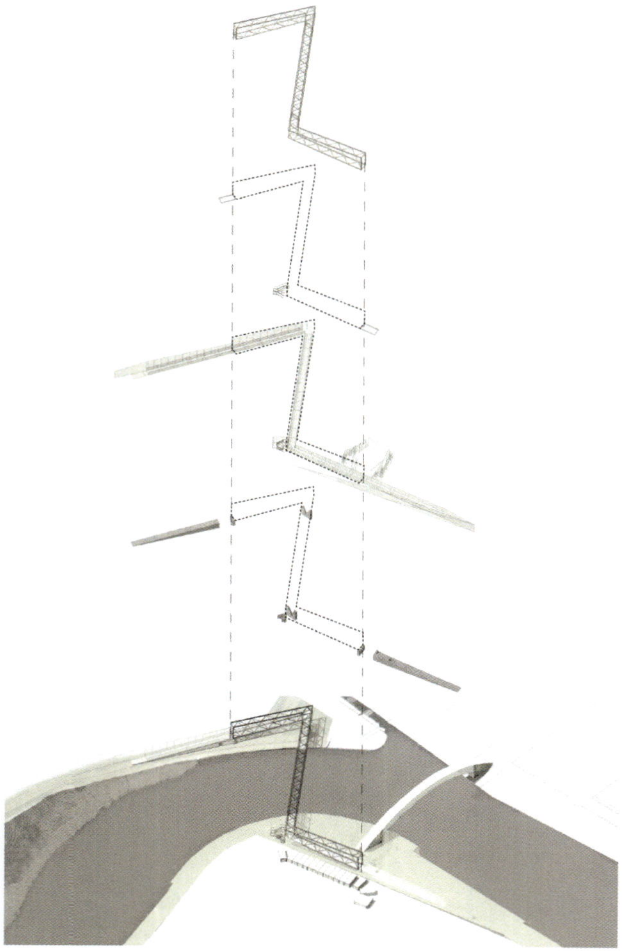

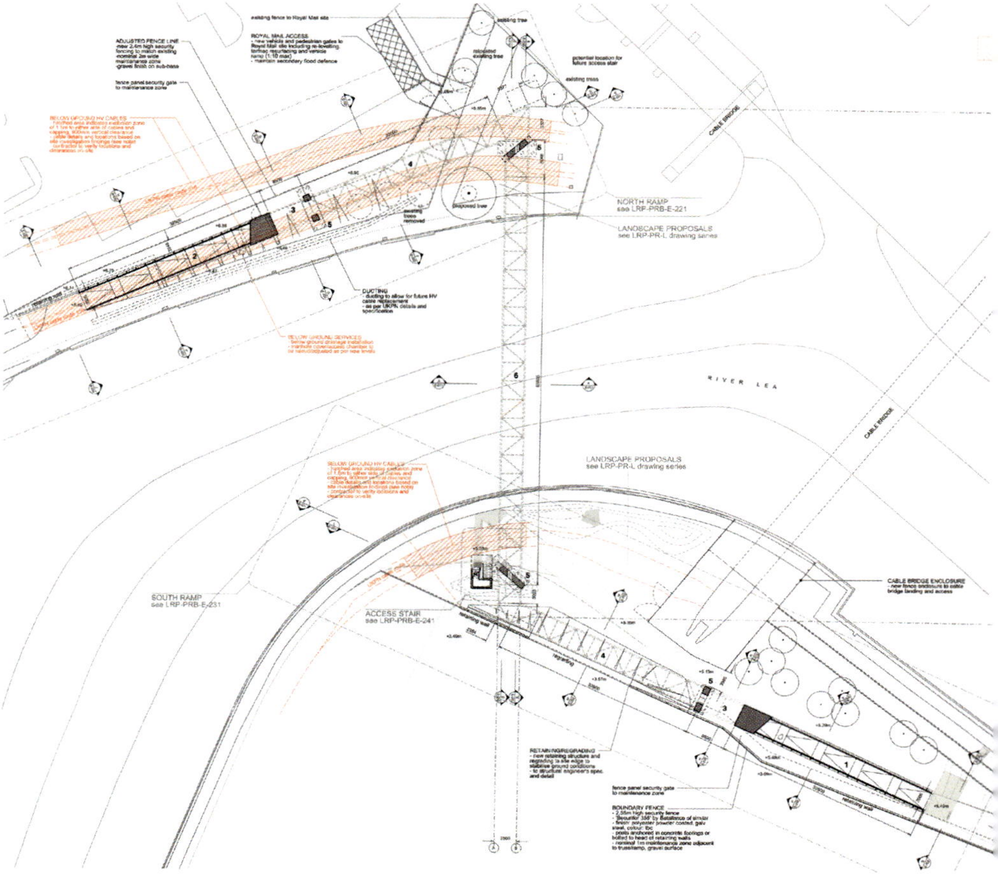

New River Crossing at Poplar Reach: exploded isometric detailing the various elements that make up the bridge.

General arrangement – the bridge avoiding high-voltage cables and other obstacles.

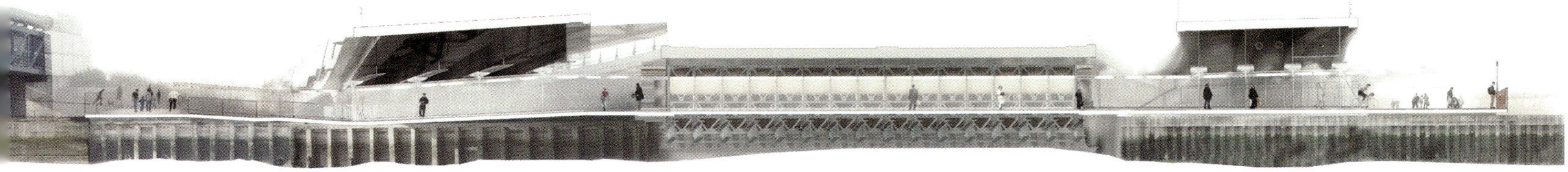

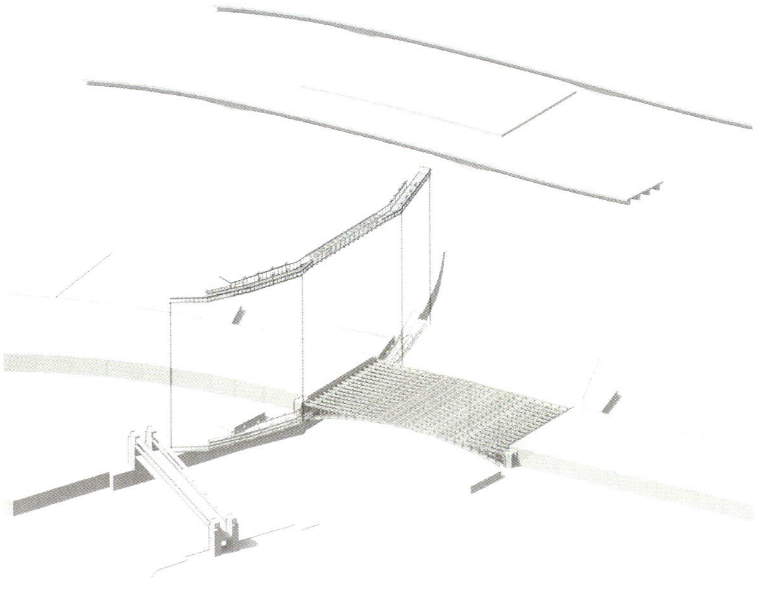

Elevations of the Fatwalk Connector under the A13 motorway, Canning Town. The Connector slings a route through the structural arches of the central river span of the original Victorian cast iron bridge, and hangs a pair of walkways from the two concrete highway ramps that run on either side.

Exploded isometric of the ensemble.

NOTES

1 Professor David Porter, Panel observation. Practice Research Symposium, Ghent, Belgium. November 2011.

2 I am most grateful to Dermot Foley for pointing out the connection to Repton, and for his essay 'The Relationship between Landscape Representation and Landscape Design', *Journal of Architecture*, Vol. 17, No. 1, 2012.

3 Evident, for example, in David Chipperfield's curatorship of the 2012 Venice Biennale, '*Common Ground*'.

4 See Leon van Schaik's discussion of this term in *Mastering Architecture, Becoming a Creative Innovator in Practice*. Wiley, Chichester, UK, 2005.

5 See Anthony Vidler, *James Frazer Stirling: Notes from the Archive*, Yale, New Haven, CT, 2010. Also, from correspondence, Vidler cites Stirling's interest in Roman remains prompted by F. Saxl & R. Wittkower's book on English classicism, *British Art and the Mediterranean*, London, 1948.

6 Robert Venturi's *Complexity and Contradiction in Architecture*, Doubleday, New York, 1966, and Aldo Rossi's writing must be referenced as part of this debate.

7 My thanks to Ellis Woodman for bringing this formative association to my attention.

8 I am grateful to Leon Van Schaik for this observation, which is also referenced in his book *Spatial Intelligence*, p. 74, and for his reference to the work of David Graham Shane illustrated here.

9 Fred Scott was Senior Lecturer at Kingston Polytechnic, which I attended between 1986 and 1990. Kingston was essentially an arts school at this time, and Scott had arrived there from a period at the Architectural Association where he taught with Robin Evans.

10 Vesely and Carl were teaching at the University of Cambridge Department of Architecture, attended from 1991 to 1993. Vesely was invited to Cambridge by Colin 'Sandy' Wilson in 1978. The combination of an art school and university education was, in retrospect, challenging, but rich.

11 Fred Scott, *On Altering Architecture*, Routledge, Abingdon, UK, 2008.

12 Ibid., p. 108.

13 Ibid., p. 113.

14 Fred Scott, 'On Architectural Recycling', *Architecture Today*, 2 November 2008.

15 See, for example, Dalibor Vesely and Mohsen Mostafavi, *Architecture and Continuity*, AA, London, 1982.

16 Ibid.

17 Dalibor Vesely, 'In Defence of Architecture', *Compendium : The Work of the University of Cambridge Department of Architecture*, p. 29.

18 Kieran Long, 'Say Goodbye to All This', *London Evening Standard*, 3 November 2010. (In response to the winding up of the London Development Agency.)

19 Richard Rogers, ed., *Towards an Urban Renaissance*; Urban Task Force, Spon, London, 1999.

20 Brigitte Schultz, Interview in *Bauwelt*, Berlin, No. 24, 26 October 2012.

21 Ibid.

22 Ellis Woodman, 'An Agency to be Cherished', *Building Design*, 29 October 2010.

23 See, for example: Richard Waite, 'Revealed: Design for London's £1.3 Million Handout to Three Practices.' *Architects' Journal*, 25 April, 2013.

24 See my and Paula Kirk's article on this: 'Energy Masterplanning and Urbanism,' *Topos*, No. 75, *Sydney – London – New York*. Munich, June 2011.

25 Professor Leon van Schaik, panel observation, Practice Research Symposium, Ghent, April 2012.

26 Tom Holbrook, 'Carlo Scarpa and the Discontinuity of Fragment'. Unpublished essay, University of Cambridge, 1995.

27 A good example of this lies in the work of Bureau Bas Smets, tasked with the creation of a new National Park in Tartu, Estonia, on the former Soviet airbase. The Estonians initially attempted to tear out traces of the airstrips but found that the runways, built for Tupolev heavy bombers, are armoured concrete 5 metres deep. Smets suggested that they leave the runways in place, and rather transform what's there, learning from local examples of what flora has managed to colonise and take hold.

28 See for example, Rem Koolhaas, *Content*, Taschen, Cologne, p. 458–461.

29 John Tuomey, panel observation, Practice Research Seminar, Ghent, November 2011.

30 Jürgen Habermas, *The Structural Transformation of the Public Sphere* (published *Strukturwandel der Öffentlicheit)*, 1962, trans.1989.

31 Robert Adam, *The Ruins of the Palace of the Emperor Diocletian at Spalatro in Dalmatia, 1757*, published London, 1764.

32 R. Wittkower and F. Saxl, *British Art and the Mediterranean*, Oxford University Press, London 1969.

33 Uvedale Price, *Essays on the Picturesque*, 1794, quoted in Mallgrave, 2005, p. 61.

34 Ignasi Solà Morales, 'Terrain Vague', in *Anyplace*, MIT Press, Cambridge, MA, 1995, p. 122.

35 Anthony Vidler, *The Architectural Uncanny*, MIT Press, 1992.

36 Ibid.

37 Irenée Scalbert, 'The Architect as Bricoleur', *Candide*, No. 4, July 2011.

38 Florian Beigel & Philip Cristou, 'Teasing Modernity', in *Ábalos & Herreros*, Editiones 2G, Editorial Gustavo Gili, Madrid, 2010.

NARRATIVES: BOUNDED OBJECTS, AGGREGATES AND MICROCOSMS; INCIPIENT URBANITY

FUCK CONTEXT?

The extension of an interventionist attitude to the very large scale seems a resilient and adaptive model. I believe that this model has particular relevance to a European topography which faces great flux, as it moves from an explicit industrialised relationship with landscape to a condition which is much more complex and yet mysteriously attenuated in terms of its physical articulation.

The adoption of former industrial structures opens the potential of another order – the inheritance of a space designed to be highly differentiated, where the removal of the original function creates a surplus. As Peter Swinnen notes of 51N4E's C-Mine project, which converts a disused mining complex in Genk, Belgium, into a cultural complex:

> At C-Mine. . .an infrastructure that had been severed from its industrial context was used to give structure to new city fabric. Perhaps it's no longer possible today to build industrial structures of this scale in an urban context. Everything about them seems just too large. . .The unrefined materials allow users to appropriate the building in a rough way. The dimensions of the interior space are pushed to the limits, as if in anticipation of continually new transformations and conversions. These buildings are made out of 'surplus space'.[1]

This problem has fascinated me in both teaching studios and in practice. I have found the fundamental disconnect between a particular building and its role within a larger intentional landscape, a constant source of both frustration and inspiration. The relationship between the immediate and the very large scale has been a key theme explored in studio teaching, as well as in practice, in response to Rem Koolhaas' 'Fuck Context': the notion that, at a certain scale, the autonomy of a project creates it own context. As Peter Carl counters:

> One may say with Rem Koolhaas' 'fuck context', but one never actually fucks context in general, only a particular context; and violation / re-interpretation is anyway more revealing than inevitably ersatz imitation. An intervention, like involvement with anyone or with anything is always a particular dialogue. . .[2]

At the University of Cambridge Department of Architecture, I ran graduate design studios based in London, Istanbul, Lowestoft and Great Yarmouth, and in Hemel Hempstead New Town. The studio looked at the role of architectural creativity in the context of very large-scale planning and the interaction of design with political and economic dynamics. John Tuomey, a visiting critic to the studio, memorably described what we were seeking to accomplish as 'thinking big, but in a particular way'.

The Swiss practitioner and external examiner Professor Marcel Meili commented:

> This studio has been working for several years now, trying to link insights and experiences on a large scale with the actual architectural project. . .. all in all, these projects integrate complex mental relationships in a compact manner into the project and in a quite amazing way.[3]

Both teaching and practice pursue an interest in the manipulation of programme as a component of an elaborate narrative strategy for a site, and in particular, the overlayering of different programmes, implied in the model of the social condenser: 'Programmatic layering upon vacant terrain to encourage dynamic coexistence of activities and to generate through their interference, unprecedented events.'[4]

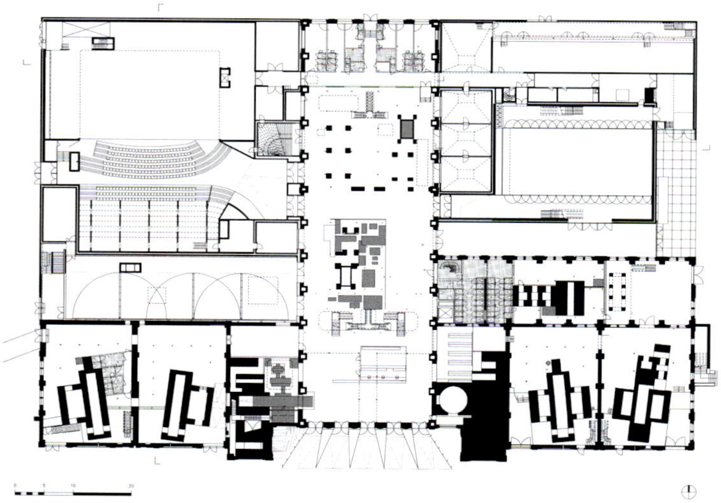

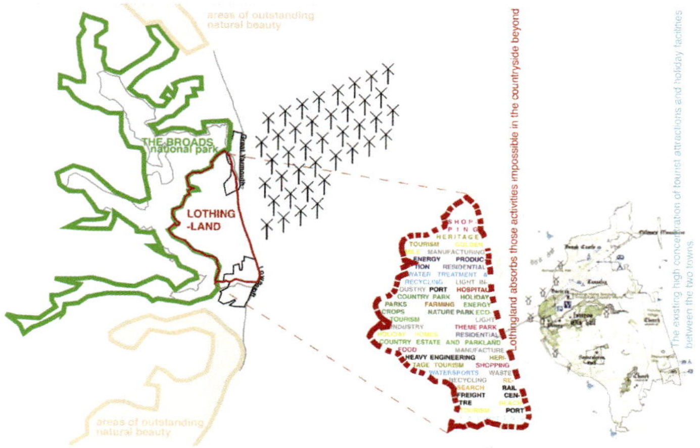

Floor plan of 51N4E's C-Mine – the reworking of a former coal mine in Genk, Belgium, to form a cultural centre. I wrote about this project in the *Architectural Review*, September 2013.
51N4E

Drawing by Kieran Perkins from 2004 diploma studio set in Great Yarmouth and Lowestoft, on England's East Coast.
Kieran Perkins

INFRASTRUCTURE

The use of the term infrastructure appears in our work in a number of ways and requires some definition. First, it is encountered quite literally in the 'contested fields' in which much of our work takes place. The Lea Valley and city peripheries, such as the northern edge of Cambridge, demonstrate the cauterization of what is potentially urban space by the instrumental thinking of engineering. The marginal status of these locations is often maintained by the abundance of active or obsolete infrastructure, and our work involves amelioration: the introduction of the ability of the territory to support multivalent, rather than singular, spatiality.

Although much of our work has been involved in the adaptation and urbanisation of existing infrastructure, there is another sense in which the term is encountered in our work: not as literal infrastructure but as a mediation between the large scale and the 'detail' of conditions on the ground. Infrastructure in these terms offers a 'third presence': a mediating framework between particular architecture and landscape or civic space. As a framework, it holds the capacity to orientate without formally determining outcomes.

As defined by Stan Allen, such infrastructures are:

> flexible and anticipatory. They work with time and are open to change. By specifying what must be fixed and what is subject to change, they can be precise and indeterminate at the same time. They work through management and cultivation, changing slowly to adjust to shifting conditions. They do not progress toward a predetermined state (as with masterplanning strategies), but are always evolving within a loose envelope of constraints … Infrastructure creates a directed field, where different architects and designers can contribute, but it sets technical and instrumental limits to their work. Infrastructure itself works strategically, but it encourages tactical improvisation.[5]

Alvaro Siza – service viaduct at Barrio da Malgueira, Evora, Portugal. Javier Sánchez -Torchondo from Wikimedia Commons https://commons.wikimedia.org/wiki/File:Bairro_Malagueira_2_(Evora).jpg

This definition offers a creative annexation of infrastructure from idealised and problem solving towards an anticipatory framework that valorises indeterminacy. Critically, in ceding total control of the environment, one moves from an a priori attitude to design as a purely formal problem towards a process of commitment over time: a role which is necessarily contingent, political and participatory. Examples of infrastructure used in this way include Alvaro Siza's thirty-year involvement in the establishment of a new town at Quinta da Malgueira, Evora, Portugal, which Siza characterises as 'forming a whole with ruins'.

Cedric Price's Potteries Thinkbelt illustrates an attempt to annexe redundant physical infrastructure (rail-lines, quarries) as an anticipatory framework for a university – a bridge between a particular landscape and a room.

Lina Bo Bardi's work offers a radically contextual way of operating as a designer and sits in opposition to what one might describe as a tyrannical tendency of architecture towards autonomy and control. Her public work has a deliberately unfinished quality – an awkwardness even – that leaves space for creativity of others.

Bo Bardi regarded her work as an interventional practice – always starting with something, and therefore complex, open and multivalent. At SESC Pompeia, she halts the demolition of a former factory, and uses her skill to instead transform it from a place of work to a setting for leisure and creativity. This translation becomes far more powerful, and more robust, than a building imagined anew. At MASP – her San Paulo museum built over a motorway intersection – she uses the project to establish a mediatory presence between infrastructure and the city, mending the wound created by highway engineering to instate a radically public space.

Bo Bardi's slow, accumulative mode of practice is highly socially engaged, and powerful, placing as it does architecture and design back at the heart of a cultural project. Her ability to absorb the contingent teaches us all about the centrality of everyday life in a useful and politically engaged architecture.

A CRITIQUE OF DEVELOPMENT MODELS

Both the public policymaking implied in planning and the private sector world of development seem complicit in their drift away from engagement with spatial intelligence towards the disciplines of management and accountancy. We have continued to attempt to articulate more precisely this critique of the flattening consequence of this drift on environments, but is certainly a tendency which our practice has evolved to resist through the way we frame, propose and participate in projects.

In the atomised model of the contemporary development industry in the UK, architects deal with buildings, their interiors are fitted out by designers, while the buildings themselves are aggregated into a masterplan developed by an urban designer. The overarching drivers for a project are invariably highly complex financial instruments rather than any coherent spatial idea, and the parameters of these instruments are discussed outside the design team and are therefore unavailable as creative tools.

This is not to say that the financial dimensions of a project are unimportant, but to acknowledge that at certain periods, development of cities has had more complex motivations than pure investment.

The financial system itself rests on a generic paradigm. Because finance is risk-averse, it prefers simple, repeatable models which can be compared and valued. While the investment 'packages' behind a project might be highly complex, their connection to a spatial problem are remarkably simplistic: based largely on floor area and highly empirical value models.

Development appraisals are built on a neo-liberal conception of the market as a magical self-regulating system in which certain models work and others fail, according to the requirements of the market at any particular time. These models operate on the basis of control. One of the problems with this paradigm is the issue of responsibility: in a project team, the appraisal will be assembled by a land agent or valuer, who might also be responsible for marketing the outcome of the project. If one of the objectives of the project is the creation of value (and one could say that one of the definitions of development is the bestowal of value on land), then one approach might be to speculate about a possible place – the valuer would prefer to leave this responsibility to the market, with the ultimate value being what a purchaser or tenant will pay once the project has been completed. The value of a site is simply what someone will pay for it.

One of the defining characteristics of development over the last decade has been the importance of site assembly and very large-scale land development. In collusion with the financial model, town planning also prefers the certainties of comprehensive development. It stands in for effective planning, it seems to have authority and it also aligns with planning as a managerial activity, with its roots in zoning, and issues of quantum rather than quality.

In a fluctuating economy, investment returns are expected in the short term and that requires that divestment of risk and the control of outcomes. What emerges from the application of this model into spatial reality is large-scale *tabula rasa* development, composed with generic models that can be valued accurately, with an emphasis on speed. Driven by the need for investor returns and lack of friction, the project manager has emerged as the '*chef de partie*'.

The model is, by nature, not negotiative: by preference, working behind the compound wall, dealing with certainties. In the disciplinary model sponsored by these development phenomena, the emphasis is on a specialist task-based contributions, with atomised consultants collaborating through complex managerial frameworks. What becomes difficult in this scenario is invention, contingency, speculation and the incorporation of particular conditions or opportunities: it is a flattened model.

More problematically, it is a model that doesn't really work very well. The outcomes are familiar: clone towns built on economic monocultures which have proved particularly vulnerable to economic changes of fortune and expensive to finance in financial slumps. Despite being risk-averse, the model tends to concentrate risk, albeit for short periods, in the hands of a few, gambling that the risk can be divested before crisis occurs. In terms of urban outcomes, this model is demonstrably problematic: a

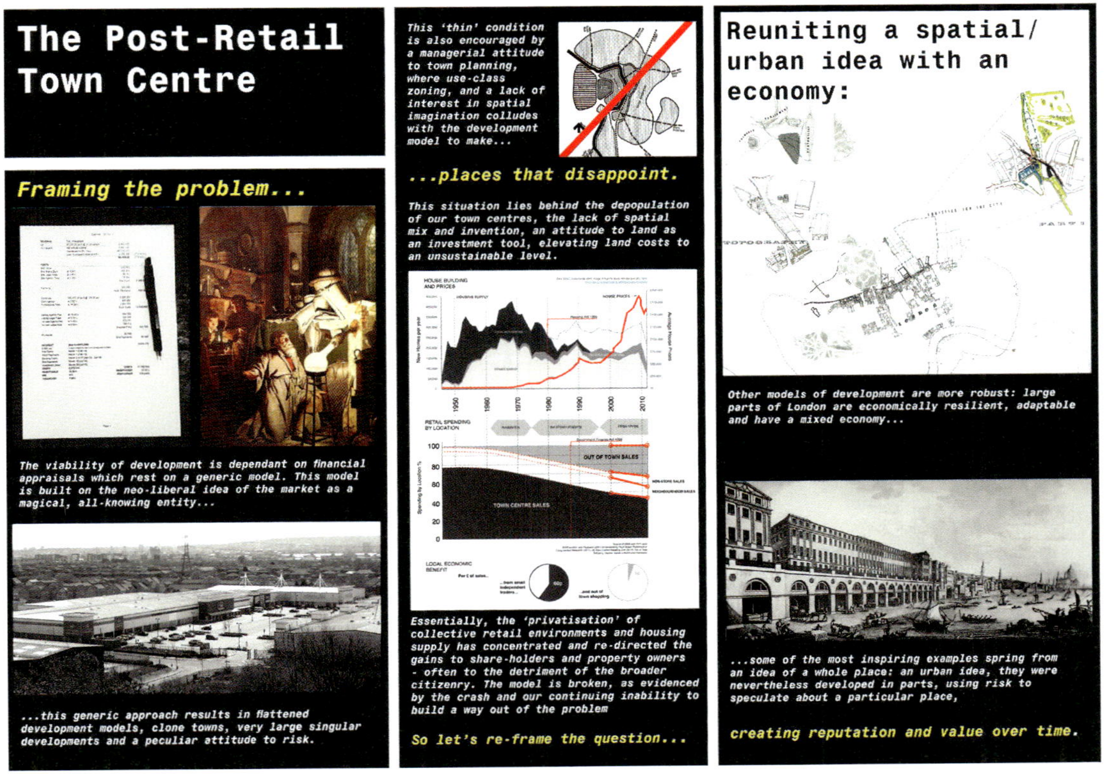

This sequence developed as a critique of development models through the research and was rehearsed in various forms as the basis for seminars: The Post-Retail Town Centre, Architectural Association, London (May 2013), and Town Centres, Incremental Transformation Design Council CABE, London (July 2013). I am grateful to Andrew Clancy and Colm Moore for bringing to my attention the painting *The Alchemist* by Joseph Wright – a depiction of the discovery of phosphorous through the boiling of urine – and a useful analogy to the magical concept of the market held by many involved in financial and property valuation in the UK.

process that hates risk and which privileges control is by definition anti-urban and unlikely to produce good public space. As the sociologist Saskia Sassen has established,[6] cities are the theatre for an increasingly globalised economy: a key driver behind the rapid urbanisation of the last twenty years. As exchange becomes increasingly virtual and geographically dispersed, the emerging 'city states' require the development of greater differentiation in terms of skill and knowledge in order to gain advantage. The dark reflection of dispersed and virtualised global trade is the establishment of increasingly concrete centres of control.

It is precisely the complex, heterogeneous structure of the city itself that provides a sufficiently variegated environment to support the interdependent ecology of knowledge and services, required by late-capitalist exchange. As the extraordinary complexity of globalised economic structures becomes physically manifest in cities, the great paradox is that the urban environment, while sophisticated in the exchange of knowledge, innovation, finance and law, actually reflect the corporate drivers of this dynamic, with their fetishisation of control, and are dismayingly simplistic in spatial terms. The resultant environments, so familiar to us all from our cities, are generic, flat and risk-averse. Rem Koolhaas' observation[7] of the emerging phenomenon of Bigness – the tendency towards very large scale development – has indeed 'fucked context', yet the resultant environments are increasingly vacuous, deterministic and less able to support the very agonic depth that defines the healthy city.

Since current urbanisation is driven by the need for control, what suffers most are the residual spaces of the city, the spaces which don't play a direct role in the new economy, but which are nevertheless affected by the associated phenomena: gentrification, the polarisation of wealth and the peripheralisation of the poor.

As global cities become more effective and politically compelling economic models than the nineteenth century idea of the nation state, urban governance itself needs to innovate and change in recognition of these emerging conditions. The last two decades has seen the establishment of the powerful city administration, but the polity has rarely grasped the opportunity of spatial planning as an extension of public policy to counterbalance the corporatisation of cities.

The idea of the public – of civic – space has been eroded for some time[8], and the role of the state as a commissioner or guardian of public space and public infrastructure is greatly diminished. The great regeneration projects in the last five years in the UK have, I think without exception, produced a privatised public realm with heavily conditional use.[9]

In writing about these new global cities, Sassen has identified that infrastructure is a primary issue with which to engage.[10] Increasingly complex and invisible infrastructures are being introduced into cities to enable and maintain their economic status.

Rather than being regarded as civic participatory structures, these infrastructures are invariably privately owned, in contrast with those introduced in the second half of the twentieth century. Their introduction is designed by engineers where the generative thinking is systematic and the resulting 'closed loop' deterministic structures are fundamentally at odds with the necessarily heterogeneous, indeterminate and messy structure of cities.

If one accepts an alternative model of infrastructure as one of the tropes of civic space – as Peter Carl says, an 'anonymous representation of collective life'[11] – then a broader, more participatory role of infrastructure is necessary.

What follows, in response to these observations concerning the creeping homogeneity of development and the privatisation of infrastructure, are a series of case studies which map out alternative strategies, in particular exploring issues of identity and structure, amplifying attenuated qualities as cultural artefacts and emphasising the particular over the generic.

CASE STUDIES

The following case studies describe three completed projects and three competition entries:

Projects:

- *Paper Trail* – a repurposed post-industrial landscape in a New Town on London's outer fringe.
- *St Albans* – a 'city vision' structure for directing change in an ancient city frozen by its own historical significance.
- *Park Royal* – a public realm strategy for locating Europe's largest industrial estate on London's 'mental map'.

Competitions:

- *Ovaltown* – using planning as a means to resist the 'entropic slide' of the market in an interesting quarter of Hackney, London.
- *Gorizia* – the reuniting of a twin city, formerly divided by the Iron Curtain, between Italy and Slovenia.
- *Andermatt* – the introduction of a new urban centre and tourist infrastructure for a demilitarised ski resort in Switzerland.

PAPER TRAIL

Hemel Hempstead, a satellite twenty miles north of London, was the third post-war New Town, launched in July 1946 as part of the government's 'policy for the decentralisation of persons and industry from London'. The New Town was designed by Geoffrey Jellicoe, a landscape architect, who described his urban vision (which engulfed a much earlier settlement) as 'not a city in a garden, but a city in a park.'

Hemel Hempstead lies in the valley of a chalk stream: the Gade, which runs off the Chiltern Hills. The stream feeds the Grand Junction Canal, which connects the Midlands with London. The proximity of London via the canal, together with the motive power of the river – the engine of a series of water mills along its length – made this location a critical one for early industrial development. The Fourdrinier brothers – Huguenot refugees – set up a workshop here in a rented corn mill and effectively invented the process that is still used for industrial papermaking.

The mill and process were bought by the entrepreneur John Dickinson at the outset of the nineteenth century, and became a vast industrial base, employing thousands. The paper that Dickinson produced was the material basis of Britain's Imperial diktat, and the canal brought both global trade in raw materials right to the heart of this Hertfordshire valley.

5th Studio were invited to develop a strategy for the remnants of this vast operation; by the 1990s, the factory had been asset-stripped and closed, with much of the land sold for commuter housing. What remained of the factory were two listed fragments – an operational paper mill at Frogmore, and the mill manager's house at Apsley, further up the canal among the remains of a much larger paper mill.

A charity – the Paper Trail Trust – had been set up to adopt these remaining elements with the intention of creating a visitor attraction around the paper mill, to maintain the remaining historic machinery, to create a research base for experimentation and innovation in papermaking, and an 'arts cluster' working on paper, printing and bookmaking.

The factory once covered the Gade Valley, with its enclosures modifying and engulfing the canal into its interior. The typology of watermills generates archipelagos (encountered again in our work in the Lower Lea Valley), with backstreams and sluices, creating a waterscape which is very hard to penetrate. This hydrology extends throughout the production process, where the addition and subtraction of water in highly regulated environmental conditions is critical. The scale and the ambiguous quality of the factory at its height indicated that the project needed to be understood as a problem of landscape.

The resulting masterplan locates itself between built intervention and landscape strategy. We recognised the importance of connecting the project with the town and Geoffrey Jellicoe's latent 'city in a park'. The project depended on conservation of the most historic elements of the Mill, while tethering that to the constant dynamic re-invention that the factory embodied. Added to that was the overarching need to break a very large project down into discrete phases that could be realised through different partnerships for various audiences, but brought together as a superimposed, coherent whole, with something of the drama of the original operation.

At Frogmore Mill, the huge Fourdrinier papermaking machine had utility not just as a working historical artefact, but as a rare means of producing short runs of very high quality paper for particular uses. The papermaking process is perhaps the most ruthless example of a production line: each element in the process being strictly sequential. We were fascinated with superimposing the tyranny of a production chain, which aspires to a perfect relationship, with a parallel sequence of spaces which allowed visitors to follow the process without having their arm torn off.

The heart of the Mill is the millrace – simultaneously the most important structure in terms of heritage, and the element which had been the most continuously transformed by adjustment to changes in technology. The race had been adjusted so many times since the original (probably the medieval race of a corn mill) that ironically, this most precious core, in terms of preservation, was also the location that had encountered the most flux.

Papermaking is an energy-hungry process, requiring vast quantities of clean water which is then polluted by the production process. The factory's intimate relationship with the canal allowed it both to draw sufficient water, and to bring into the pulping rooms raw material by barge. Further downstream (for though it is a canal, the Grand Junction is intimately entwined with two rivers at this point, giving it a clear flow towards London) were the remediation beds of the mill. These beds, which were part of a complex hydrological system controlled by the factory, had been abandoned.

We persuaded the Paper Trail Trust to add this extraordinary landscape to their project, in partnership with the local council, who had inherited much of the land, and by this means connect the project back along the river to Jellicoe's water gardens in the heart of the New Town.

The remediation beds – a picturesque example of the decay of human ingenuity to nature – created the perfect landscape for the project to locate its environmental intentions as part of the animation of a public garden built around a dramatic hydrology. The paper mills had a long tradition of making

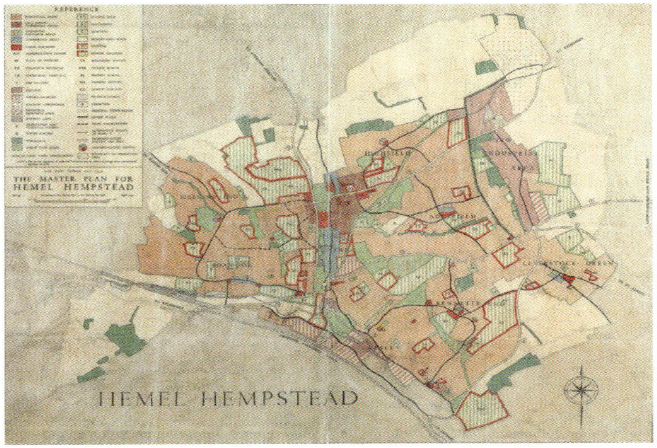

Aerial photograph of the paper mill at its height. The canal flows through the middle of the factory complex.

Jellicoe's plan of the New Town of Hemel Hempstead, organised around the canal and the River Gade.

Mapping of topography – 'city in a park'. The mills cluster along the canal on the bottom right of the mapping, as it flows towards London.

The growth of the Apsley mill complex from the 1817 watermill, to the factory's height in 1968, to its contemporary reduced state.

An early collage plan exploring the linear process of production, and entwining that with other parts of the project programme.

The components of the whole project mapped across the two mill sites. The canal has been foreshortened. The canal provided a means of connecting the sites via a wilderness, rather than the banality of town fringe retail parks.

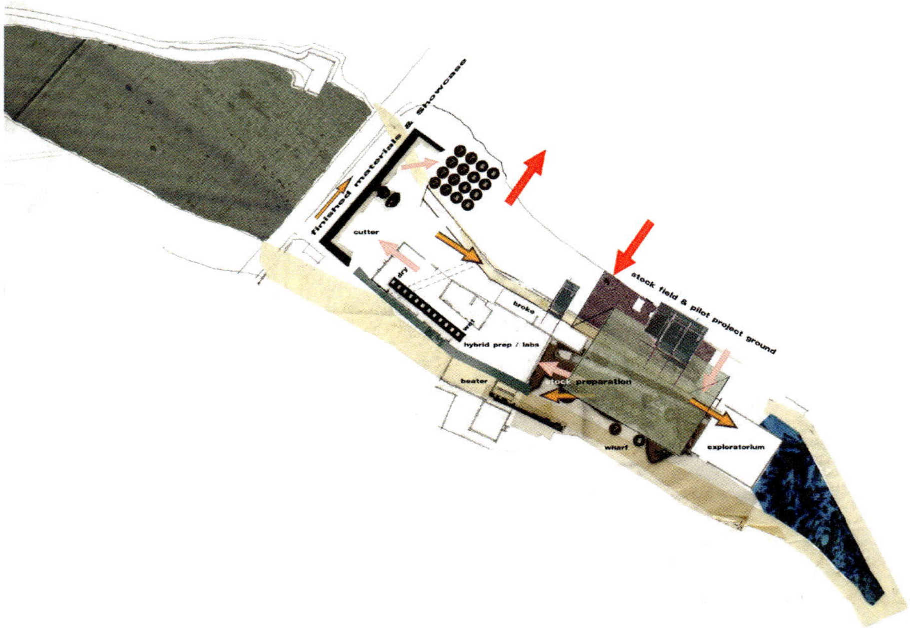
finished materials & Showcase
cutter
dry
wet
broke
hybrid prep / labs
stock field & pilot project ground
beater
stock preparation
wharf
exploratorium

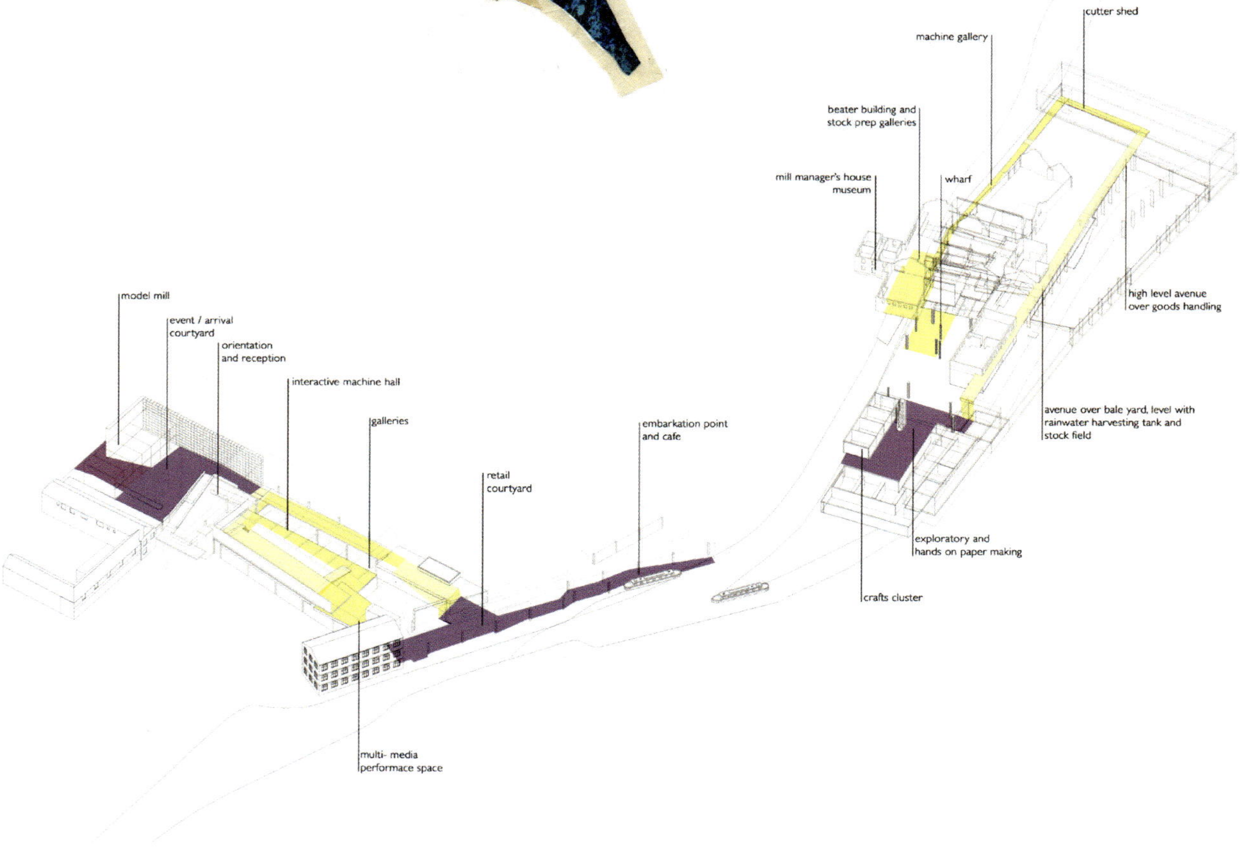
cutter shed
machine gallery
beater building and stock prep galleries
wharf
mill manager's house museum
high level avenue over goods handling
avenue over bale yard, level with rainwater harvesting tank and stock field
model mill
event / arrival courtyard
orientation and reception
interactive machine hall
galleries
embarkation point and cafe
retail courtyard
exploratory and hands on paper making
crafts cluster
multi- media performace space

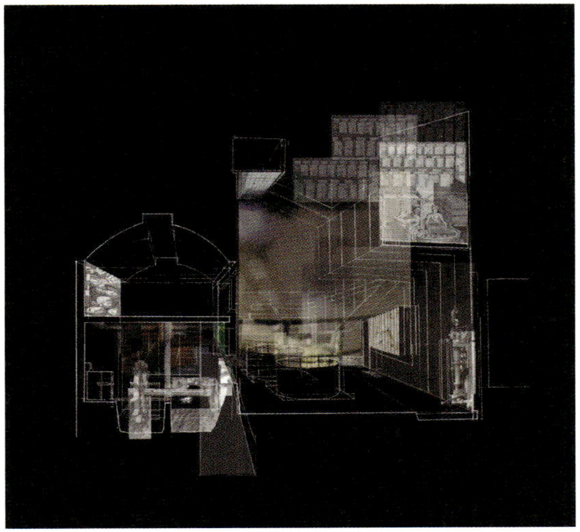

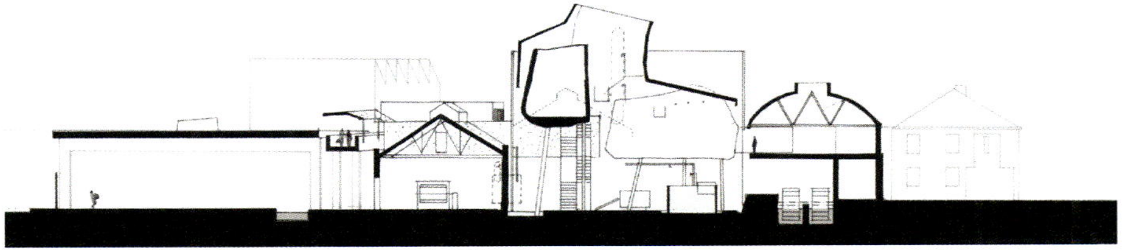

Collage through the mill race at Frogmore Mill – the atmospheric conditions of industrial papermaking brought together with studio papermaking above.

A section of the same set of spaces as in image 4.11.

A new quay – we enjoyed the intimacy between built form and the canal, and reproduced it with this space to disembark from a riverboat.

Another interface – here an automated room allowed people to drop off their paper for recycling and watch it transformed into pulp for papermaking.

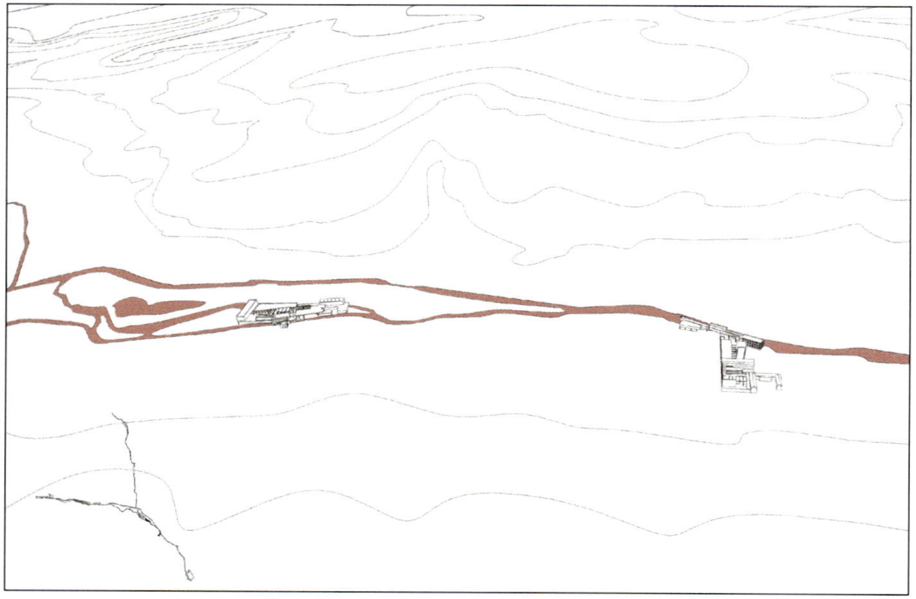

A series of diagrams were developed to capture the various things that we had learnt about critical aspects of the various sites, and their relationship to the wider landscape. The operation of the Fourdrinier papermaking machine and its hydrology was also mapped. Both mills and remediation beds follow the contour of the canal. This drawing relates the key sites of the project, united by the hydrology of the canal and parallel process of papermaking.

paper from waste – both from rags and recycled paper – and the trust set up on the factory's demise included the establishment of testbeds to develop processes for papermaking that used less energy and water, or that created fewer pollutants.

Our instinct when beginning a project as complex as this is to widen our gaze and to take on more. This tactic surprised our client, who, like many specialist trusts, on inheriting a rich but seemingly insuperable problem, had spent a few years looking with closer and closer focus at the remaining artefacts of the great lost industry. The wider landscape gave us critical clues for how to address the void left by the attenuation of the process – so legible in operation, but so difficult to reconstruct without the industrial activity that formed it. Our role in this project was primarily to construct a new narrative framework to support multiple new ways of using this landscape.

This construction of a narrative was played out against a critique of the New Town itself, and the post-war suburbanisation of the margins.

Extended from project to teaching studio enquiry in 2006, the introduction brief set out the following task:

> The periphery of London is seen by many as simply latent space for the city's own inexorable expansion. Indeed, the population shift towards the south-east has already resulted in suburbanisation of much of the territory now marked by the M25 – London's orbital road, completed in 1986.

London has constantly been defined by its periphery – by the sense of what is not London. The landscape that lies without the city has been key to the development of its particular urbanity – beyond the city lies a topography of possibility, of invention, provisioning, play, negotiation, madness.

Among this mundane outer ring are the seed-beds of the future, rapidly being subsumed by the evenness of suburbia . . . Amid the end of foxhunting and riots at IKEA, the studio have been encouraged to question 'what is this territory for?' and to develop ideas of new or latent topographies to develop a critique of this rather jaded and unfinished New Town.[12]

ST ALBANS TO LONDON'S WORKSHOP

Strategies of differentiation can be seen in two projects that find quite different territories in the north-western periphery of London, through documentation of what is already there.

St Albans is a cathedral city with a substantial Roman foundation, now a wealthy commuter

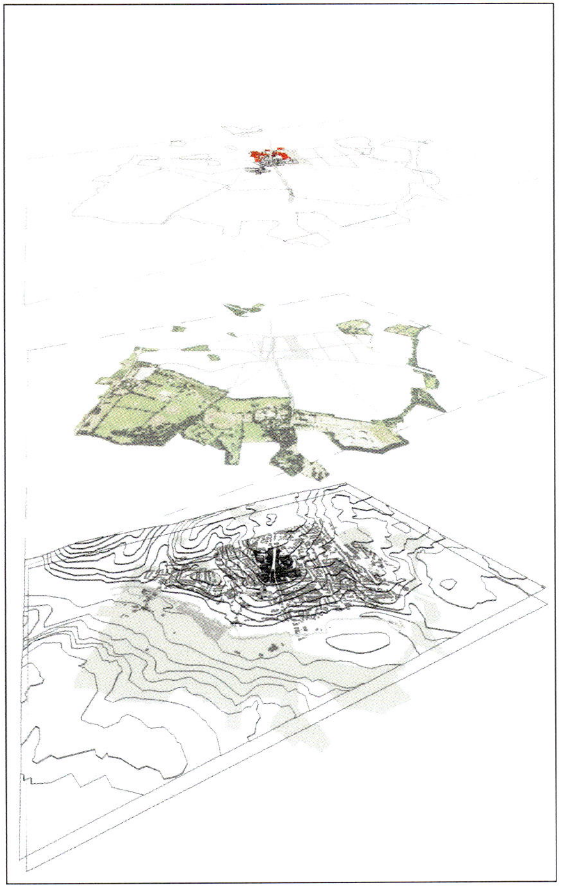

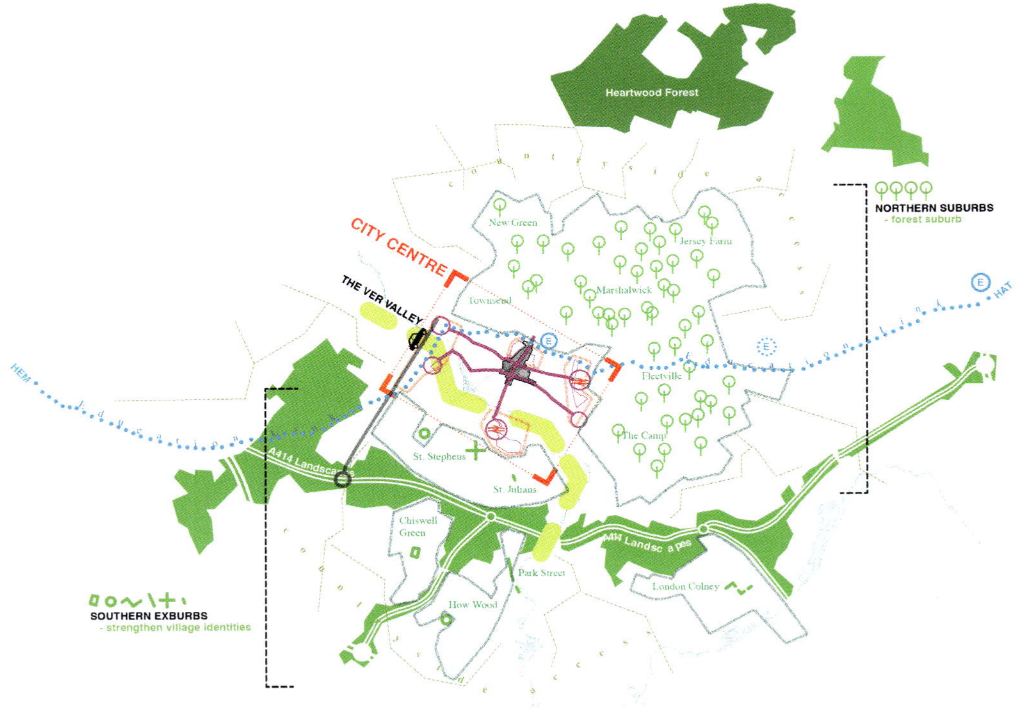

A pop-off mapping which draws the structure of the city, highly linked to its underlying topography, and intimately connected to surrounding parkland, protected by its archaeological significance.

Plan of the urban structure proposing a relationship between a latent surrounding landscape ring and the centre, with a clear central focus for reinvention, which we dubbed 'the spider of change' (shown in pink) linking the centre to the points of entry, including the station. The blue line locates a latent educational corridor running between satellite towns of Hemel Hempstead and Hatfield, and their varied grain of education and training institutions. The yellow line marks the river valley.

satellite just beyond London's orbital motorway. Park Royal – known as 'London's Workshop' – is a critical 'just in time' service area for central London, and Europe's largest industrial estate, positioned just a few miles west of the centre of London.

These two places would seem to have very different issues: the former one of the UK's most prosperous towns, the latter a critical city servicing resource, regarded as having something of a lawless environment.

In St Albans, we were appointed by the town council to develop a thirty-year 'vision' for the city, where conservation and heritage protection had led to a negative, reactionary planning culture. Since the 1970s, the city's development has been compromised through poor planning, which sought to prevent physical change. Lacking a sense of a contemporary identity and a prospective idea of a how to guide inevitable flux, the city has had development imposed through the planning appeal system. The town council had realised this when their planning team turned down the council's own proposals to modify the town hall.

PARK ROYAL PUBLIC REALM STRATEGY

In a similar way, Park Royal can be said to have lost a sense of place. Park Royal is an area of 700 hectares which constitutes Europe's largest industrial estate. Located halfway between Heathrow and Central London, it plays a key role in the city's strategic service and employment system. But Park Royal is a victim of its own success as 'London's Workshop' – with a congested road network and a low quality public realm presenting challenges to its thriving economy.

Although vast, there is almost no public space, and the generic quality of the roads and residual spaces between anonymous big sheds and workshops has created a dangerous 'white van' road culture. This hard environment has made it difficult for firms to attract and keep employees, and numerous road accidents had only reinforced the sense of placelessness. Workers tend to drive to work, even though many live relatively locally. A better set of routes and spaces would enable walking or cycling from the residential neighbourhoods that surround the quarter.

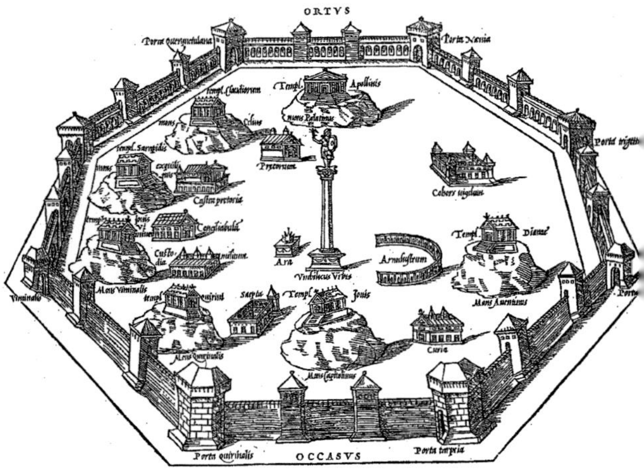

Engraving of the Servian walls and gates of Rome, enclosing the instruments of identity of the city: the seven hills, and key monuments.

With very different means, both projects pose the question 'How does one extend the public domain, and reinforce a sense of an urban public identity?'

In the context of these problems, 5th Studio were commissioned to develop a public realm strategy that could achieve a radical uplift in the environmental quality of the area.

Given the impossibility of comprehensive change on this vast scale, the proposals offer a tactical response which considers how to maximize the impact of investment: a strategy of targeted intervention. The strategy articulates a clear spatial reading of Park

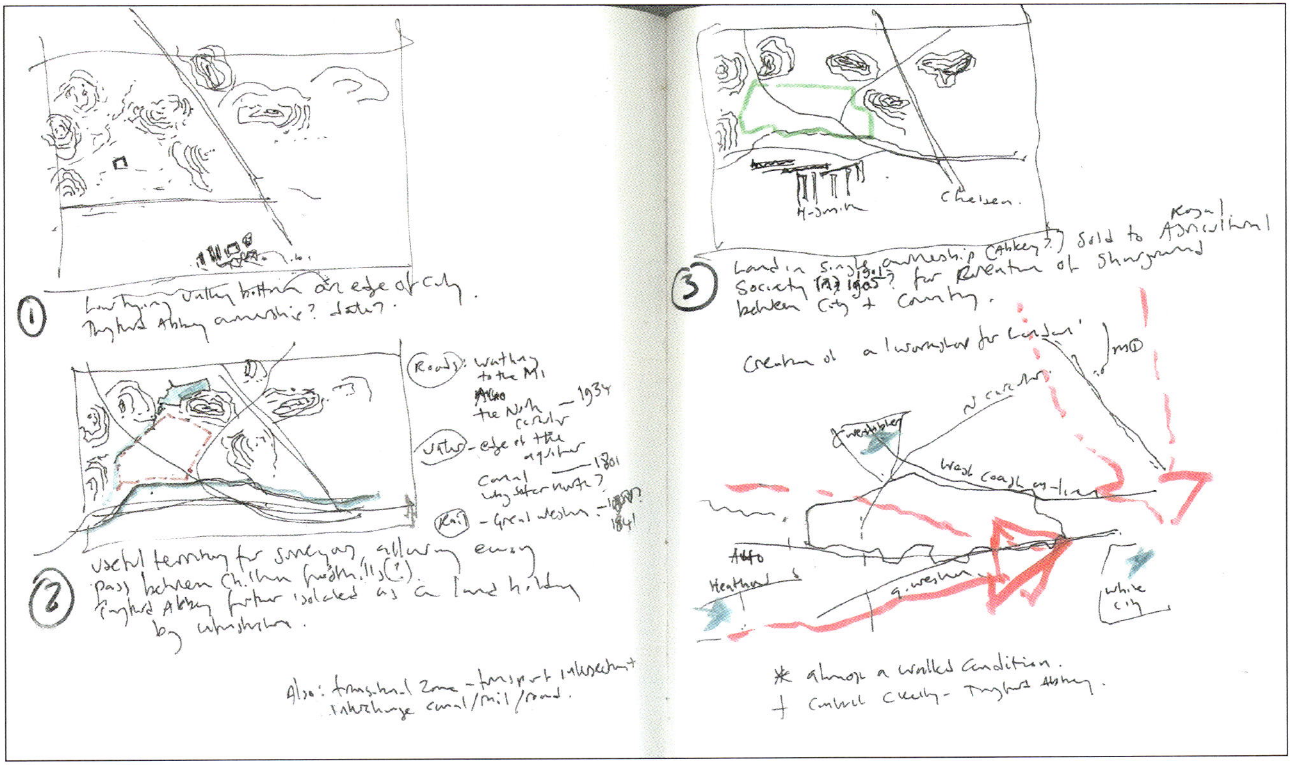

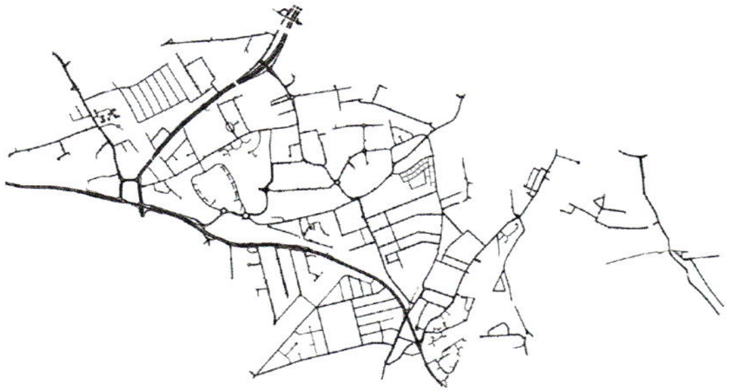

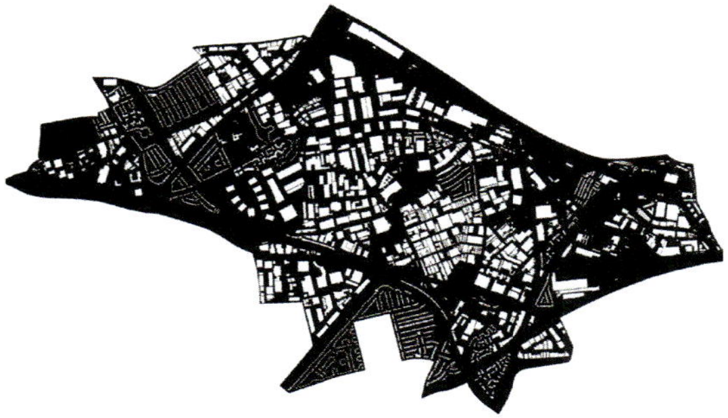

Early sketchbook notes, relating a topography bounded by infrastructure, with a need for a distinctive and positive identity.

Definition of what constitutes public space in a place like Park Royal was one of our first questions: Is it just the road network? (illustrated in 4.20) Is it all the space left between buildings? (illustrated in 4.21) The proposals operate selectively in the space between two extreme definitions of the public realm.

Royal as a place – understanding it as a distinct city quarter defined by a perimeter wall of transport infrastructure – in order to guide the geographical logic of proposals.

Working with a 'toolkit' of tactics – from big-scale moves to bottom-up local projects – it proposes a spectrum of projects within three spheres of action: network, gateways and districts.

Overall strategy – assembling the different layers of the proposals.

Gateways are the points of entry to Park Royal, coincident with rail and underground stations, where it is possible to cross the infrastructure that establishes it as a distinct territory. The proposed interventions seek to strengthen the identity of Park Royal and the sense of its boundary by reinforcing the unique qualities of these edge spaces.

The 'network' describes a series of road corridors that are almost the only way to traverse Park Royal. The strategy proposes to improve their functional operation, safety and spatial quality through the integration of a system of off-road cycle paths and a consistent materiality – as well as seeking to maximise use of the Grand Union Canal.

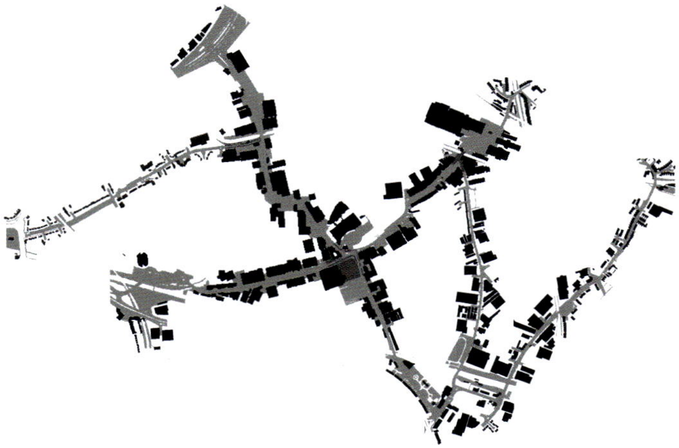

A series of distinct pieces of urban fabric whose diversity is critical to the economic operation and urban character of Park Royal. To support this richness of place, and fit with the reality of what would make sense on the ground, the strategy proposes a number of small-scale interventions which respond to specific local conditions.

OVALTOWN 'zone of tolerance'

London Festival of Architecture 2012

The English Planning tradition is bureaucratic, not spatial, controlling use, rather than directing spatial opportunity. This concern with separating use prevents the creation of a **'rich mix'**.

What could **'tolerance'** provide in Ovaltown?

Ovaltown is a hole between major East London **agents of change** - Crossrail, the Hack-sea or Chel-ney Line, the reinvention of the Overground, the Olympics.

Yet it does have the 'urban assets' needed by any self respecting town: a station, a canal, urban utilities. It is located between busy London **high streets**, the **quiet canal** and the ancient route of the **'Black Path'**, which connects a string of markets.

Ovaltown is fascinating precisely because it is a significant area of town which **remains available to plan** in **contrast** to the stuff around it. Land ownership is in relatively few hands.

With the gasholders now decommissioned, little prevents this area from an **entropic slide**: loosing the particularity that makes it an interesting place. Unfettered, market forces will generate a housing monoculture - with the land ownership atomising into a thousand individual mortgage securities

Of all property conditions in a city, private accommodation is the least available for change - both the complexities of ownership, long-term investment, and high value for area mean that once urban land reaches this condition, a certain **stasis** is inevitable.

We ask: "what alternative urban landscape might **resist the laissez-faire creation of housing monocultures**, and so retain the capacity for change / variety of use over time? What land ownership mechanisms might present as alternative to the entropic fragmentation of many tiny flats, or student rooms?"

Ovaltown might develop some resistance to the 'three magnets' of its neighbouring communities...

Planned development for the site is already highly generic

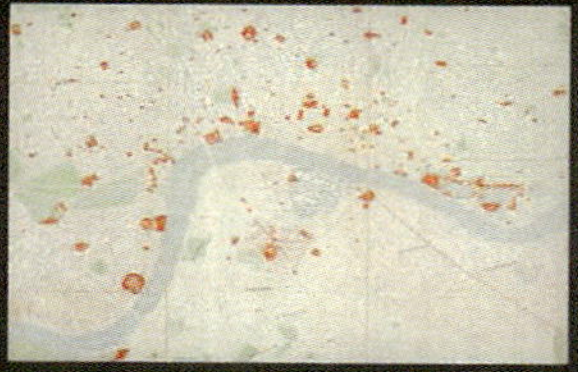

ENCLAVE

We are interested in the 'sui generis' planning precedent of the enclave or precinct - allowing, for example, a university to develop a range of accommodation from cultural spaces, teaching hospital, nuclear laboratories and student housing within its boundaries.

Tower of Babel - the love-child of the gasholder and railway viaduct

Adelphi - housing above a plinth of industry

..... an idea that operates at a singular level between infrastructure and architecture.

URBAN SPLASH

Re-use of the existing infrastructure of the Park Hill estate, Sheffield, which is of a similar scale to the Ovaltown site.

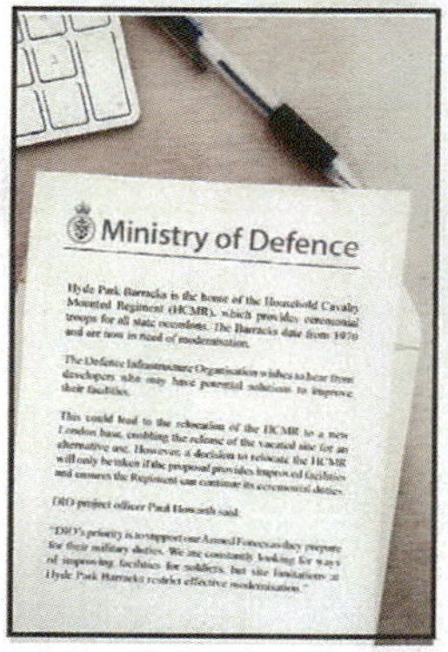

Ministry of Defence

Hyde Park Barracks is the home of the Household Cavalry Mounted Regiment (HCMR), which provides ceremonial troops for all state occasions. The Barracks date from 1970 and are now in need of modernisation.

The Defence Infrastructure Organisation wishes to hear from developers who may have potential solutions to improve their facilities.

This could lead to the relocation of the HCMR to a new London base, enabling the release of the vacated site for an alternative use. However, a decision to relocate the HCMR will only be taken if the proposal provides improved facilities and ensures the Regiment can continue its ceremonial duties.

DIO project officer Paul Howarth said:

"DIO's priority is to support our Armed Forces as they prepare for their military duties. We are constantly looking for ways of improving facilities for soldiers, but site limitations at Hyde Park Barracks restrict effective modernisation."

The Failure of the planning authorities to retain a 'rich mix' in **Knightsbridge** has resulted in an anchor tenant becoming available - the Household Cavalry are to be evicted from Hyde Park Barracks

We propose to bring the **regiment to Ovaltown**, providing stables in the undercroft ...

... on top of which, at viaduct / station level, is built a **curtain enclosure**: about 850 places to live.

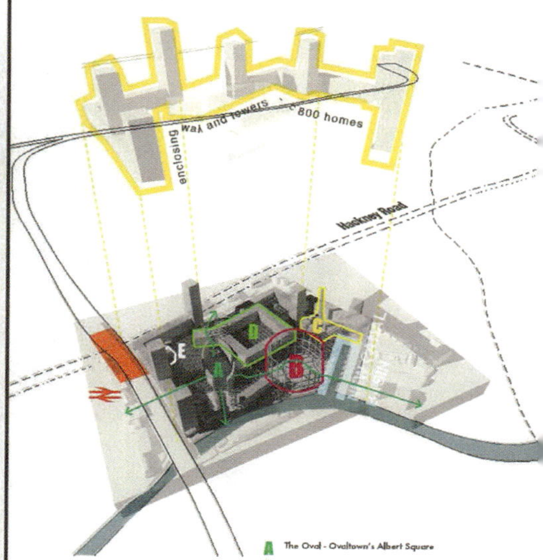

A The Oval - Ovaltown's Albert Square

B gasholder glasshouse and park - using low grade heat from the

C ...waste to power plant that takes the surrounding city's waste and sells it back as power and heat

D The Household Cavalry barracks, stables and parade ground relocated from Hyde Park

E The Brewery

Undercroft
- industry, workshops, stables, warehousing, stores, parking, waste transfer, baths, clubs, cinema etc.

... Ovaltown, equidistant between the Regiment's ceremonial duties and the equestrian landscape of the Lea Valley, including our Fatwalk project.

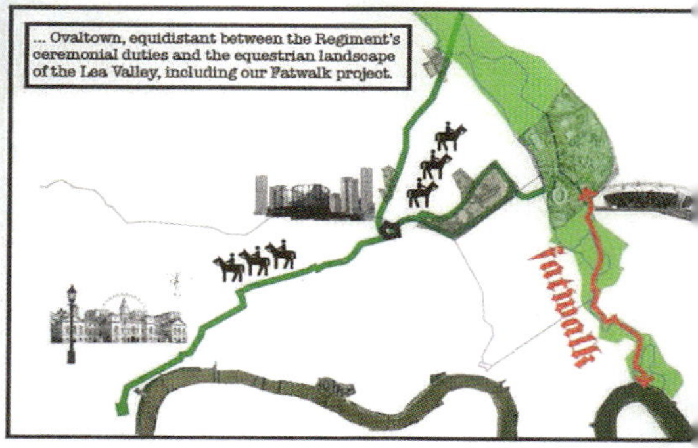

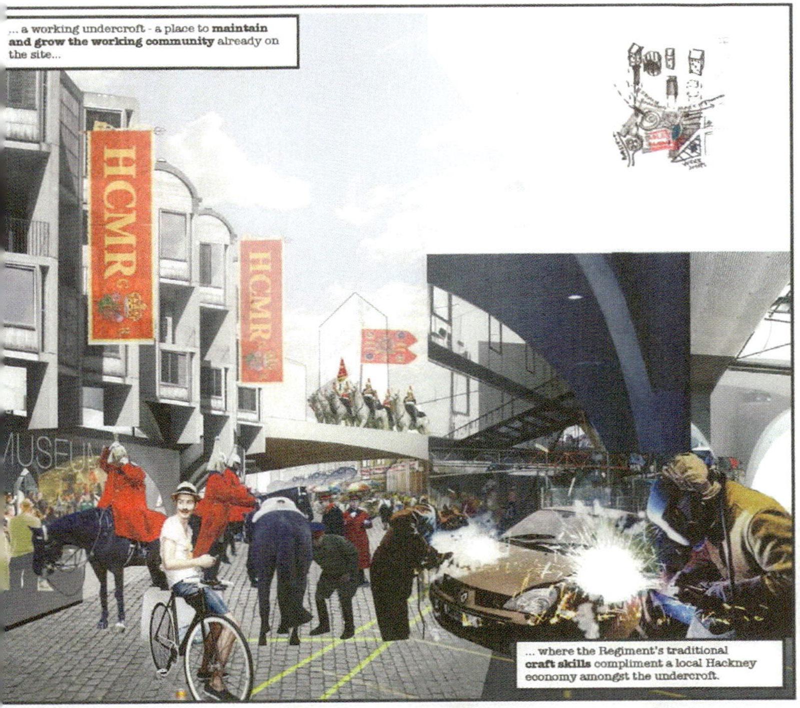

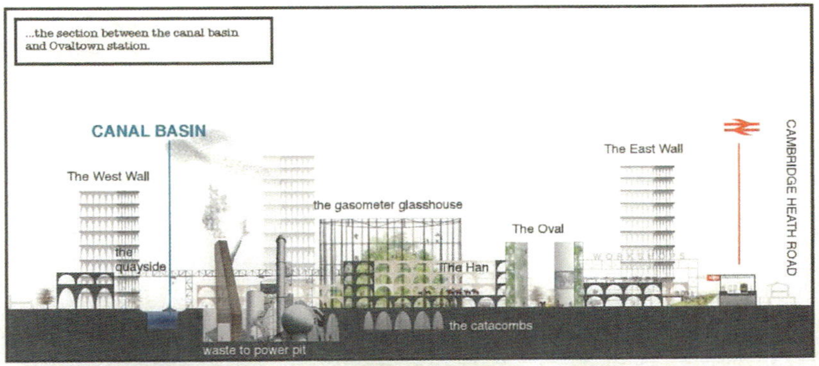

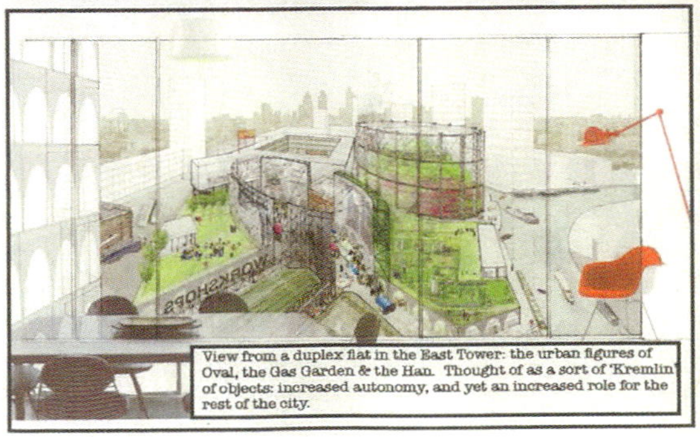

In terms of '**tolerance**' - the point of planning is to create something different from laissez faire - something of **itself**

5th studio

in collaboration with **urbansplash**

GORIZIA

Gorizia lies at the heart of the upper Adriatic, between the regions of Friuli-Venezia Giulia and Zahodna Slovenija. The town is set in a rich landscape, between the Julian Alps to the north and the Adriatic coast to the south.

The Schengen Agreement has brought down the 'Iron Curtain' border between Italy and Slovenia. The formerly divided city of Gorica/Gorizia is at the centre of a potential 'knowledge corridor' linking Udine, Gorizia, Trieste, Koper and Ljubljana. This corridor is like a golden thread through a very particular and productive landscape. Our proposals for the competition 'Il spazio giovani alla frontiera' grows from this geographical and economic reality.

A DIVIDED CITY

For over a millennia Gorizia has had a defensive character. It is border country . . .

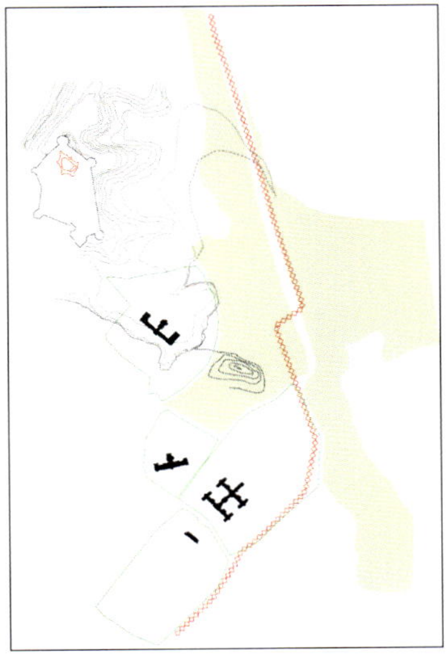

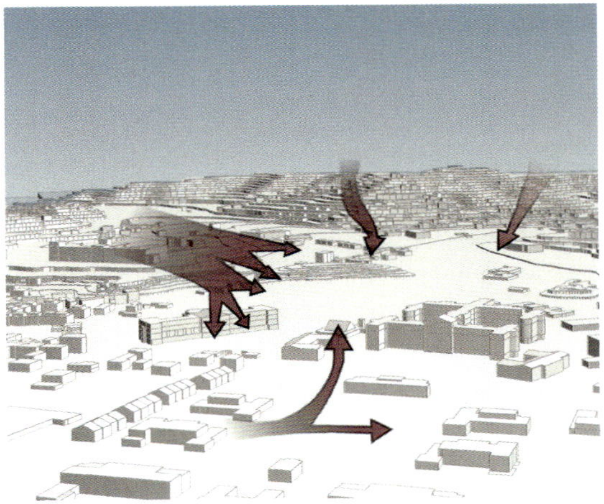

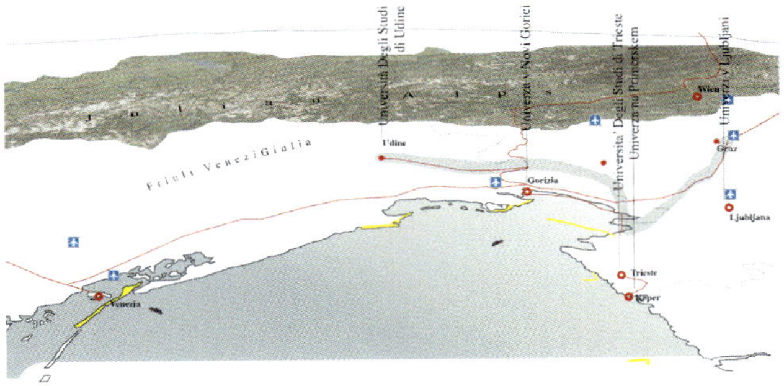

IRON CURTAIN

. . . from medieval castellations which exploit the terrain, to the Iron Curtain which once divided Italy and the former Yugoslavia. As is characteristic of a border zone, the adjacent territory has become a 'terrain vague' fuori le mure; a place for singular institutions within defined enclosures. Natural features have been coerced into a systematised landscape.

DEMILITARISATION

With European integration, a relaxed border offers the opportunity for vibrant renewal of this middle ground. A space for hospitality can be created in place of the inhospitable systems of division; a rich mix of activity where there was rigid singularity.

CATALYST

What is the catalyst for this re-occupation of the valley? We propose that regional investment in infrastructure is used to create a point of intensity: a new centre in what has been a peripheral zone. . .

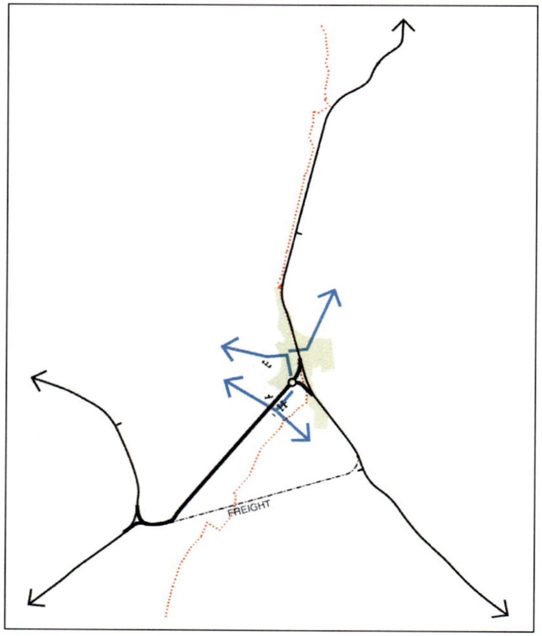

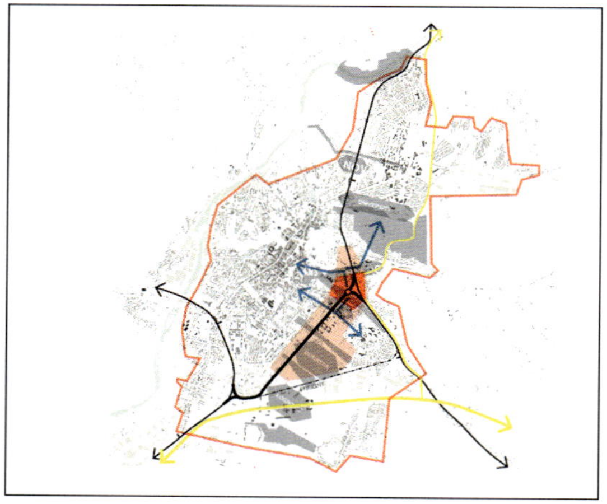

. . .creating a rationalised rail system and a central station for the twin cities. The new station will provide direct train services between the university and research nodes across the region. A 'treno natura' will connect the mountains with the coastal resorts.

A series of overlaid topographies stitch together the old borderline and make spaces for play, sport and hospitality. A former hospital estate is re-occupied and thrown open for culture and creative enterprise. All the riches of the upper Adriatic region are represented here for the use of young citizens. The masterplan identifies a latent university, research and enterprise quarter.

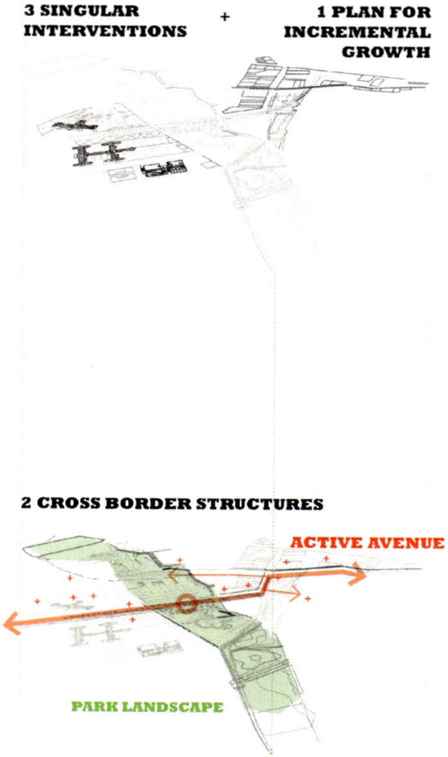

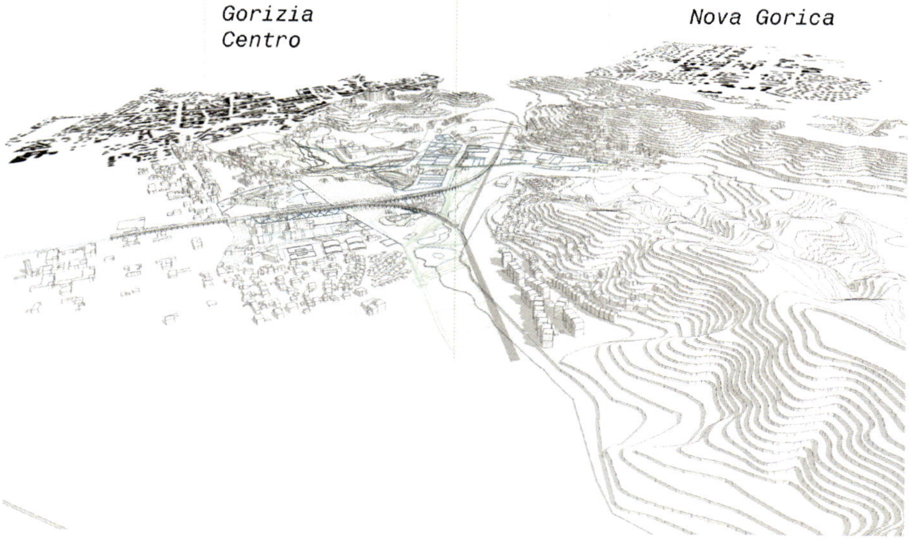

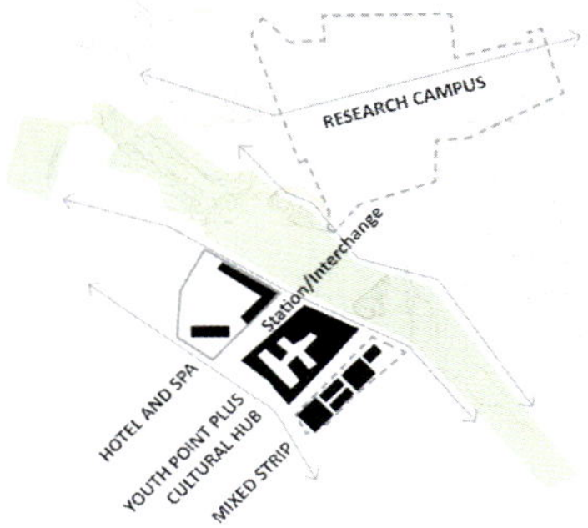

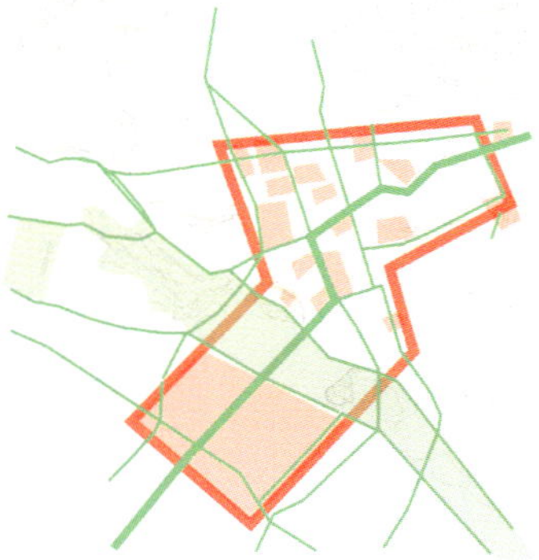

Rather than demolish the great institutional buildings of the former sanatorium and hospital (Croce di Lorena), we have proposed treating these in different ways to help structure this new urban quarter.

The opportunity of the existing slack areas and generous infrastructure left following the disassembly of the border is utilised as the basis for a newly intensified urban quarter. This is focussed on research and accommodation – around the Piazzale della Casa Rossa and linking across the border as an urban continuum.

The proposed station is at the centre of a great new urban space between the two towns, and is the beginning of an intensive area of development.

The site also realises a major park space, and the existing web of footpaths and cycleways are enhanced and expanded, encouraging non-car use.

View of the new centre of Andermatt from the Gurschen lift.

EIN SCLOSS FÜR ANDERMATT

Andermatt is a Swiss resort which has experienced dramatically changing fortunes. As the last stop before the St Gotthard pass, the village flourished economically and became a popular spa. Andermatt also became the garrison town and command centre of the Swiss Federal Army.

By the 1930s, the town's income from tourism had seriously declined, and by 1990 the grand hotels had been abandoned and were eventually demolished with explosives.

With the departure of the Federal Army, Andermatt is undergoing much speculative building. Egyptian billionaire Samih Sawiris intends to invest $500 million on doubling the size of the resort and on improving its ski infrastructure. We took part in a competition in 2011 to establish a new urban centre for the resort.

Our competition proposal read:

> Each period of Andermatt's development is distinctive – the original village around the pass road, the chalets of the post war period, to the highly differentiated object-ground of the contemporary podium development.

What is missing from this picture? With the demilitarisation of the village, what should be created as the middle ground between the existing and proposed quarters of Andermatt?

We imagine the new intervention as a singularity – a generous volume that operates as a hospitable gathering space for the village. We see the opportunity for a hybridisation of architecture, landscape and infrastructure: in short we propose A CASTLE FOR ANDERMATT.

Taking inspiration from structures such as Le Mont St Michel and Hadrian's Mausoleum, the proposition superimposes a number of different topographies to create a public space at the heart of the village:

- An extensive botanic garden and arboretum as a microcosm of Swiss landscape, creating river and lake topographies, high alpine gardens, alpine meadow, forests and erratic fields. The entire site is treated as a landscape.
- A transport interchange for effective arrival, departure and movement within Andermatt.
- Four season visitor infrastructure, enabling visitors to access the surrounding landscape on foot, horse, cycle and ski.
- Local services, education and living accommodation to support the village economy and to ensure that local skills are enhanced, including a brewery.

LANDSCAPE ECOLOGIES

The landscape presents a didactic microcosm of Swiss ecologies, from High Alpine rock gardens through to mixed forest and native prairie

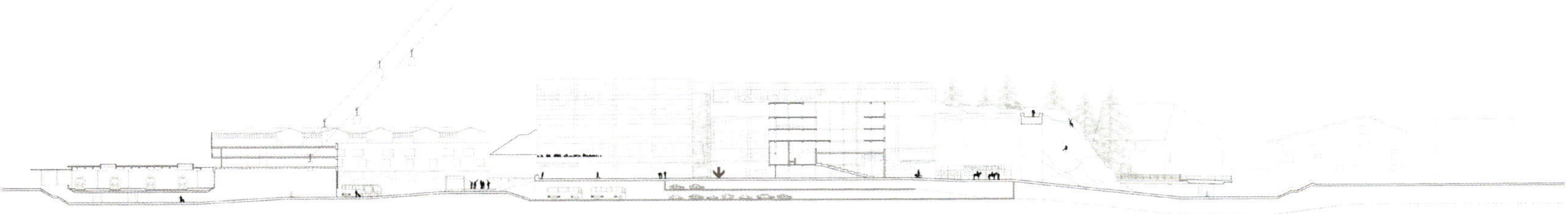

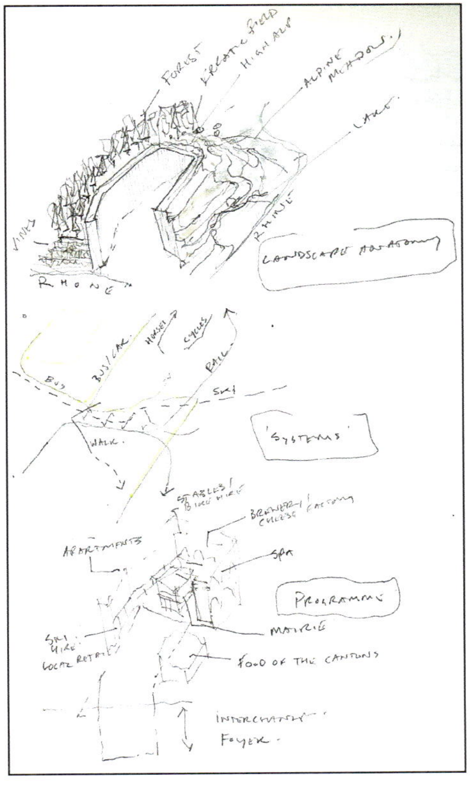

Sections through the proposal.

Sketchbook investigation, overlaying landscape microcosm, transport systems (rail, ski lifts, busses) and a mixed programme, from tourism to local economy.

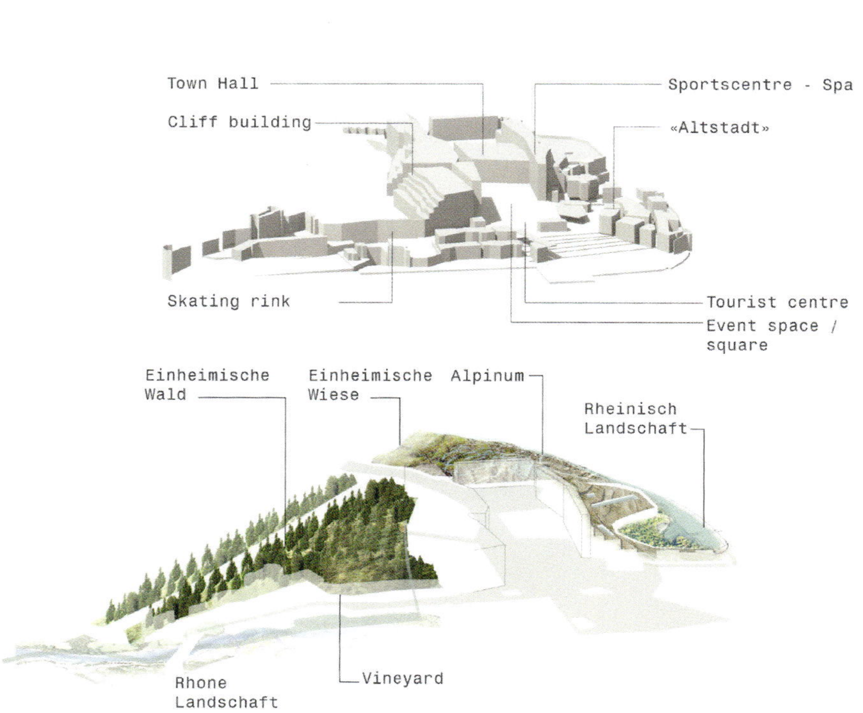

The various elements of the proposal – both landscape ecologies and programme.

The new urban centre in its valley setting.

topographies. These topographies are also keyed to water systems and orientation – which has a great effect in the extreme climate, sheltering from winds and offering access to sun or shade.

NOTES

1 Swinnen & Van Den Driessche in conversation, Anrys et al., *51N4E: Double or Nothing*, AA Publications, 2011.

2 Peter Carl, 'Praxis: Horizons of Involvement', in *Common Ground*, reader of the Venice Architecture Biennale, 2012.

3 Marcel Meili, External Examiner's Report, University of Cambridge.

4 Rem Koolhaas/Office for Metropolitan Architecture, *Content*, 2004, p. 73.

5 Stan Allen, *Points + Lines: Diagrams and Projects for the City.*, Princeton Architectural Press, New York, 1999.

6 Saskia Sassen, *Why Cities Matter*, in *Cities. Architecture and Society*, catalogue of the 10th Architecture Biennale Venice, Masilio, Venice, 2006.

7 Koolhaas, *op. cit.*

8 This erosion has been well documented and discussed as a phenomenon by sociologists such as David Harvey, Richard Sennett and Edward Soja.

9 See Anna Minton's book *Ground Control* for a discussion of this tendency.

10 Sassen, *op. cit.*

11 Peter Carl, *op. cit.*, p. 81.

12 Diploma Studio brief, University of Cambridge Department of Architecture, 2006.

INTERVIEW WITH ELLIS WOODMAN

This interview with the architectural critic Ellis Woodman took place at the Boot & Flogger in Southwark, London, in March 2013. The conversation addresses three 'exegetic' propositions put forward in the closing stages of my doctoral research. These propositions – established in three books – span from the scale of a large building through to a whole city quarter, to the consideration of a trans-national topography: the productive landscapes bordering the North Sea.

Tom Holbrook – 'The research has split into these three prospective projects, taking a more direct path out of the thesis.'

Ellis Woodman – 'So the *North Sea Dialogues* work you've talked about is part of that?'

T – 'Yes, there is a singular topography between Lincolnshire and Schleswig-Holstein, which you notice from the window of the Eurostar train: similar conditions whenever you look up. Various kinds of logistic worlds are determining these landscapes: the serial airport schemes for London, for example. These are enormous projects which remain undiscussed in cultural terms. The book we made[1] frames the dialogue, essentially addressing this cultural gap.

I'm interested in exploring these found conditions, in making observations on the upheaval that's going on from the North Sea back to the first major motorway inland, with the aim of bring that into a spatial discourse with some connection to the discipline. We're interested in seeing how these monocultural conditions might become ameliorated, richer. We have been talking of the project as a contemporary

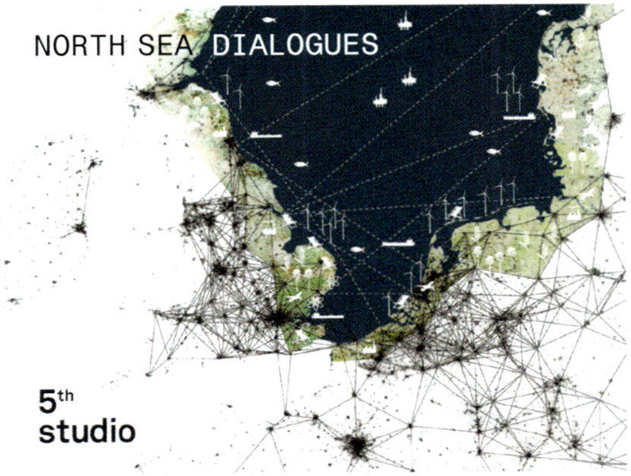

The cover of the book for North Sea Dialogues.

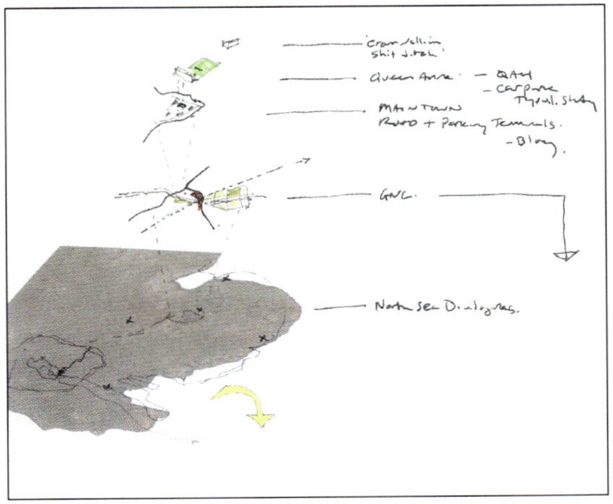

Sketch interrelating the various nested 'exegetic projects'.

"*Rural Rides*":[2] going through this trans-national topography, looking very carefully at the similarities, and at the differences.'

E – 'The Patrick Keiller film *Robinson in Space*[3] seems to be all about that – putting a lie to the idea that Britain is no longer a manufacturing nation. There's also a Rayner Banham essay – *Flatscape with Containers*,[4] written at the time as Cedric Price's Thinkbelt project,[5] which is also one of the references.'

Eric de Maré: St Edward's, Brotherton, North Yorkshire, with Ferrybridge B Power Station behind (1960s) RIBA British Architectural Library Photographs Collection. Eric de Maré / RIBA Collections

T– 'It's really interesting how that generation were so tied into ideas about landscape.'

E – 'Yes, one thinks of the *Architectural Review*'s ideas on re-visiting the picturesque, Eric de Maré's photographs, for example. . .'[6]

T– 'There's that and there's Colin Rowe's connection with Wittkower. Anthony Vidler talks about a strong strand of thinking that Stirling is introduced to through Rowe, all about burial mounds and castles.[6] He references the Saxl & Wittkower exhibition *British Art and the Mediterranean* which came out of the Warburg Institute.'[7]

E – 'They did a lot of going away at the weekend – Gowan photographing Restormel and Dover Castles. And there was the NW1 Group, including people like Paolozzi, that met and discussed slides of landscapes and so on in Gospel Oak.

So we've talked about the largest of the three projects, what about the other two?'

T – 'Of the other two, the intermediate-scaled project takes North Cambridge as one of the last quarters of that city to be urbanised, and the third project involves the re-invention of a multi-storey car park in the middle of the city.

North Cambridge is interesting as it has a rare bit of infrastructure investment by government – a new rail station – but the station lands at the moment in this nothingness of the city's sewage works, and extensive car parking around the Science Park. We think it's an opportunity to review the Science Park model, which is fifty years old, and to retrofit it – to start using the station and these various other elements as "agents of change".'

E – 'Right.'

T – 'There's an interesting hybrid that comes out of creating a landscape that can deal with extensive remediation of water management, using that and the arrival of the station to help form something very urban. And then there's the potential to re-think the spaces for science and technology – entrepreneurial culture – that isn't like Palo Alto.

It's really fascinating territory: the spatial requirements of the knowledge economy is so underexplored. The land is in really few ownerships, so it's really possibly to talk about an orientating plan. Because it's to the east of the city, there are lots of city utilities – the national electrical grid arrives here, and this great Victorian sewage work which cauterizes the site. It's a huge site and has shockingly low density in terms of land use: almost none of it's built on. Twelve percent of it is blacktop: car parking and road. It has this suburban quality to it.

Meanwhile, at a global scale, the Science Park is trying to attract a global audience of bright graduates, and the only social infrastructure it has is a sandwich van in the car park, and that just doesn't work anymore. And of course the "cluster" phenomenon depends on people meeting – but here there's no stuff in between to support this.'

E – 'And do you see this project as a model or a case study that might reflect something back to the bigger territorial study?'

T – 'I think this project is about differentiation: you make one part more urban, and the other more extensive. You build an edge to something that's thought of as city, rather than as an intermediate world. And then finding these quasi-infrastructural moments where the sewage works is made into a piece of landscape that does various things, that supports development, generates power and so on. Trying to use the infrastructure as a catalyst that is also the beginnings of an urban model.'

E – 'And the third architectural scale project is what?'

T – 'The third project involves the re-fitting of a car park in the middle of Cambridge: a car park which came out of a plan for the city from 1966. At that point in time, the typology of the car park was seen as a civilising interchange between the private motorist and the city, the point where they emerge into the city and become citizens.

So there's this '60s car park which needs investment because it's falling to bits through concrete cancer. It was built on the edge, and now it's in the middle of the city – land values have exploded. It forms one edge to Parker's Piece – it's an impressively scaled building – a piece of scenography.'

E – 'Is it a live project?'

T – 'It's building into a live project. We've got a bit of it as a live project, we hope, and we're hoping to extend that into the bit that the City owns. They have this quandary about having to spend millions repairing this car park which they'd rather get rid of, which is completely blind to Parker's Piece.'

E – 'And do they still need the car park?'

T – 'No, they probably need a proportion of it, but because of land values we could put that underground. What we've said is that it should be a "city building", rather than it being a car park with a gymnasium. It should be lots of things – that builds into this terrace that has sufficient scale to address Parker's Piece. Part of that is mapping how Parker's Piece was on the edge of the city – where the town gaol was, and then it became one of the first pockets of agricultural land to be enclosed.

Over time if you keep looking at it, the position on a map where the Ordnance Survey writes "Cambridge" gradually creeps over it, so if you Google "Cambridge" now it drops a pin right on Parker's Piece: it's become the middle, while it once was on the edge. There's a whole rash of civic development from the '70s – the police station, the fire station, the car park – that's now being re-made as something much more valuable in economic terms. So it's a continuation of that narrative.'

E – 'It feels like one of the things that connects the three projects is roads and car infrastructures: from the scale of a car park to the blacktop terrain of the Science Park, to the motorways of the big territorial scheme. The question is how you make functional urban value of that landscape.'

T – 'It's really fascinating looking at some of those Smithsons' engagements with roads, which were bonkers. . .'

E – 'As in "*AS in DS*".[8] They did a Cambridge scheme, didn't they?'

T – 'They did a Cambridge scheme, yes. They were really interested in roads. Look at the *New Ways for London* – Peter Smithson lays down this huge interchange number which goes right through Soho, taking out everything we hold dear. . .'

E – 'That's the National Theatre there. . . and Centrepoint?'

T – 'Yes. Peter Smithson says: "*Seen from the year 2002, the net of roads is too tight, too destructive*".[9] Ha ha! It was interesting because they thought roads were what architects should be talking about, and they talk about road infrastructure as being like a river, or the Acropolis, having this topographic status as something you could build meaning around. Other people like Louis Kahn were also looking at these interchange points – the Philadelphia work – where car parking has got this status – terminals, the extensity of moving around, and there's the point of urbanity where you change that, somehow. Like a great rail station does for nineteenth-century infrastructure.'

E – 'That's interesting, no one's ever done a car park that's generated that sort of urban presence – Preston Bus Garage[10] perhaps.'

T – 'Well, exactly, these are incredible structures. There's this great article in the *Architectural Review* from 1960 by Michael Brawne on "parking terminals",[11] with key examples of a new typology, and bits of Neufert-type metrics – how various systems of slotting cars in work – and yet there's also this incredible feeling of it as a new public typology, like a city gateway or something like that.'

E – 'Brian Richards was the member of Team X who was a road expert: he collaborated with James Gowan and the Smithsons, and taught at the AA, but his work is not that well known. That's a fascinating problem, how you could make something on an urban scale out of traffic. . .'

T – 'Well, it's an interesting scale "in between". As with the North Sea conversation, there's a world that architects don't really occupy: one that's located somewhere between the urban and the infrastructural. A condition that's at the edge, with an interest in differentiation: between one side and the other of an urban condition.

New Ways for London: Alison and Peter Smithson.
Drawing: Alison & Peter Smithson;
© The Smithson Family Collection

Their Citroen DS19 at Upper Lawn.
Photograph: Peter Smithson
© The Smithson Family Collection

E – 'Is OMA's Zeebrugge Terminal[12] an example of that?'

T – 'Yes, exactly, and I think that Kollhoff's Atlanpole project[13] has that kind of interesting connection to something that feels like a piece of infrastructure, and yet has an urban density, an obvious public presence. An institutional presence, I suppose.'

E – 'Kollhoff has this thing he takes from O. M. Ungers, the idea of *grossform*. Both Kollhoff and

Rem Koolhaas were both students at Cornell with Ungers. Kollhoff developed this idea for archipelago urbanism where he stopped believing that a city can be reconstructed – which was his position until the reconstruction of Berlin became available! Projects like the Piraeus building in Amsterdam[14] were a manifestation of this idea: something with a massive and a singular form, off regular scale, and speaking for an archipelago object in that dimension.'

T – 'And I guess trying to make sense of that problem of how we bring meaning to those post-industrial scales of space – whether that's the Amsterdam dockside, or with something like a mining landscape, as with 51N4E's C-Mine project.'[15]

E – 'Your Creative Exchange project has something of that. . . it feels like it has an aspiration to suggest a different scale, a more urban idea than what's around it.'

T – 'Yes, definitely. There's a weary feel in any of those towns that we tend to work in, that are becoming dormitory towns, too close to London. Their market – in the case of St Neots – had some connection with agriculture or manufacturing, and now is all about housing. Housing is the only game in town.'

E – 'A dormitory operation. . .'

T – 'The government growth agenda or economic agenda just produces reams of little housing boxes, from which to send people to London. That project came from a brief where the council were trying to cement a home-grown economic culture in the town, so that kids didn't grow up and automatically leave. Instead they might find a cheap place to set up a company, and do something locally. And we felt it was really key that it was a reminder, but also a prospective idea, about how it wasn't just a dormitory town, but was something more urban. In reality, it's getting more and more suburban. So a sort of awkward building that is compact, and talks about a different sort of economy, was the intention.'

E – 'I'm just thinking about your territorial scale investigation, where presumably these different sites that you're identifying between the North Sea and the motorway, their employee base is primarily within a ten-mile radius, so they become magnets for people living locally, whereas there's this other story, which is probably much more dominant, about commuting suburban centres. There must be a graphic where you can overlay those two points of attraction – the big one from London and the local one?'

T – 'That's really interesting – because there is this sort of placelessness to the locations that are growing up as places to work or industrial settings. That's something we came across at Park Royal, in the Lea Valley, and on the periphery of Cambridge – because they're on the edge of something, they're devalued and they're seen as problematic landscapes that people don't want to walk through. The perception of them is as low-value places, when they're actually not – they're of critical importance, and are quite well used, but there's something in the association of places to do with making that isn't valued. That perception may be a residue of planning and zoning;

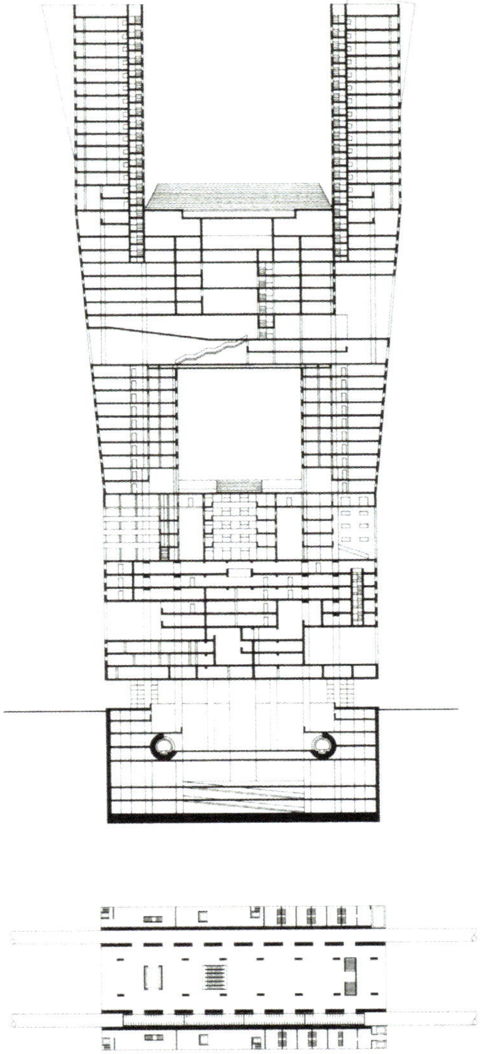

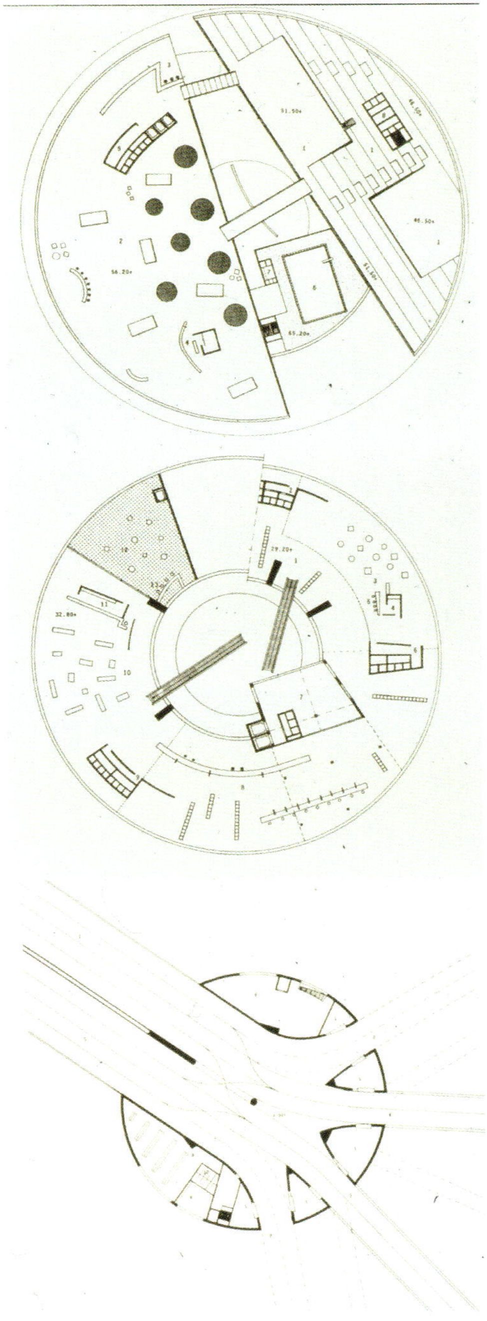

Hans Kollhoff's Atlanpole project, competition entry, Nantes, France, 1988.

OMA's Zeebrugge Sea Terminal, competition entry, Zeebrugge, Belgium, 1989. Office for Metropolitan Architecture these places should never be as monofunctional as they are. Yet, even if they live quite close to them, people tend to drive to access them, because there's some sort of disconnect, a proximity issue.

Take something like London Gateway[16], which is the new port out in the Thames. It will employ about 12,000 people, but they will all drive in, work and then go away. Compare that to the heyday of the Port of London where there's a completely different idea of those proximities: you don't get an enduring culture out of that, you just get the efficiencies of forklift operations or Fordist planning of a process, with no residue or grit.'

E – 'But there's almost two landscapes overlaying, there's this commuting landscape – people who aren't actually invested in the place, beyond their garden or the shopping centre. And then in terms of your desire to make these compounds less monofunctional, there aren't too many ingredients available – empty landscapes. It'd be interesting to see how one connects those worlds more directly, the commuter world and the more localised world.

Do you have any places which you do think are models that are achieving something more purposeful in relation to the landscape, and are more socially integrated?'

T – 'I suppose that I'm interested in stuff that has come together over a longer period of time, so bits of Cambridge, Massachusetts, or funny edge situations that have had such extreme conditions that they've ameliorated those over time, and become more successful urban spaces. Ameliorating things inherited from engineers for example, like the Victoria Embankment: an incredible, brilliant project, in engineering terms, but with horrific implications for anything urbane, compared to what was there, and the vibrancy of that river edge.'

E – 'But I guess I meant in the more perforate landscape that you're looking at, are there solutions – are there better out-of-town shopping centres or militarised zones, or. . .'

T – 'I think it's such an unremarked phenomenon that actually it hasn't got that awareness – amelioration hasn't really kicked in yet. But there's definitely work that needs doing. I think it's interesting that there's a whole generation of architects dealing with these things, but it hasn't been explicit in its conceptualisation yet as a landscape problem. It tends to be on the basis of individual projects, so something like the C-Mine project, or a whole number of projects which one can think of that essentially stem from this issue, and end up tackling it through a model of a back extension, or a new industrial building, or a single project. The issue is that not many people are talking about a larger crisis, so those things aren't located in some sustained bit of thinking. Belgian practices are alert to these conditions – for example, Jan van de Vylder, and a lot of Bas Smet's work[17] are looking at those conditions because they're so prevalent in Belgium.'

E – 'So it's the existing condition, and how you transform it is what you're particularly interested in, rather than developing the new model: how you cultivate a more urban condition in places with a lack.'

T – 'I suppose the north Cambridge stuff is looking at something where, without planning in a spatial rather than bureaucratic sense, it will just end up in a series of incremental projects, and will miss the opportunity to re-think that edge of the city as something that's more "thick", more multivalent.'

E – 'Do you think something like Paju Book City[18] is a model?'

T – 'Yes, possibly. Certainly Florian Beigel has been talking about this condition for a long time. The idea of a masterplan that doesn't over-determine – what's his phrase? "*Design the rug, but not the picnic*" – a kind of orientation towards something where you lay down certain conditions and realise that you can't control everything. That's really fascinating in terms of thinking about what one's role is as a masterplanner: whether it's a formal idea, which is Richard Rogers' generation's approach, which rapidly becomes almost completely obsolete, because it doesn't adapt very well to events. Or something that's more sequential or able to deal with contingent stabilities, but which still is clear about what the essential ingredients of what one's trying to achieve.'

E – 'And it feels when you talk about masterplanning, your interest is always about edge conditions, about encounters between things with different functions or different scales, and with the Rogers' plan, one's looking at something formally fixed. There's a difference in sensibility – you're relaxed about what the disposition, the dimensions of what the various elements might be, but you're interested in the relationship between one thing and something surprising adjacent to it.'

T – 'I think that's right, and I've realised through the process of doing the PhD that there are flaws in that approach – that our attitude to masterplanning is very sequential and it depends on an idea that things never happen at once, or even in an ideal way at all, so is pessimistic about the level of control you can operate with.

I think that's quite a good thing. But, there's also, countering that, an interest in the very large scale and the singular object, something like Kollhoff's *grossform*: those things so rarely come off, because they're based on a "Napoleon", or a top down idea of planning resembling the Smithsons' imposition of a motorway system through Soho. Really interesting things come out of that, but it's kind of catastrophic at the same time – particularly at a time when planning is at a nadir, and *laissez faire* is the preferred mode.

This developer I was talking to today said you might have a great plan: "I like the plan, I can see what you're talking about in North Cambridge, absolutely get it, but of course, when the customer comes along and says they want a 20,000-square-foot floorplate, that's what the customer gets." I find that really problematic at one level, but on the other hand, some of the stuff I admire has come out of a meeting point of control and freedom, as with the analogy of the rug and the picnic. But to have that conversation you have to have a level of sophistication, and a cultural level of engagement in what you're trying to achieve, that isn't available here at the moment.'

E – 'Your impulse is always towards making sensitive juxtapositions between slightly nebulous, defined quantities; in America, an urban planning strategy

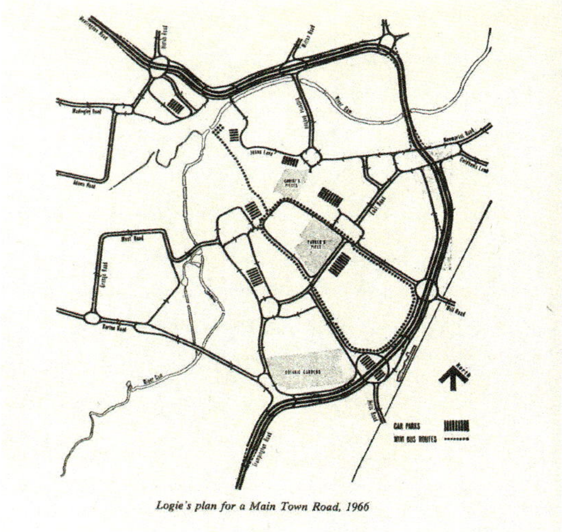

Design collage study, drawn by Florian Beigel, view of the large Book Distribution Centre conceived as an artificial hill in the wetland with the Simhak Mountain in the background. Florian Beigel & Philip Christou with Architecture Research Unit, 'Paju Landscape Script', Paju Book City Landscape and Urban Concept Design, 1999.

Logie's 1966 plan for Main Town Road, Cambridge.

might be a grid plan. And maybe that's a more robust way of making order out of the ebbs and flows of late capitalist society.'

T – 'That's true. Although you could look at Cerda's Barcelona plan, which is somewhere in between: it is a grid plan, but you've also got chamfered corners where other things can happen. There's a sort of built-in uncertainty principal in that planning which is really rich.'

E – 'And it's interesting that you're looking at the Smithsons – there's probably a gap between them and you – they're the last British architects who were interested in planning before a generation who weren't. I don't know if they were very effective in their engagement with planning, but it was certainly on their agenda.'

T – 'Yes, at a time when planning was a really strong and powerful, politically supported arm of policy – an extension of policy. Whereas the stuff we've done with Design for London has felt like guerrilla tactics: *despite* politicians and policy, we've managed to do something good. I think that's really problematic.

Design for London, and the Architecture and Urbanism Unit before,[19] were incredibly good clients, who brought urbanism back into architecture: bringing the idea that you can design a city, and architects had a place at that planning discussion – the bit that didn't really work was convincing the politicians that this was a powerful model. Curiously, Richard Rogers got it, quite a lot of planners got it, but I'm not sure Livingstone did. I'm not sure Johnson does.'[20]

E – 'Do you feel as an architect-planner you bring a different sensibility from someone who has come from a purely planning background? Does the creative planner really exist anymore? It's a hard one to ask.'

T – 'Well, for instance, the Smithsons did plans for Cambridge and the planning at that time was incredibly powerful and top-down: people like Holford[21] were involved, in the days when planners got knighthoods, and there was a top-down expectation that the state would guide. Looking back, those plans did understand what the issues were facing the city: mostly to do with cars, the challenges of private motoring, and the introduction of shopping. And they got it pretty much right, although their implementation was never really tested on the ground, so the reality of it was very crude. Raised highways, or the Smithsons' imposed motorway phenomena was never really imagined spatially or adequately judged in spatial terms. And yet the counterpoint of that now in reaction is that everything is about ameliorating very local conditions. There's no sense of the town as a whole, what you might do strategically.'

E – 'I think one of the things you've clearly identified as an area of interest is the motor car and its implications, which is absolutely the engagement which discredited a generation of planners thirty years ago. Almost to the point where it's become dubious to be thinking on that sort of scale. The planning we associate with Design for London it is at a much more micro scale, and I haven't heard anyone talk about what the nature of Eastern England, from London to Lowestoft, should be. If that feels like a spatial problem, it's one that's not been addressed for many decades. Do you feel you're consciously re-visiting a problem which has got a history?'

T – 'I think for us, those phenomena have become a marker, a laboratory marker, for places that we become interested in. So if there's been a big piece of infrastructure from the Embankment, through to bits of regeneration like the Eastport scheme in Great Yarmouth, or High Speed 2, or any sort of "redemptive" infrastructure, then we're interested. I think what was interesting in the 1960s was the redemptive quality of thinking about roads and infrastructure, as something that had a civilising possibility, and that would come with new typologies that would be civilising, something in which architects would find the new challenges, like great rail termini were in the nineteenth century. I find it fascinating that, over a century on, one can still find scar tissue at engineered places like King's Cross or St Pancras, or on the Embankment where the infrastructure is only just being re-assimilated into the city.

Down the Lea Valley, there's lots of this stuff that's been dreamt up by engineers – bits of the London motorway box, the Eastway and the Greenway, are hugely problematic because they're not urban, and – like a magnet the wrong way around – they repel urbanism. It takes a long time to address this phenomenon. The north Cambridge project is all about looking at railway sidings and sewage works, and pretty aggressive road engineering that's also expected to be the heart of England's creative industries, and those two things just don't work, they're repellent to each other.

So how do you take these things on? You've got to know something about roads. And I suppose in many ways the agenda which that generation set in the '60s – of shopping, and roads – is still with us. The shopping thing is now about the decay of high streets, the road thing is about trying to re-think some of those problems of discouraging private motoring – having paid off its utopian expectations. We suddenly got really excited that there are certain buildings which are going out of fashion, becoming markers for new interventions – so whether that's petrol stations, or gasometers, or the multi-storey car parks built in the 1960s, each one of those becomes a potential future project, becomes a typology for revisiting and translating into something that's no longer just doing one technical thing.'

E – 'I'm intrigued, looking at the Louis Kahn project in Philadelphia.[22] What's interesting there is this change that happens between an infrastructural scale and an architectural scale. There's a point at which he takes the infrastructural network and brings it into an architectural conclusion. And you could definitely think of projects where that line is much more blurred: the characteristic 1960s car park is an example. One is resistant to think of most car parks as architecture because they feel like a vertical extrusion of road. I wonder how as an architect-planner one is thinking at both scales – how you see that interface. How does the journey evolve from the motorway to where someone is standing on a pavement? How is that termination ideally modulated?'

T – 'I suppose – like looking at those Kahn drawings – that it feels very much thought of as a problem of landscape. So, much like Stirling and Gowan looking at castles and landforms as a way to form their competition project for Churchill College as an autonomous object on the edge of Cambridge, that tries to express what the college needs in terms of connections and autonomy. There was a sensibility at that time, it seems to me, that was about something scenographic, about landscape. They were looking for models – like castles – which are huge in East Anglia, and finding a new architecture that came out of that funny hybrid between those two things. That's really interesting because some of those car parks have that quality. Quite a lot of brutalist architecture like the South Bank and Preston Bus Garage also has that unfinished quality that's really ready to go back and re-visit, finish. Instead they are often torn down. I mean, Robin Hood Gardens is being torn down just before its quality is finally realised! Perhaps it does take fifty years to realise something that started off as landscape, and finishes as a proper building. The same with the Hayward Gallery.

The discussion behind the Preston Bus Garage is fascinating because there's this structure, which is pretty much the only thing that Preston has that has that openness and sense of possibility. And that's really exciting – we don't think or build like

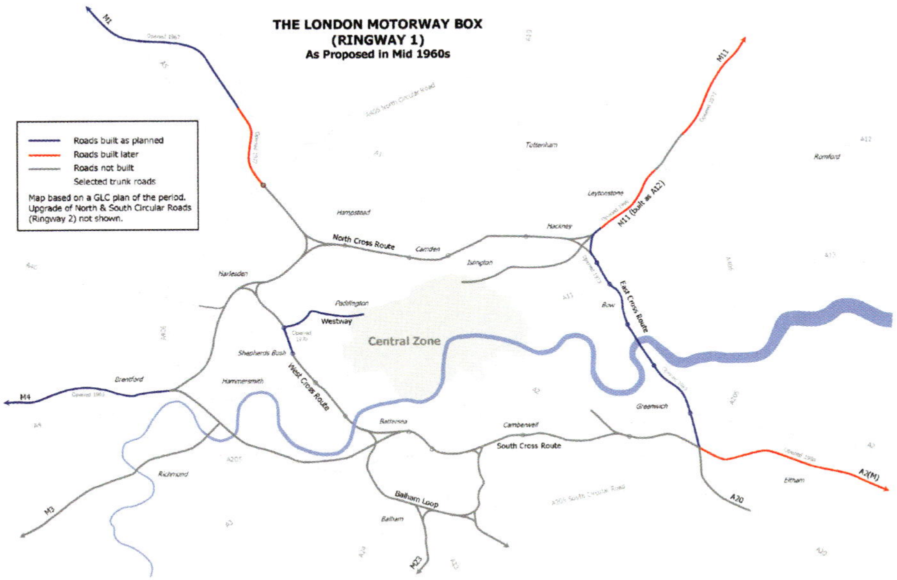

London's unrealised Motorway Box from the 1960s.
David Cane-Wikipedia, GNU Free Documentation License

that anymore, but the scenographic scale, I think, is quite deep in the English psyche – the sort of thing Vanbrugh was talking about: a way of building big and worrying about how it's occupied later – it becomes filled with stuff. But it has an idea of duration, so you build this thing and gradually it becomes absorbed and useful.'

E – 'That feels like your interest in the Adelphi: something about building at an infrastructural scale which can be occupied in many different ways.'

T – 'All that Thames edge held a sequence of projects that had that quality of being like open code, it had a fuzziness at a certain level, but at other levels was incredibly refined. At the Adelphi, you got some of the best plaster workers in Europe finishing the rooms to a high level of order, but it stands on a podium of stuff that's completely unfinished, and has the Thames washing in at the bottom. I suppose that spectrum of "completeness" to "availability to be occupied in different ways" or to be more contingent I find really fascinating. And there's not just the Adelphi on the Strand, but Hungerford Market, and various other bits, such as the Savoy: it seems like that bit of the Thames at the time was a piece of an infrastructure like our motorways. At that time, it attracted this weird intermediate scale of thinking: like a laboratory for London urbanism.'

E – 'Often your interests come back to these big infrastructural-scale projects, that have a certain scale, a certain ruthlessness. The largest building I've seen of yours is the Creative Exchange, which is also the most monumental in a way. . . but it's not a monumental language. . . it's more like. . .'

T – '. . .assemblage?'

E – 'Yes, absolutely. And I guess I wonder if. . . At what point does the language of a building a kilometre long become different from the language of a house? How do you negotiate those transitions of scale? How do you find an appropriate scale for the language you're working in?'

T – 'I think that's a really interesting issue. The first time I presented in Ghent it was one that John Tuomey picked up. He asked something like, "If the things you love are so singular, why is your architecture made of bits. . . why is it assemblage?" I've been really struggling with that question, because it's certainly true that some of the stuff that I most admire in terms of urbanism comes out of the Adams' idea, the idea of the terrace, say. To get down to the scale of a house, the terrace is the perfect model of a repetitive and yet fairly contingent structure where you can change stuff all the time: it can be a posh house, or it can be divided into five tenements depending on fortune. And yet the projects we've done tend to be made out of bits. The intention at St Neots was to make a singular building, and there are certain singular bits of it: there was a desire for it to be "monumental for St Neots", for it to be awkward. And yet also its counter-intention is to represent the number of people, of occupants, who would have a stake in that, as a kind of stepping off point from their spare bedroom to something bigger. So it's also a sponge-like building, or a building that's designed to take everyone's crap – twenty different firms starting up with their funny furniture. It needs to be generous for that sort of occupation. It's not for a single occupier, it felt like it needed a more open structure.

Again, my model is in the Stirling world of bits, of putting stuff together from bits. I think he and Gowan certainly had a sense of the whole, which I think we are still looking for: "the style for the job", something that appears very singular but is also interested in articulation or invention: you know, the funny hanging stairs at the Florey Building, or. . . one thinks of any number of examples from the "Red Series".'

E – 'The first works of yours that I knew of were some very beautiful house conversions that were published, with an obsessiveness about how two bits of wood were put together. But you're also an architect who talks about work on a territorial scale. There's a point along that spectrum where one abandons certain preoccupations and becomes more effective in making more ruthless interventions in the world.'

T – 'It's true. Although a lot of those domestic projects were not really detailed, many were detailed on site in quite a contingent way, because they tended to be for clients who didn't have quite enough money, but had a lot of ambition. We were always trying to do more than was strictly possible. We spent a lot of time on site with dodgy builders trying to just make stuff happen. And I guess from that point, even the domestic projects came from a certain "staginess". My background was in the theatre, and stuff "having to go on", even if you ran out of money, or there wasn't enough time. There's always been an interest in pragmatism in that way. There's an interest in entrepreneurialism – in the older sense of the word, in the sense of putting something on, acting as an impresario, getting something to come off in a certain way.'

E – 'So that's where the ruthlessness is?'

T – 'That has its own ruthlessness. And it's maybe a ruthlessness that reflects an age where actually the architect has very little power in the dynamics of development or planning. But what you can do is put together fragments of "what could be". . . and hope that bits of it come off. It goes back to that thing about control: unless you have a status in the process – which I don't think we really do anymore – what is it that you care about? It's about choosing your battles, and articulating those as well as you can.

Actually, one of the really interesting things we've been doing is in Soho, which is mostly crumbly

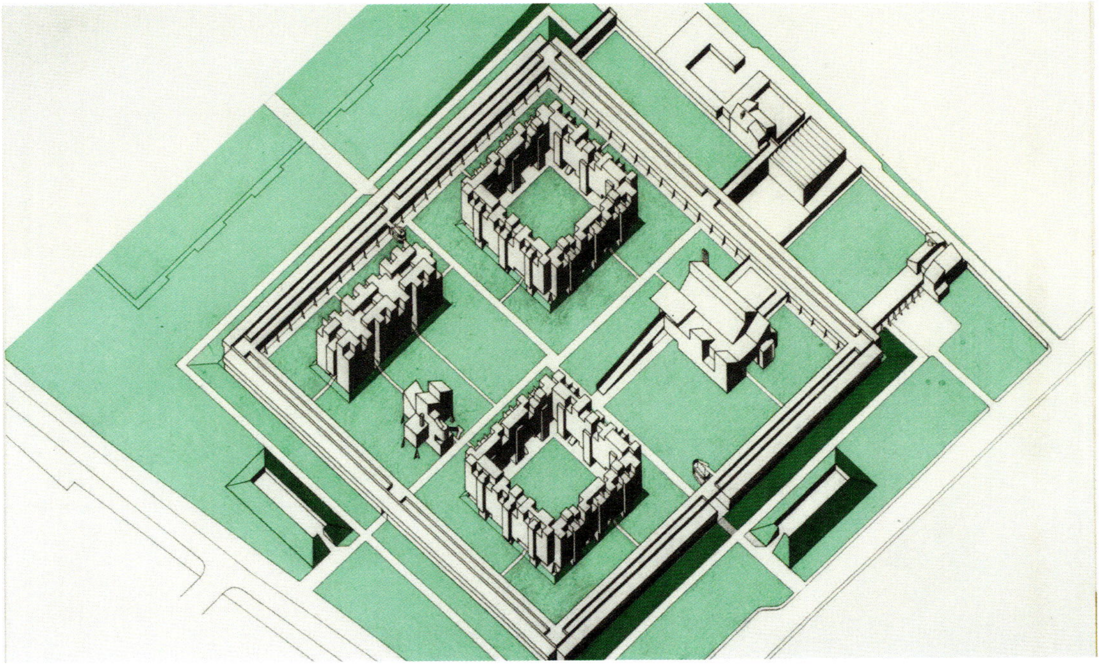

Stirling and Gowan, Churchill College competition entry, axonometric, 1958. James Stirling/Michael Wilford, Centre Canadien d'Architecture (Canadian Centre for Architecture), Montréal.

eighteenth-century marshland property, now worth a fortune. Two things have happened. First, it's occupied by very high-value media companies, who need to be in that location, but would probably be better off in an "out of London" location – Pinewood Studios, say – with soundstages and technical space. The other thing that's happened is conservation, which was actually a kind of co-product of the world we were talking about earlier, of the Smithson generation. On the one hand was that world of architects talking about *tabula rasa* or imposition, and the other product of that was saving Covent Garden and a very creative or politicised conservation. In Soho you can't go in and impose in the way that was possible in the '60s – so it has to be much more tactical and sequential.'

E – 'And can't demolish anything. Everything is "existing fabric".'

T – 'You can't knock down anything. And so everything has to be on a basis of a narrative about value and how you can use the qualities of existing stuff, and how you might identify the soft tissue, where you can start to introduce stuff that's really needed by the people who are trying to occupy those structures. So projects in Soho, as with a lot of those college projects in Cambridge, have been about fabric that's incredibly precious, both in terms of its institutional history, and in terms of what's too difficult to knock down, and being very pragmatic about stuff that works or is required, and isn't yet part of that picture. So how the modern and contemporary intersects with the existing is really deep in our culture in that way. You end up through that, negotiating little bits of stuff: ruins, that are kept, fabric that you really can't damage any further, but you've damaged as much as you can. And then adding an intervention – something that's in dialogue.'

E – 'St Neots maybe stands out as an oddity, but I think pretty much everything else I know of yours works with existing fabric.'

T – 'Well St Neots does too. I mean, with its landscape, the fact it replaces a country house which was demolished in the '50s. It intends to re-make a relationship between a building and its lost landscape.'

E – 'So everything's implicated somehow. You can think of celebrated architects who have never in their lives had those sort of conditions to work with. I mean, I can maybe think of a couple of Richard Rogers' buildings which deal with existing fabric, but it is a rarity. And is that a choice?'

T – 'Yeah, definitely, it's a choice. I mean, it goes back to the whole thing about really finding the monofunctional, the univocal, a problem. And we've always found it more interesting to have a debate – even if it's a row – with stuff that's there, rather than construct our own autonomous reality. My problem with the whole idea of "fuck context" is that actually it's really dull. Euralille is really dull. . .'[23]

E – 'But Euralille is dull not because it "fucks context", but because there's not enough programme perhaps?!'

T – 'Well, yeah, but there would be more programme if you started with some context! I think we're more interested in the other side that Koolhaas talks about, which is the social condenser:[24] that you take everything that's there, and all you do is add. The frustration is with autonomy: making your own reality is a real problem for twenty-first-century architecture.'

E – 'Well, you can make your own reality, but maybe it has an antagonistic relationship to an existing situation, and at least that's a relationship.'

T – 'Yes. For example, the Smithsons were wrong in so many places, but at least they were wrong in an interesting way, and it's a place to start from. Robin Hood Gardens would have been a fascinating location for a critique of all that, and everything we're doing is a critique of a different generation's idea of what planning was, or what architecture was.'

E – 'And at the current culture of planning – the CABE-approved idea of what urban development might be – do you have a critical take on that? Do you feel a distance from what Allies & Morrison might do for example?'

T – 'I guess there's a blandness to it which I find unchallenging.'

E – 'Which is to do with the mantra about density?'

T – 'Which is partly to do with the mantra about density: there's a sort of comfiness to it. I guess, as with Rogers, there's a sort of lazy cosmopolitanism – that density on its own will create place. And that seems to me to be too close to the market – the *laissez faire* condition – and is just convenient to developers. Kollhoff, when he decides he's going to be dense, is dense in an uncompromising, purposeful manner – there's a density of program, rather than a density of floor plate. I think that's our frustration – it does lead to a very formalised way of planning that, as with the Rogers' plan for Cambridge Station, becomes really problematic, and leads to "shorthand urbanism". Like Station Square, that doesn't seem to have any animation, but that has very dense corporate buildings all around it. And I guess that's very different from the spikiness of a Smithson or Stirling building, which has a critical response to context. I don't know, it just seems a bit redolent or bland.'

E – 'With a Rogers' masterplan, one feels a sort of beaux-arts sensibility undercutting all the high-tech imagery, where there's a circus there and a building here, and there's one to match it on the other side. And actually one feels the masterplans are gigantic buildings. It's an urbanism at an architectural scale, while a New York grid plan is an urban idea – the barbershop and the skyscraper next door to each other. The plan can accommodate that, while the Rogers' plan can't accommodate difference in that way.'

T – 'Your talk about the Manhattan grid and the barbers' shop makes me think about that Saul Bellow novella, *Seize the Day*. The way in which connection to authorship of the realization of just writing the equivalent of a short story for each of these projects, it's a really interesting way to think of one's role. One's also not just responding like a Pavlov's dog, waiting for the phone to ring. And, of course, looking back over all the projects and finding continuity between them is really good.'

E – 'What is the time frame for the next bit of the research process?'

T – 'The projects have their own trajectory. The car park project starts and stops. So the relationship between the research and reality is not really controlled. But certainly the thinking is different. Just assembling stuff in the way the research process has dictated brings a kind of self consciousness, which has re-framed these three projects in a totally different way.'

E – 'The project in Cambridge feels like something that will generate an architectural image most directly – the others feel like the outcomes will be maps and quite disparate analysis.'

T – 'I don't know – the trick is always to find some mediation between the universal and particular. The North Cambridge project could generate some retrofitting hybrid infrastructures that we want to start drawing, about the urban edge, and the way you might see it as you drive into the city from Points East, and then how you might deal with all these kind of technical issues that come together. That put together might generate the equivalent of Kahn's Philadelphia scale of consideration.

Even with the North Sea Dialogues project, we want to look at the physical outcomes, implications on the ground at an immediate scale: what sorts of room come out of this critique? Or what could come out of this found reality?'

E – 'Have you seen this publication that came out of TU Delft called '*Over Holland*'?[25] It is very good at bridging between the territorial scale of investigation and local individual projects. They commissioned individual research projects from people like Office KGDVS, Neutlings Reidijk and other interesting Dutch academic practices, who are proposing speculative projects, grounded in a sense of reality for particular situations in relation to the railway system. It might be worth looking at as a sort of model. There's a mapping element, and there's a proposition. I can imagine from your territorial scale work you are going to want to bring it down to something architectural.'

T – 'Railways are certainly rich territory, the way that East Anglian railways were extended into the territory as a sort of entrepreneurial way to make places.'

E – 'Actually when one starts thinking at an infrastructural scale, then there's real political will that one can harness. These are projects that would win votes. Something like your Fatwalk project: if you could implant an idea like that into the public imagination, then it's got traction. But it seems that nobody feels that political resonance now; in many of these schemes from the '60s' you could find an incredible sort of weight of political or popular support.

T – 'In a way, it's a cultural question of finding confidence in being modern again, which was the case in the 1960s. So much of that was tainted subsequently – as you say, has been made problematic territory.'

E – 'New York's High Line is a good example, isn't it? An idea which, a very dramatic change to the city found a popular support in a way that a more disparate idea about how to redevelop that territory might not.'

T – 'That's really true. As with the ecology debate, these themes are so explicit in the US – whether you're in a cabin on your own going through an autonomous condition of being in nature, which is one tradition – Thoreau's *Walden* – or alternatively, you're building infrastructure with the US Army Corps of Engineers.'

NOTES

1 *North Sea Dialogues* is a research proposition produced by 5th Studio and available on the practice website.

2 *Rural Rides*, written by the English pamphleteer William Cobbett in the 1820s, documented agrarian change caused by the agricultural revolution.

3 *Robinson in Space*, feature film; director, Patrick Keiller (1997).

4 Reyner Banham, 'Flatscape with Containers', *New Society* Vol. 10, No. 255, 17 August 1967, p. 231–232. Subsequently appeared in *Architectural Digest*, November 1968.

5 Cedric Price, Potteries Thinkbelt Study, 1964.

6 Anthony Vidler, *James Frazer Stirling: Notes from the Archive*, Yale, New Haven, CT, 2010.

7 Saxl & Wittkower's exhibition, and accompanying book of the same title, *British Art and the Mediterranean* was held at the Warburg Institute during the Second World War.

8 *AS in DS*, published in 1983 by Alison and Peter Smithson, records the drive from their London office to Upper Lawn, their Wiltshire cottage, contrasting the mechanical slickness of their Citroen DS19 to the picturesque countryside encountered on the journey.

9 Peter Smithson quoted in Alison and Peter Smithson, *The Charged Void: Urbanism*, Monacelli Press, New York, 2005.

10 BDP's iconic Preston Bus Garage was under threat of demolition at the time of this conversation.

11 See Michael Brawne, 'Parking Terminals', *Architectural Review*, August 1960.

12 OMA's Zeebrugge Sea Terminal competition, 1989. '*How to inject a new "sign" into a landscape that, through scale and atmosphere alone, renders any object both arbitrary and inevitable? To become a landmark, this project adopts a form that resists easy classification to free associate with successive moods the mechanical, the industrial, the utilitarian, the abstract, the poetic, the surreal. It combines maximum artistry with maximum efficiency.*'

13 Hans Kollhoff, Atlanpole competition proposal, Nantes, France, 1988. The competition brief was for a communications centre as the centrepiece of the developing high-tech hub in the Loire estuary economic zone, bringing together the local authority, university and commerce. Kollhoff stacked the programme vertically, as "*a large house containing the whole of a city*". Floors 2 to 10 would house production areas; 11 to 15 would house exhibition spaces; 16 to 25 would be a hotel.

14 Piraeus Building, Hans Kollhoff, Rapp & Rapp, Amsterdam, Netherlands, 1994.

15 51N4E C-Mine, Genk, Belgium, 2009. See my discussion of this project in a former coal mine in Holbrook, '*Kraftwerk*' *Architectural Review*, August 2013.

16 D P World London Gateway Port. See: http://www.londongateway.com/the-port/

17 See Bureau Bas Smets. http://www.bassmets.be

18 ARU: landscape and urban design of the first phase of Paju Book City, a new 'City of Publishing' on a very large site next to the Han River north-west of Seoul, 1999.

19 Design for London (2007–2012), and the Architecture and Urbanism Unit before it (2001–2007), were exceptional clients and exemplify a more careful mode of urban planning.

20 Ken Livingstone was London's first mayor, followed by Boris Johnson – in 2015, the incumbent.

21 William Graham Holford, (22 March 1907–17 October 1975) was a British architect and town planner.

22 Louis Kahn's Philadelphia project.

23 OMA's project in Euralille, 1994–2010.

24 Rem Koolhaas, 'Patent for a social condenser' from *Content*, accompanying plan of Parc de la Villette competition entry 1982. 'Programmatic layering upon vacant terrain to encourage dynamic coexistence of activities and to generate through their interference unprecedented events'.

25 http://www.bk.tudelft.nl/en/research/publications/publicaties-boeken/over-holland/

ON INFRASTRUCTURE: A CONVERSATION WITH SHELLEY MCNAMARA, GRAFTON ARCHITECTS

This exchange took place through email between January and March 2013, following a number of conversations. During that period, Shelley delivered a lecture at the Architectural Association, London, titled *Architecture as New Geography*.

The conversation forms part of the process of defining a potential bridge between the scales of infrastructure and architecture in my own work.

Tom Holbrook – 'I'm interested in why the qualities of infrastructure are so resonant in the thinking of certain architects, including our own work!

I first came across this tendency in your work when I saw Yvonne Farrell lecturing on the building you completed for Bocconi University, Milan. What it is about the infrastructural scale that Grafton Architects find so compelling? What are the roots of that fascination?'

Shelley McNamara – 'A number of things and influences come to mind in relation to this. I remember reading an essay by Stan Allen many years ago where he was describing the qualities of "architecture as infrastructure". He says something like, "infrastructures are flexible and anticipatory. . .they work with time and are open to change. . .by specifying what must be fixed and what is open to change they can be precise and indeterminate at the same time". (We used this quote in our Bocconi competition report.)

We were fascinated by this idea of the possibility of making buildings which might not be completely prescriptive or finished. Walter Benjamin also talks about "the capacity of certain structures to act as a scaffold for a complete series of events not anticipated by the architect." I have not investigated the connection between these influences and that of the Smithsons' definition of a "conglomerate" in that essay "Conglomerate Ordering" in their book *Italian Thoughts*. I must look at that piece again. And on a different note and even further back in time, probably around 1977, I remember being completely intrigued by an essay written by Alan Colquhoun in a book called *Le Corbusier in Perspective*, which I have just miraculously put my hand on! The title of the essay is "Formal and Functional Interactions". He compares the French Embassy project in Brasilia with the Venice Hospital project. From memory, at least what I took from this essay, was that Corb had a dynamic "form free"way of organising space irrespective of whether he was proposing an "object" type building like the Embassy as opposed to the more organic open form of the Hospital. The term infrastructure is not used here I think, but many of the qualities in Stan Allen's essay would relate to the Venice Hospital project in particular.

So in a sense, I think our interest in infrastructure does not initially come from dealing with the large scale but more from a characteristic that a project might have, and from the liberation that the ideas inherent in the term infrastructure could bring to design of a building at whatever scale perhaps.

In terms of the big scale, projects that catapulted us into this realm would probably be those of the Brazilian Architects I referred to in the AA lecture. We were inspired by the spatial potential of large scale structures. That together with the fact that we have worked with structural engineers on the design of motorway bridges.

Somehow when we were making a plan or section of a bridge, and physically experiencing the huge dimensions of the elements of column and beam, it shifted and focussed our awareness of structure.

But the Brazilian architects, especially Vilanova Artigas, can make a tennis club or house feel like a bridge!

And, of course, there is the capacity within thinking about "infrastructure" of getting away from the isolated object as the only intention. . . that idea of connecting to the bigger context, supporting or contributing to the bigger context, and architecture as something that can underpin and support human endeavour.'

T – 'I think it's really interesting that you go directly to the issue of determinacy – architectural culture seems to be going through a period where so much revolves around formal issues and an over-determinacy of form.

At a research seminar last year, John Tuomey said that while he once subscribed to Hermann Czech's notion of "architecture as background", he was now convinced that his interest lay in an architecture of "vital presence". Are the qualities of a strongly characterised, yet "unfinished" infrastructure a means of achieving both? I am struck by the way the Bocconi can be so muscular, and yet at the same time can become so localised, so much part of an everyday Milanese street corner.

Your reference to the Smithson's notion of "Conglomerate Ordering" is revealing – Peter Smithson illustrates what they were referring to with the analogy of "building like a farmer": with each element expected to act in a multiple way, both field boundary and shelter, and so on. It also urges a more visceral relationship with built form, which resonates with both your buildings and your references to projects by Bo Bardi, Vilanova Artigas and Mendes da Rocha.

The liberation that the notion of infrastructure from a completed position to something more anticipatory brings to mind Rem Koolhaas' essay on urbanism from *S, M, L, XL*:

> If there is to be a 'new urbanism' it will not be based on the twin fantasies of order and omnipotence; it will be the staging of uncertainty; it will no longer be concerned with the arrangement of more or less permanent objects, but with the irrigation of territories with potential; it will no longer aim for stable configurations but for the creation of enabling fields . . . it will no longer be about meticulous definition, the imposition of limits, but about expanding notions, denying boundaries . . . it will no longer be obsessed with the city but with the manipulation of infrastructure for endless intensifications and diversifications, shortcuts and redistributions — the reinvention of psychological space.

Koolhaas' infrastructure inevitably irrigates what for him is a *tabula rasa*, while you seem interested in a more engaged and urban milieu. To what extent does "Architecture as a New Geography" or the interest in infrastructure as a mediatory position differ from urbanism?'

S – 'I find your questions and comments extremely interesting. I agree with John Tuomey's comment about architecture having a "vital presence" but I am not sure that this rules out the "architecture as background" idea.

I love an essay by Alvaro Siza on "Making Walls". He talks about the wall of the Monasterio de San Paio de Antealtares, in Santiago de Compostela. He says something like, a magnetic and vibrant wall finishing the square, wavers between nothing and magnetic presence . . .it makes him angry because it has such presence and yet it is just a virtually solid wall with what must be one of the longest public benches imaginable.

Is that a piece of infrastructure?

The difference between the Smithsons' Conglomerate Ordering and Rem Koolhaas' interpretation of "infrastructure" for me, is that the Smithsons' make the case that the specificity of a building is actually the quality that makes it generic and flexible! I love this idea in terms of urban forms and typology. Stan Allen's definition of infrastructures would also be close to the Smithsons' view.

The idea of infrastructure being related to the *tabula rasa* actually frightens me. We think about it in a completely different way as I will try to describe in answer to your final question:

"To what extent does 'Architecture as New Geography', or the interest in infrastructure as a mediatory position, differ from urbanism?"

Architecture as new geography, for us, relates directly to urbanism. It is the idea that we as architects have the responsibility to build places and spaces which have a richness which can somehow compensate for the fact that so much of the natural world is disappearing, and more and more people are living in cities. It is also the idea that architecture grows out of physical and cultural ground.

An architectural "infrastructure" can "hold" culture. It is not neutral. It might be big but it needs to also have spaces which engender intimacy, security, identity, conviviality, community.

Hugh Campbell, writing about Bocconi, encouragingly says, "the heroic scale and sureness of purpose of the architecture transfers itself to the occupants, so that they too feel bound together, part of some larger social order".

By virtue of the sheer scale of many urban developments, architecture *is* at the scale of pieces of geography. We need to make spaces where inhabitants can tell where they are, the time of day and the seasons. Not much to ask for?!

Paolo Mendes Da Rocha is good on this. . . He says, "We need to get architecture out of making and thinking of isolated objects and show it as an inexorable transformation of nature".

I remember that great lecture you gave at University College Dublin and your sense of geography, landscape and the delicate balancing of intervention with the given conditions. You showed a depth of knowledge, sensitivity and awareness which was really admirable and enviable.

So we are talking about the same thing I hope!'

Index